D0907219

Israel into Palestine

GWYN ROWLEY

Israel into Palestine

I know you two are rival enemies;
How comes this gentle concord in the world,
That hatred is so far from jealousy
To sleep by hate, and fear no enmity?

WILLIAM SHAKESPEARE
A Midsummer Night's Dream

MANSELL: LONDON AND NEW YORK

Mansell Publishing Limited
6 All Saints Street
London N1 9RL, England

First published 1984

Distributed in the United States and Canada by
The H. W. Wilson Company, 950 University Avenue
Bronx, New York 10452

British Library Cataloguing in Publication Data
Rowley, Gwyn
  Israel into Palestine
  1. Israel—History
  I. Title
  956.94   DS125
  ISBN 0-7201-1674-0

Printed and bound in Great Britain by
Butler & Tanner Ltd, Frome and London

To Katie, with love

Contents

List of Figures

List of Tables

Preface

For over fifty years and increasingly so since 1948 the Middle East has been divided and constantly locked in combat on the question of Israel. Many view the problems as complex, deep rooted and basically incomprehensible, yet the conflict remains at or near crisis point, threatening not only to erupt again but to spill over into a far wider, general war. Surely at some time in the near future reason must prevail and compromises must actively be sought. The alternative is for further and mounting crises that would lead on inexorably to world war.

This book, which draws together material from both published and unpublished sources, including field work within the West Bank, incorporates material from such disparate areas as religion, philosophy, geography, sociology, economic and social history, economics and political science. It provides a much needed base from which more fully to understand and consider the evolving problems, the complexity of competitions and alternative strategies about the locale of Israel. It presents pointers to certain of the potential scenarios that seek to transcend and overcome some of the present uncertainties of the Middle East. The specific premise from which this book is written is that any potentially durable settlement *must* consider the problem's four cardinal features: the Palestinians, Israel's right to exist, territory and peaceful relations. A sense of hope might then replace despair for all communities within this critical region.

To undertake to write a book on such a sensitive area as the Middle East poses a number of difficulties, not least being how to deal with the almost daily changes that occur through the region. I recall Elspeth Huxley's apposite remarks on a similar theme, 'Writing about modern Africa is like trying to sketch a galloping horse that is out of sight before you have sharpened your pencil.' It is partly for this reason that I have concerned myself not only with the facts but also with an evaluation of specific scenarios into which the possible changes might be slotted. Thus, although the book is of necessity time specific, it does attempt to envisage the range of options that will present themselves, and the reader may consider these against the historical backcloth presented within the earlier chapters. Any one of the supposedly 'new dramatic' developments arising from 'new initiatives', that appear every so often may thus be set into the considered format presented in the penultimate chapter and evaluated accordingly.

A few words are necessary on the historical background that is provided to enable even the general reader to appreciate the development, in space and through time, of certain specific ideas relating to territoriality and to existing conflicts. The brief evaluation of certain philosophico-theological considerations, particularly the relationship of both ancient and present-day Israel and its territory with the Torah and interpretations of the Oral Law, may allow certain insights to be developed. Whereas Rodinson (1982) provides a broad picture of the Israeli–Arab conflict in its historical setting, an essential feature of the first part of this volume is to paint an historical backcloth to the developments, both those in process and those envisaged, in and about the confines of Israel.

I have attempted to keep a strict rein on the development of tangential subjects; the bibliography, however, points to the larger body of relevant literature available for further study.

The constant endeavour has been to present a balanced view; although the book is opinionated, it is not intentionally biased. Though a difficult task at the best of times, it is far more so on a subject where the various writers have usually written from entrenched Arab or Zionist perspectives. The British have much to answer for in their attitudes to the native peoples of the Middle East, and I share some of the shame of T.E. Lawrence in the broken and contradictory promises, conspiracy, intrigue and insincerity that have for long characterized British, indeed Western, dealings with the region.

By and large publications on the region fall into two basic types: scholarly work on quite precise and specific subjects, and far more general and broader 'journalistic' volumes. *Israel into Palestine*, it is hoped, will provide a much needed addition to the existing literature by tapping the insightful approaches of both types of research, while at the same time considering the broader realities, the likely possibilities and developments within the sensitive and critical region.

My special thanks go to Dr Bakr Abu Kishk, Director of the Research Centre at Birzeit University, and to Nabila Brain and Ibrahim Dakkak for providing me with up-dated material on Israeli developments within the West Bank and East Jerusalem; to Paul Harper of the Council for Arab–British Understanding; and to the staffs of the Jewish Library in the Manchester City Library, the university libraries in both Sheffield and Cambridge, the British Library in London and the National Library of Wales in Aberystwyth. David Jones of the University of Sheffield Library has always been of particular help in his guidance and forbearance. The Israeli and Saudi Arabian embassies in London and the United Nations Relief and Works Agency in Geneva have provided me with prompt and interested services. A number of individuals, especially Professor Lowell Schecter and Dr Soleiman El-Hamdan have helped to focus my attention upon alternative viewpoints, although my deficiencies and continuing problems of transliteration still manage to show through. In a similar vein I also wish to thank Dr Stanley Waterman, Dr Nurit Kliot and Dr Moshe Inbar of the University of Haifa. My sincerest thanks go to each of my long-suffering colleagues within the Department of Geography, the University of Sheffield. I cannot think of a friendlier environment in which to work. I thank Dr Rick Cryer of that department for his insightful advice and help on matters relating to Litani waters, and both Tony Arblaster of the Department of Political Theory and Institutions and David Clines of the Department of Biblical Studies for some useful and stimulating suggestions. Special mention needs to be made to Rosie Duncan and Sheila Ottewell for their cartographic skills and John Owen and David Maddison for their photographic expertise. The assistance of Dr Verity Brack in reading the proofs and compiling the index is gratefully acknowledged. I also thank those who have assisted me but who wish to remain unnamed. Above all I thank Katie for her love, forbearance and understanding. I also wish to record my special thanks to John E. Duncan at Mansell for his encouragement and assistance in seeing this volume through to its publication.

Acknowledgements

The author and publishers wish to thank the following for permission to reprint or modify copyright material: Kollek & Son Ltd for the two parts of Figure 21, from *Stay Kosher in Israel* (1981); John Wiley & Sons Ltd for Figures 9, 14, 15 and 16, from 'The *Land* in Israel' by G. Rowley, in *Political Studies from Spatial Perspectives: Anglo-American Essays on Political Geography*, ed. by A.D. Burnett and P.J. Taylor (1981); and John Wiley & Sons Inc. for Figure 11), modified from *Systematic Political Geography* by H. de Blij (1967).

Introduction

No other comparable region in the world, by spatial area, population size or resource base consistently achieves such a continuous and full coverage in the national and international press, on radio and television, as the troubled Middle East about Israel. *Israel into Palestine*, it is hoped, will enable the reader to understand more fully the reasons for this importance.

The term 'Middle East' is said, erroneously, to have been coined by the American naval historian Captain Alfred Thayer Mahan, during a discussion of British naval strategy in relation to Russian activity in Iran and a German project for a Berlin to Baghdad railway (Lewis and Holt, 1962, p.1; Beaumont, Blake and Wagstaff, 1976, p.1). Captain Mahan asserted that the Middle East embraced the territory between the Mediterranean and the Indian Ocean. In fact, as revealed by Koppes (1976), the neologism 'Middle East' had been used two years earlier by General Sir Thomas Edward Gordon in a paper on the increasingly tense British–Russian rivalry within the region at the century's end (Gordon, 1900, p.413). Koppes (1976, p.96) suggests that Gordon's almost casual off-hand reference to the 'Middle East' may be taken as implying an earlier, more general use of the term than has previously been assumed, and that it is likely that the origins of the designation 'Middle East' have yet to be traced. Professor E.A. Bayne speculates, however, that the term may have arisen in the India Office in the mid-nineteenth century (Koppes, 1976, p.98).

The Middle East, as referred to in this book, embraces that area fringed by five seas: the Mediterranean, Black, Caspian and Red Seas and the Persian or Arabian Gulf, nowadays increasingly referred to simply as the Gulf (Fogg, 1950, p.51). The broad region extends to include Turkey in the northwest, Iran in the east, and Egypt and the northern Sudan in the west, although a more specific Arab realm would exclude both Turkey and Iran. Several physical and cultural features serve to isolate and present certain general congruencies within the region: its position through time immemorial as the link between Asia, Europe and Africa; its pervasive Islamic religion and culture; the dominance of Semitic peoples; the prevailing and unifying Arabic language; and the constant physical effect and perceptual characteristics deriving from the juxtaposition of the desert and the sown. It is this proximity of the desert, with its aridity providing sustenance to the founders of the three great monotheist creeds and to its inhabitants, the nomadic Bedouin, that despite supposed development and change represents and will forever represent the underlying constancy of the region and its peoples. Furthermore, it is against and within this broader context that we should situate the question of Israel's entry into Palestine.

Four states now occupy the area of the eastern Mediterranean: Israel, Jordan, the Lebanon and Syria. Syria, a province of the former Turkish Empire, later became part of the French Mandate, and since 1941 has been an independent republic. Lebanon, previously a part of southern Syria, became independent in 1941 as well. To the east of the Jordan River is the Arab state of Jordan.

The area of Israel within the boundaries as set by the 1949 armistice agreements with Egypt, Jordan, the Lebanon and Syria is 7,993 square miles (20,700 square kilometres). Over 50 percent of Israel so defined is comprised of the Negev Desert. In addition, the West Bank has an area of 2,200 square miles (5,900 square kilometres). Israel approximates in size to Wales' 8,016 square miles. By contrast, Great Britain is 89,038 square miles (Fig. 1), Vermont is 9,267, Vancouver Island in British Columbia is 13,049, and Tasmania is 26,215 square miles. In January 1979 Israel's population was estimated at 3.82 million, and the populations of areas under Israeli administration as a result of the Six Day War of 1967 are estimated at about 1.2 million: c.800,000 residing in Judea and Samaria, c.420,000 in the Gaza Strip and Northern Sinai, and c.2,000 in the Golan Heights.

The general physical structure and configuration of the Holy Land is quite simple, yet the details are complex (see Beaumont, Blake and Wagstaff, Ch. 16, 1976). There are four parallel, approximately north-south zones. A discontinuous Mediterranean coastal plain is where two-thirds of the country's population reside; three major urban blocks are located in this coastal region: from north to south, Haifa-Acre (264,000), Tel Aviv-Yafo (1.3 million) and Ashkelon-Ashdod (110,000). The overall impression of the region is of an alternation of towns, agricultural villages, private farms and citrus groves. On the landward side of the coastal plain is a plateau region comprised of a series of mostly limestone hills and fertile basins, divided into two sections by the Plain of Esdraelon: in the north, the hills of the Galilee, and in the centre and south, the hills of Samaria and Judea. Further east and still parallel to the coast is the downfaulted Jordan rift valley, while the uplands of Jordan lie farther east. To the south lies the Negev Desert, geographically a northern extension of the Sinai. Since 1981 the Golan Heights, a steep, sloping and elevated basalt plateau,

Vermont, USA

ISRAEL

| 0 | 100 | 200 | 300 | 400 | km |
| 0 | | 100 | | 200 | 300 | miles |

FIGURE 1. Israel, the United Kingdom and Vermont

has been included within the Israeli state.

Climatically Israel is transitional between a Mediterranean climate in the west and north and the more arid deserts of the south and east. Characteristic over the northern and central regions is a winter rainfall of rather more than 600mm, a rainless summer ameliorated by heavy dews and much humidity, and a relatively small range in mean temperature and an absence of killing frosts. The Jordan valley has a quite regular rainfall of about 500mm, although the value of this precipitation is limited by an excessive mean summer temperature, lower humidity and reduced dew-fall. The south receives an average of between 400 and 300mm of rainfall, yet suffers from prolonged periods of drought.

A central thesis of this volume is that any understanding of the recent colonization and settlement of the Holy Land by Zionists should be based not only upon an appraisal of the territorial aspirations of the colonists but also upon a deeper appreciation of the fundamental Hebrew system of beliefs in which *land*, the Promised Land, plays a central if not the central and crucial role. The modern development of Zionism is viewed as an outgrowth of this latent Jewish nationalism which for long had remained as an enshrined and symbolic yearning for a special place. Maier (1975), considering Jungian psychological and Lorenzian ethological concepts, considered Jewish history in terms of territorial symbolism, suggesting that the Torah became the conceptual substitute for the Promised Land as a type of movable, indeed abstract territory. However, here it will be demonstrated that Torah was never and never could be a substitute for real land. Rather it must be seen as a deed of title between Israel and God with solemn obligations on behalf of both parties (Newman, 1962; von Waldov, 1974). We would here suggest some comparison with the ideas of Gwyn Williams who has demonstrated, in a quite different context, the historic necessity for an element of fabrication in romantic nationalism (Williams, 1982). No real understanding of the development of historical Israel, nor of the modern state of Israel, is possible without an appreciation of land, God-given land as *storied place*.

Israel into Palestine is in three main parts. The first three chapters provide a background to and promote an understanding of both the region and Israel: the dispersal of Israel from out of the land of Israel, the emergence of Zionism in the later nineteenth century and its developing colonial activities within the Holy Land. The end of the Ottoman Empire, the quickening of Arab nationalism and the mounting crisis of Jewish immigration are seen to link, inexorably, with Western colonial ambitions within the Middle East, the so-called 'Cross-Roads'. Chapter 4 provides a brief presentation on the place of region, its geopolitical context, and considers the emerging relationships within the region between 1948 and 1967. The further expansion of Israel after the war of 1967 is considered in Chapter 5 together with an evaluation of Israeli settlement policies. This section includes reports of continuing personal field enquiries within the West Bank and East Jerusalem. The penultimate chapter focuses attention upon the potential bases for agreement and the possible future scenarios that present themselves. The final chapter, both an epilogue and postscript, brings the volume right up to date at the time of going to press.

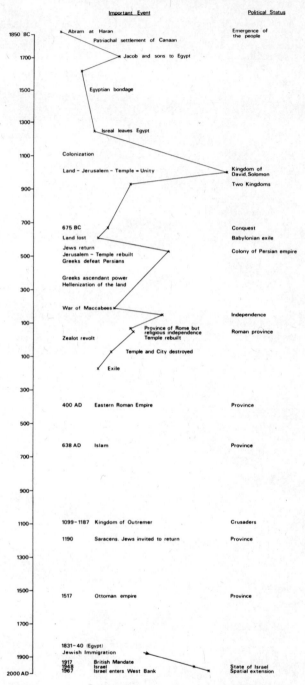

Important Event   Political Status

Time	Important Event	Political Status
1850 BC	Abram at Haran	Emergence of the people
	Patriachal settlement of Canaan	
1700	Jacob and sons to Egypt	
1500	Egyptian bondage	
1300	Isreal leaves Egypt	
1100	Colonization	
	Land - Jerusalem - Temple = Unity	Kingdom of David, Solomon
900		Two Kingdoms
700	675 BC	Conquest
	Land lost	Babylonian exile
500	Jews return Jerusalem - Temple rebuilt Greeks defeat Persians	Colony of Persian empire
300	Greeks ascendant power Hellenization of the land	
	War of Maccabees	Independence
100		
	Zealot revolt	Province of Rome but religious independence Temple rebuilt
100	Temple and City destroyed	Roman province
300	Exile	
400 AD	Eastern Roman Empire	Province
500		
638 AD	Islam	Province
700		
900		
1100	1099-1187 Kingdom of Outremer	Crusaders
	1190 Saracens. Jews invited to return	Province
1300		
1500	1517 Ottoman empire	Province
1700		
1900	1831-40 (Egypt) Jewish Immigration	
	1917 British Mandate	
	1948 Israel	State of Israel
2000 AD	1967 Israel enters West Bank	Spatial extension

FIGURE 2. The Jews in the Promised Land

CHAPTER 1

Historical Background
to the Holy Land

Arabia and the development of Israel

Basic to any understanding of present-day Israel is the need to be familiar with the emergence of this part of the Middle East, the Levant or Sham; to know the movements and discern the differentiation of the peoples; to recognize the forces that served to evolve the Jews into a people associated with a specific land; and to appreciate the durability of such sentiments despite the passage of time and the dispersal of the Jews from the land of Israel. In this chapter we shall consider briefly the development and progressive separation of the Hebrews from the larger group of nomads, their emergence as the *chosen people* that enabled them to attain a special identity.

In ancient times the region referred to as the Arabian peninsula or Arabia generally comprised the peninsula itself and an area extending northwards and eastwards in an arcuate form from Egypt in the west to include Mesopotamia in the east (Zeidan, 1922, p.29). This region possessed a certain overall unity of ethnic stock, Semites, with a primarily desert-peninsula heartland as the origin of peoples who migrated outwards to its peripheral crescent (Fig. 3). It was to this so-termed Fertile Crescent that the cyclical movement of peoples, the first commencing in c.4500 B.C., was largely directed and which, in turn, was to nurture the development of the great civilizations, particularly in Egypt and Mesopotamia, that in time were to lay the foundations for Western civilization.

By the middle of the fourth millenium B.C., with the creation of large agricultural surpluses, specialization of occupations, increasing diversification within and stratification of a society headed by a literate élite who possessed and were fortified by religious beliefs, the lower Euphrates–Tigris basin contained a large number of prosperous, walled cities. With their adjacent irrigation systems, fields and villages, these became organized into such independent, self-contained, theocratic states as Ur, Kisiga, Larsa, Isin and Eridu which according to legend is the earliest city in history (Lampl, 1968).

1

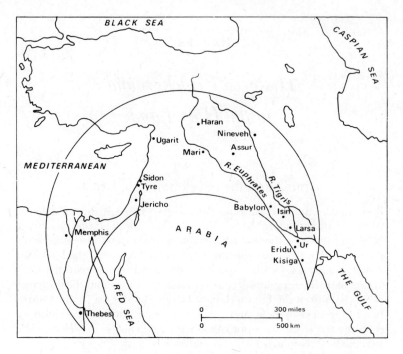

FIGURE 3. The Fertile Crescent: an inseparable part of Arabia and the
'Cradle of Civilization'

In about 2500 B.C. a further wave of Semitic wandering shepherds,
the Arameans, previously located in northern Arabia, settled along
the Euphrates and spread their clans throughout the region. Abram
was, apparently, of one such clan that settled about Ur of the Chaldees. Early in the nineteenth century B.C., Terah, Abram's father, led
his nomadic band with its herds out of Ur to Haran in the northwest,
necessitating a journey of some 800 miles. At that time Ur and the
region in general was experiencing a period of prolonged inter-city
hostilities, often referred to as the Isin-Larsa period (1955–1755 B.C.).
Isin and Larsa were the two rival city-states locked in combat for
control over the surrounding cities and their tributary areas for most
of the period. At this time other groups of these wandering Aramean
shepherds left the Euphrates to settle in Syria and Jordan and some
even entered the margins of Egypt.

The sojourn of the Terah clan at Haran in upper Mesopotamia
(Genesis 11:31) probably allowed the flocks and herds to recover and
replenish from the ravages of the lengthy journey from Ur. At that
time Haran was an important Aramean centre, possessing good pas-

2

tures; the various Aramean deities were worshipped, including Te-
menos of Nannar, the Moon-god. In about 1850 B.C. Terah died at
Haran and Abram, his son and heir, became leader of the clan. Quite
suddenly a previously unknown, powerful God revealed himself to
Abram saying:

> Get thee out of thy country, and from thy kindred, and from thy
> father's house, unto a land that I will shew thee: And I will make
> thee a great nation, and I will bless thee, and make thy name great,
> and thou shalt be a blessing. (Genesis 12: 1–2)

The particular importance of this covenant is that the Lord promised
these wanderers alone a specific land, nationality and distinctive
separateness. Abram left Haran to journey 700 miles westwards to the
land of Canaan, the Promised Land. It should be noted that the
Abramic clan was still nomadic, differentiated from the Semitic Canaanites who occupied the land of Canaan by little more than religion.
Yet this religion and the distinctiveness of the people, the *chosen people*,
was to be of particular importance: 'And the Lord appeared unto
Abram and said, Unto thy seed will I give this land' (Genesis 12: 7).

The specific and precise separation of the Jews from the Arabs
occurred, supposedly, through the two sons of Abram, Ishmael and
Isaac. Whereas the covenant between God and Abram asserted, 'And
I will give unto thee, and thy seed after thee ... all the land of Canaan'
(Genesis 17: 8), Ishmael, Abram's first born son by Haggar, his second
wife (Genesis 16), was specifically dispossessed of this covenant by God
(Genesis 17: 19). God is quoted by Jewish historians as having specified
that Abram's second son, Isaac, born to his first wife, Sarah, and
Isaac's issue would inherit the covenant. The reported subsequent
lack of concern for Ishmael, despite Abram's intercession with God on
his first son's behalf (Genesis 17: 18) is summarized in Genesis 17: 20
and 25: 12. The rapacious, bitter, grasping Sarah, we are told, caused
Abram literally to force out Haggar and Ishmael into the desert,
admonishing Abram, 'Cast out this bondwoman and her son for the
son of this bondwoman shall not be heir with my son, *even* with Isaac'
(Genesis 21: 11). Ishmael, reputedly the father of the Arab race, is
blessed and made fruitful. Indeed God is quoted as promising that, 'I
will make him [Ishmael] a great nation' (Genesis 21: 18). But nothing
approaching the Covenant is offered to Ishmael. This Old Testament
theological story again serves to reinforce the notion of the physical
and the spiritual separation of Israel from the rest of mankind and to
establish a particular fidelity between the Israelites alone and a particular place. Even this brief philosophico-theological inquiry into the
mystery of Ishmael and Isaac reveals a particular, irresistible and
indeed awful significance that may not be lightly dismissed as

simply another ordinary politico-economic struggle.

After entry into Canaan the Abramic clan continued on in its nomadic ways and in one specific famine entered Egypt, later returning to Canaan (Genesis 12: 10–20). Various documentary sources such as the Petersburg papyrus tell us of the waves of nomads who endeavoured to enter Egypt in search of water and grazing lands, particularly in times of drought. It was a further migration of the descendants of Abram, suffering from drought and famine in Canaan, who entered Egypt at Joseph's behest in about 1706 B.C.: 'And they took their cattle, and their goods which they had gotten in the land of Canaan, and came into Egypt, Jacob, and all his seed with him' (Genesis 46: 6). Genesis 45: 10 recounts how the sons of Jacob, Israel, came to live in the land of Goshen, that area to the east and southeast of the Nile delta, to the west of the Bitter Lakes, now forming part of the Suez Canal, and to the north of present-day Cairo. The important point is that even in its Egyptian exile of some four centuries, Israel not only maintained but increased its identity and distinctiveness: 'And the children of Israel were fruitful, and increased abundantly, and multiplied, and waxed exceeding mightily: and the land was filled with them' (Exodus 1: 7).

It was, however, the departure of the Hebrews from Egypt in c.1275 B.C. and the Sinaic covenant under Moses, that served to separate further these people from the larger Semitic group of wanderers in the Middle East, generally termed 'Apiru (Greenberg, 1970). This covenant possessed certain antecedents in the earlier Noahic covenant and in that between God and Abram (Genesis 15: 18).

At Kadesh-Barnea in the Sinai, that 'great and terrible wilderness' (Deuteronomy 1: 19), in the first half of the thirteenth century B.C. these Hebrews entered with a far more specific covenantal obligation with Yahweh. The Mosaic covenant was clarified when God said:

'Behold, I make a covenant: before all thy people I will do marvels ... Observe then that which I command thee this day: behold I drive out before thee the Amorite, and the Canaanite, and the Hittite, and the Perrizite, and the Hivite, and the Jebusite. (Exodus 34: 10–11)

In exchange for His side of the bargain, God required, 'For thou [Israel] shalt worship no other god: for the Lord whose name is Jealous is a jealous God' (Exodus 34: 14).

There follows in the subsequent nine verses of Exodus the specific covenantal details and duties that the Israelites must undertake. Later God again reassured Israel that acceptance and adherence to these strictures would earn for Israel its desired result, that is distinctiveness and possession of its land: 'For I will cast out the nations before thee, and enlarge thy borders' (Exodus 34:24).

The overall importance of this covenant was that a forlorn, despairing, landless people were given hope, particularly a hope for possession of land. The desert thus symbolized the wilderness, aridity, wanderings, uncertainties, privations and fear. 'The Bible is addressed to the central human problem of homelessness (*anomie*) and seeks to respond to that agenda in terms of grasp and gift' (Brueggeman, 1977, p.187). No real understanding of the development of Israel can be forthcoming without an appreciation of the impact of the covenant of land on a lost, displaced, afraid and homeless people wandering in a wilderness (Davies, 1974, p.194; *see also* Tuan, 1979, p.6).

The basic human need for security was to be attained by God's offer of land (Exodus 31:10-11).

> The [Mosaic] covenant is characteristically about land, about the promise of land not given, about retention of land now possessed, and about land loss because of covenant breaking. Israel never had a desire for a relation with Yahweh in a vacuum but only in land. (Bruggeman, 1977, p.188).

This special relationship between Israel and Yahweh itself did much not only to create and differentiate Israel but also to maintain its unity and corporate identity even in periods of wandering and dispersal. Indeed, it may be suggested that this *chosen people* deserved and needed this further traumatic 'wilderness experience' in the Sinai where God was again to provide care and guidance (*see* Hosea 2:14). The cult established by Moses in the desert recognized a Yahweh who would accept no rival; therefore, Moses reacted with fury when the people worshipped the golden calf, for long a fertility symbol in Egypt (Exodus 32). This bowing before an idol was not just the breaking of the first commandment; for a terrible moment, Israel lost her distinctiveness from the rest of mankind. Such a catastrophe to the developing national consciousness caused Moses to order the killing of about 3,000 men who refused to adhere to the strictures of the commandments. Recognizing the need for a visible and constant focus of God's presence in their midst, Moses established the tabernacle and various sacrificial, fasting requirements; God again pledged land as the reward to his chosen people for service (Exodus 33:1).

The Israelites, both while in Egyptian bondage and in their wanderings within the Sinai wilderness were without home territory and lacked the essential basis for security (*see* Hall, 1966, and Jakle, Brun and Roseman, 1976, pp.37-49). The real contribution of Moses, in gaining release for the newly differentiated people who clearly believed they had been 'chosen', was the promise of land.

C.G. Howie shows how the Mosaic covenant conforms to the format of the suzerainty treaty widely used within the Hittite empire, such a treaty having six parts (1967, p.9):

1. Preamble, naming the speaker
2. Historical prologue, tracing history
3. Stipulations and requirements
4. Provision for deposit in temple
5. Gods called to witness
6. Curses and blessings

The first three parts are clearly seen in the following:

1. Preamble: 'I am the Lord thy God' (Exodus 20:2)
2. Historical prologue: 'Who brought you out of the land of Egypt, out of the house of bondage' (Exodus 20:2)
3. Stipulations and requirements (Exodus 20:3–17):
   a. Thou shalt have no other gods
   b. No image of God
   c. No vain use of God's name
   d. No breach of the Sabbath
   e. Honour parents
   f. No murder
   g. No adultery
   h. No stealing
   i. No false witness
   j. No covetousness

To these several stipulations must, of course, be added the most important, the worship of God by His people.

Yet, surprisingly, perhaps revealing the depth of suspicion of the covenantal promise, these Hebrews still had doubts and hesitated. Moses, at the Lord's command, instructed Israel to march directly into Canaan via the Negev, 'Notwithstanding ye (Israel) would not go up, but rebelled against the commandment of the Lord your God' (Deuteronomy 1:26). For this refusal Israel was condemned by a patient deity to wander in the desert for the next thirty-eight years until virtually all of the adults had died.

At about that time the emerging concept of monotheism, that there is but one supreme being, was becoming inexorably intertwined with the land theme. In the sixth chapter of Deuteronomy both concepts appear together:

Now these are the commandments, the statutes, and the judge-ments, which the Lord your God commanded to teach you, that you might do them in the land whither ye go to possess it. (Deuter-onomy 6:1)

6

Hear, O Israel: The Lord our God is one Lord. And you shalt love the Lord thy God with all thine heart, and with all thy soul, and with all thy might. (Deuteronomy 6: 4–5)

These historic words indicate that the Hebraic understanding of God, which continues in Christianity, is emphatically monotheistic:

The God of the Hebrews was originally worshipped as a tribal god, Jahweh of Israel, over against such foreign deities as Dagon of the Philistines and Chemosh of the Moabites. But the insistent, though at first incredible, message of the great prophets of the eighth, seventh, and sixth centuries before Christ (above all, Amos, Hosea, first Isaiah, Jeremiah, and second Isaiah) was that Jahweh was not only the God of the Hebrews but the Maker of heaven and earth and the Judge of all history and of all peoples. (Hick, 1973, p.5)

Despite the great impact of such a recognition of the universal deity, the base theme of land appears of almost equal importance:

And it shall be, when the Lord thy God shall have brought thee into the land which he swore unto thy fathers, to Abraham, to Isaac, and to Jacob, to give thee great and goodly cities, which thou buildest not. (Deuteronomy 6: 10)

What we are witnessing in this man-land relationship, in social anthropological terms, is a fine example of a specific totemic relationship: 'A totem is something which is exclusively regarded as the property of a particular clan and which plays a crucial part in its identity' (Hicks, 1976, p.26). Here we have in juxtaposition *our* God, Israel and *our* land, a notable example of the sacred and secular that would serve to seal with reverence an unbreakable unity.

Later, prior to their momentous entry into the Promised Land, they paused with the wilderness behind them and the land before them. God unequivocally related again the basis of the covenantal details:

See, I have set before thee this day life and good, and death and evil, in that I command thee this day to love the Lord thy God, to walk in his ways, and to keep his commandments and his statutes and his judgements, that thou mayst live and multiply: and the Lord thy God shall bless thee in the land whither thou goest to possess it. But if thine heart turn away, so that thou wilt not hear, but shall be drawn away, and worship other gods, and serve them; I denounce unto you this day, that ye shall surely perish, and that ye shall not prolong your days upon the land, whither thou passest over Jordan to go to possess it. (Deuteronomy 30: 15–18)

The position is clear. Possession of the land was and must always be conditional.

7

The Israelites' entry into the Promised Land commenced about 1240 B.C., although this was the same land entered by Abram some seven hundred years earlier. The colonial activities of these Israelites again emphasized a separatist consciousness from the original 'unclean' people of the land and 'their abominations' (Rowley, 1981, pp.446-8):

> And I [the Lord] brought you into the land of the Amorites, which dwelt on the other side Jordan; and they fought with you: and I gave them into your hand, that ye might possess their land; and I destroyed them from before you. (Joshua 24:8)

Although the conquest of the land proceeded, the earlier inhabitants remained:

> And the children of Benjamin did not drive out the Jebusites that inhabited Jerusalem; but the Jebusites dwell with the children of Benjamin in Jerusalem unto this day. (Judges 1:21)

In fact, there were few Israelites in the land (Kenyon, 1967, p.62), 'and there remaineth yet very much land to be possessed' (Joshua 13:1). Later we are informed that, 'The children of Israel dwelt among the Canaanites, Hittites, and Amorites, and Perizzites, and Hivites, and Jebusites' (Judges 3:5).

Yet the purification of the land required an alternative separatist consciousness. Those who had entered into marriage with non-sectarian Israelites were admonished and instructed by God to:

> Separate yourselves from the people of the land, and from the strange wives . . . that ye may be strong and eat the good of the land, and leave it for an inheritance to your children for ever. (Ezra 10:11-12)

The overall impression gleaned from the various references is that the Israelites never appeared to be in sole occupation of the land; indeed some suggest that Israel never attained a numerical majority within the area (Glubb, 1971, p.52).

Whereas Moses had united a people, gained their release from Egypt and obtained a covenantal promise for the future in a special relationship with Yahweh, it was Joshua who was the guiding force in subduing the newly entered land, who presided over the transformation from a desert, nomadic people to a settled, agricultural community. Yet, throughout, Joshua had to maintain the spiritual leadership and allegiance to Yahweh in the face of the fertility cult of the sedentary Canaanites. He renewed the covenant between God and his people at Shechem (Joshua 24:25) and gained for the Hebrews the promised homeland while maintaining the identity of his people through their faith in Yahweh. There are, it is true, problems con-cerning the factual nature: did all these events actually take place? See discussion in some detail by Eichrodt (1961, p.37) and Newman (1962, pp.29–38). However with the Israelites, 'We are dealing with traditions cherished and handed down by people transmitting in the most solemn way their view of their own origins, not with history as such. What is important is what remained engraved on the national memory' (Daiches, 1975, p.7).

Although nationalism is usually considered a quite recent post-Renaissance development, the Hebrew notion arose from a clearly defined consciousness of being different from other peoples, the Gentiles or pagans. This national character and enduring spiritual creative energy of the people came to form a cultural continuity that was to prove stronger than racial, political or geographic continuity. Israel in those far-off times came to represent the strong consciousness of a cultural mission, possessing three of the essential traits of modern nationalism: the idea of the *chosen people* (Covenant), the emphasis on a common stock of memory of the past and of hopes for the future (destiny), and national messianism.

Throughout this initial section we have examined the emergence and differentiation of a people in relation to their deity. By contrast, a Marxist theory of historical materialism would suggest that history is made by man, not by destiny or the so-called 'Hand of God'. In essence history is the life of the people. The Marxist view of religion is as a combination of beliefs and cult-practices that subordinate human existence to a divine super-order, appearing in history as a form of opposition of the people by a ruling 'class'. Marxism thus sees in religion the exploitation of human ignorance and credulity. However, some would suggest that although such religions as Judaism, Christianity and Islam have subordinated people to the devine super-order, they are not in and of themselves exploitive.

It was under David (c.1000–c.961 B.C.) and Solomon (c.961–922 B.C.) that Israel flowered. Jebus, an important Jebusite town dating from c.4000 B.C. was taken by David as his capital and renamed Jerusalem in c.1000 B.C.; under David the tribes of Israel became united in the land. During the reign of Solomon the territorialization of conceptual space became a reality, with Israel achieving its maximum territorial extent and the Temple constructed.

David, the warrior king, is followed remarkably by his son Solomon, the stabiliser, the result of David's adulterous relationship with Bathsheeba, wife of Uriah the Hittite who was indirectly killed at the behest of David (II Samuel 11:15). Thus Solomon, although Jewish, was not a Jew. It is interesting to note how this enduring story fits into the diptych format suggested by De Jouvenal, 'Every people has its "foundation-legend", in which a forceful hero appears and the forces of chaos are tamed. This legend, be it noted, seldom lacks its crime' (1957, p.45).

Paradoxically from this position of strength and attainment of Israel came discord, disunity and the division of the kingdom. In the aftermath of Solomon's death in 926 B.C. and following a period of internecine tribal quarrels Israel became split into two kingdoms. The ten northern tribes seceded under Jeroboam as Israel, being in an almost constant state of conflict with Judah, ruled by Rehoboam from Jerusalem in the south (Fig. 4).

By 675 B.C. both kingdoms had been conquered, Israel by the Assyrians and Judah by the Babylonians. By 660 B.C. the Assyrians had extended their empire to Thebes, the capital of Upper Egypt No-Amon, and Ur of the Chaldees (Fig. 5). With the death of the Assyrian king Ashurbanipal in 626 B.C. a coalition of Medes and Neo-Babylonians succeeded in defeating the Assyrians. At the turn of the sixth century B.C. Judah refused to pay tribute to and rebelled against the ruling Neo-Babylonians. Then, some six hundred and fifty years after

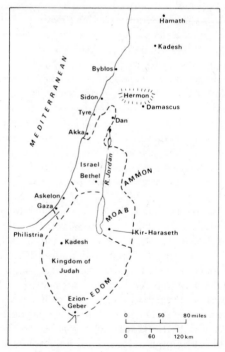

FIGURE 4. The divided kingdom of Israel and Judah, c.850 B.C.

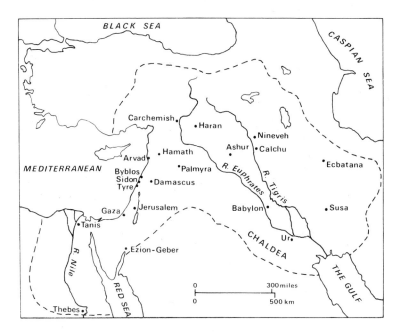

FIGURE 5. The Assyrian Empire, c.660 B.C.

Joshua had led Israel over the Jordan into the Promised Land, the greater part of the population of Judah was 'deported into exile to Babylon' (II Kings 24: 10–15). The vassal state of Judah was greatly reduced in territorial size.

In 538 B.C., after fifty years of exile, Cyrus, King of Persia, conquered Babylon and a year later allowed the Israelites, about 42,000 in number, to return to the land (Ezra 2: 1–3 and 64–7). By 515 B.C. King Solomon's Temple and much of the city of David in Jerusalem had been rebuilt and Israel settled down as a small theocracy within the Persian empire. The Persian defeat by the Greeks at Marathon in 491 B.C. heralded the eventual demise of the Persians, the replacement of the previous eastern and southern, primarily continental, controls by a western maritime influence. In 333 B.C. at Issus, near present-day Alexandretta in Northern Syria, the Macedonians under Alexander the Great became the ascendant power and the theocracy of Judah was quietly absorbed into the Hellenistic realm.

Upon the death of Alexander in 323 B.C., Judah was incorporated into the kingdom of the Hellenistic Ptolemies centred in Egypt and the foreign influence became increasingly manifest in Judah. By 195 B.C. the expansionist Seleucids of Antioch, one of the other successor states of Alexander's empire, had pushed west and south and taken

11

over Judah (Fig. 6). Direct Hellenization of the land of Judah was prompt, forthright and vigorous. The Temple was plundered and desecrated in 168 B.C. and an edict was published to destroy the faith of Israel. These actions led directly to open resistance in the War of the Maccabees.

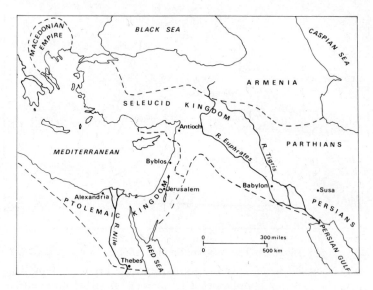

FIGURE 6. The Hellenistic Empire, 300 B.C.

After a series of remarkable guerilla attacks Judas Maccabaeus liberated Jerusalem in 164 B.C. and reinstated the old order in the Temple. Despite Judah's eventual defeat in 162 B.C., the Seleucids offered surprisingly favourable terms to the vanquished. Liberty of worship was guaranteed and the religious community at Jerusalem was again recognized. Not content with religious freedoms alone, however, the Maccabees strove for political independence which they achieved in 142 B.C. (I Maccabees 15:8-9). By 100 B.C. the borders of Judah were extended almost to the area covered by the earlier Israel and Judah (Fig. 7). In 63 B.C. the political independence of Judah came to an abrupt end and it was incorporated as a province within the Roman Empire. In 40 B.C. Herod, with Roman support, became king of Judaea and rebuilt the Temple for the second time. In 70 A.D. the Zealots or Sicarii (Assassins) revolted against Imperial Roman rule, only to be quashed by Titus who savagely destroyed the Temple, virtually the entire city of Jerusalem and much of its population. Under the Roman Emperor Hadrian Jerusalem was designated a

12

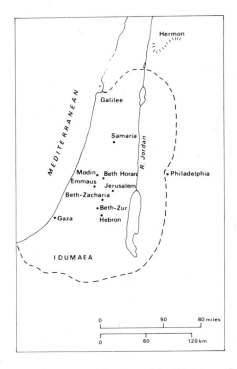

FIGURE 7. Greatest areal extent of the Kingdom of the
Maccabees, 100 B.C.

Roman colony, Aelia Capitolina, in which Jews were forbidden either
to reside or enter, and in an attempt to blot out Jewish identity in the
land Judah was renamed Palestine, supposedly after the Philistines,
an Aegean people. From 135 A.D. the Jews were dispersed from out of
the land. The crisis of the dispersal into the Diaspora was to prove
somewhat similar to the entrance of Israel into the Promised Land in
c.1250–1200 B.C. It was a further test of the people's fidelity to the
faith. In this the Law was to be the central guide and honoured above
all else, and in this manner the identity of the people would be
preserved in distant lands. This basic function of the Law was the
same for the time of Sinai wanderings and colonization of the Promised
Land.

Following the division of the Roman empire in c.400 A.D., Palestine
was governed for over 200 years as part of the Eastern Empire from
Constantinople. In 638 A.D. it came under Islamic Arab rule and
remained so for eight centuries, except for a short break of 88 years
from 1099 when the Crusaders Christian Kingdom of Outremer ruled

13

from Jerusalem. Palestine, or in Arabic, Filastin, thus became a pre-dominantly Arab and Islamic region by the end of the seventh century (Fig. 8). Saladin, the Saracen ruler, defeated the Christian Kingdom in 1187. In 1190 Saladin invited the Jews to return to the land and in 1517 Palestine was conquered by the Ottomans and remained within

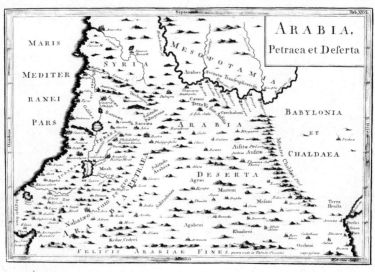

FIGURE 8. W.H. Toms' map of *Arabia Petraea and Deserta* dates from the period 1723-58

that empire for some four hundred years to 1917, except for a brief interlude in 1831–40, when Palestine came under Egyptian suzerainty. In 1917 Palestine was captured from the Ottomans by British forces and Arabs under Faisal and placed under British military administration, the period of the Mandate. At this time, according to the 1914 census, the total population of Palestine numbered almost 690,000, of whom 56,000 (8.83 per cent) were Jews. The majority of Jews resided within Jerusalem.

The end of the Ottoman Empire— imperial objectives and counter proposals

The period of the death throes of the Ottoman Empire witnessed the emergence of a vital Arab nationalism. Early in the second decade of the twentieth century Jamil Mardam Bey, a Syrian, and Hamdy al Pachachi, an Iraqi, founded *Al Fatat*, the Young Arab movement. During World War I the British Government sought an alliance with

14

the Arabs to defeat the Turks, and in return the Arabs were given definite assurances of self-government. Duplicity, trickery and chicanery characterized British dealings with the Arabs throughout the period of waning Ottoman rule. Arab help was thought necessary to 'Our cheap and speedy victory in the East, and that better we win and break our word than lose' (Lawrence, 1978, p.24). However, Lawrence clung romantically to a mistaken belief that following upon the victory, 'expediency would counsel to the Great Powers a fair settlement of their [the Arabs] claims' (Lawrence, 1978, p.24). But the secret Sykes-Picot Agreement had already divided the area into British and French spheres.

The Sykes-Picot Agreement suggested a partitioning of Iraq and Syria between a French sphere of influence in the north and a British sphere to the south, with a Palestine under international administration. This agreement only came to light after the Bolsheviks made it public in December 1917. The shocked British and French governments simultaneously issued a joint Anglo-French statement in November 1918, which sought to reassure the native peoples of the region that:

> The goal envisaged by France and Great Britain ... is the complete and final liberation of the peoples who have for so long been oppressed by the Turks, and the setting up of national governments and administrations that shall derive their authority from the free exercise of the initiatives and choice of the indigenous populations.

In fact a mounting and direct British interest in the general area about Palestine developed from the second half of the nineteenth century. Until the construction of the Suez Canal (1869), for example, the almost uninhabited Sinai desert was regarded as of little political consequence. Following the British conquest of Egypt the first British Governor, Lord Cromer, in 1892 interpreted the border as running from El-Arish to Aqaba. However, it appears that Britain, with an eye to its Indian Empire, became increasingly apprehensive for the Suez Canal–Red Sea with the progress of the Hejaz railway in 1905 and the alleged plan for a branch line to Aqaba. Pressure was brought to bear on Turkey to sign an agreement that fixed the Ottoman–Egyptian boundary in an almost straight line from Rafah to Ras Taba, excepting the Gaza Strip. The subsequent British move into Palestine was a continuation of this concern with the Suez Canal in particular and the Middle East in general.

The San Remo Conference, which assembled in April 1920, clearly disregarded the Covenant of the League of Nations of January 1920. That Covenant contained specific provisions for the Arab countries, stipulating that the wishes of the populations concerned were to be a principal consideration in the selection of the Mandate. In his seminal study, G. Antonius has shown that, in reality, each power grabbed as much territory as the other would allow (Antonius, 1938, p.353). Relating to Syria the powers went further in their disregard of this pledge of the 'well-being and development of its people' by deciding upon a dismemberment and partition into three separate states, Syria, Palestine and Transjordania.

The British sought to undermine the Arab nationalist movement by buying over the desert chieftains, the parvenu Hashemites, who became puppet kinglets of the imperialists, Abdullah in Transjordan and Faisal in the client state of Iraq. The colonialist territorial division between Britain and France artificially split up the previously integrated area of Sham, that is Syria and Palestine and its cities of Jerusalem, Damascus, Haifa and Beirut (Amin, 1978, p.45), although:

> The country had a unity of its own in more ways than one. In spite of the great diversity of its physical features, it was geographically one and formed a self-contained unit enclosed by well-defined natural frontiers. In the economic field, it had developed its agricultural and commercial life on a foundation of natural resources, and the whole country was criss-crossed with a close network of interdependent lines of activity, linking region to region, the countryside to the towns and the coast to the interior. It had also cultural and historical traditions of unity: ever since the Arab conquest, except for the interlude of the Crusades, it had formed one political unit and kept the language and customs which it had begun to acquire in the seventh century. On every essential count, it was clear that the well-being and future development of the country were bound to be retarded if its unity were destroyed. (Antonius, 1938, pp.352–3)

An alliance already existed between British imperialism and a western-orientated Zionism to create what Winston Churchill saw as a European-type buffer state in Palestine to maintain a presence in the Middle East in general and the Suez area in particular (Gilbert, 1975, pp.594–5). The basic Zionist thesis, as developed by Theodor Herzl in the last decade of the nineteenth century, sought to free Jews and solve problems of anti-Semitism in the West. Such a need was foreseen in the writings of Moses Hess who, in the third quarter of the nineteenth century, was suggesting that:

> It is only with a national rebirth that the religious genius of the Jews, like the giant of the legend touching Mother Earth, will be endowed with new strength and again be inspired with the prophetic spirit (Hess, 1943, p.77) ... What we have to do at present

16

for the regeneration of the Jewish nation is first to keep alive the hope of the political rebirth of our people and next to reawaken the hope where it slumbers (p.146).

Hess sought to further his notions of a Jewish nationalism amongst the pious and more scholarly Jewry of Eastern Europe, particularly of Russia and Poland, including those who had moved into Western Europe from the East. Indeed it was the widespread and vicious pogroms against the Jews in Russia that finally brought to an end the illusion of assimilation that is said to have characterized much of the nineteenth century as a period of enlightenment and provided a particular and immediate impetus and catalyst both to the debut and development of Zionism (Birnbaum, 1982; Halevi, 1981).

This influx of Eastern Jewry with its superior standards of religious scholarship, Epstein suggests, saved Western European Jewry from distintegration and extinction through assimilation and acculturation (1959, p.30). However, Herzl translated this germ of an idea on Jewish nationalism into a vital world movement possessing specific political aspirations; his rhetoric and vision were inseparable from and should be considered against the background of the recent unification of Germany under Bismarck. Later refinements realized the notion of the Jewish state, *Judenstaat*; locations in Latin America and British East Africa were considered, but Palestine was finally accepted as the area in which the historic foundations of a Jewish homeland could be recognized.

In Basle in 1897 Herzl convened the first Zionist Congress which formulated the specific intent and purpose of political Zionism concluding that 'Zionism aims to establish a publicly and legally assured home for the Jewish people'. The agenda sought to establish a renewed Jewish nationalism throughout the Diaspora by providing a focus for world Jewry at a time of mounting crises for religions in general and particularly where the religious Law was of fundamental importance as the bond to a *chosen people*. Max Nordau, converted to Zionism by Theodor Herzl in 1895, became one of Zionism's chief leaders. His ideas of Reconstructuralism, based on a faith in rationality, viewed Jewish 'peoplehood or nationhood' rather than religion as the central aspect of Judaism (Baldwin, 1980). Zionism thus became a further point of unification for Jews in the post-Darwinian age; Zionism, aided by and a facet of Western imperialism, gained in momentum to become, 'A movement looking toward the segregation of Jewish people upon a national basis and in a particular home of its own' (Singer, 1939, p.666).

Opposed to these positive decisions that led to Zionism and the notion of a Jewish state is a negative aspect: Western European countries were increasingly loathe to accept the multitude of Jews fleeing the Russian pogroms and persecution in all Eastern Europe except Hungary. The response of the British government was the Aliens Act of 1906, enacted in the period of the Campbell–Bannerman Liberal administration that is considered to have been one of the greatest social-reforming British governments of all time.

The Times, 1 May 1905, set the background to the Aliens Bill by quoting from a Board of Trade report and commenting on the problem:

> The immigration of Russians and Poles, nearly all of whom are said to be Jews, amounted to 28,511 in 1902, to 30,046 in 1903, and to 46,095 in 1904. It is at least probable that it will reach 50,000 in the year now proceeding ... Apart from the seething mass of poverty and of criminality which has thus been forced upon the attention of the public, it is well known to all who have inquired into the subject that the Russian and Polish immigrants as a rule consist of persons who are habituated to a lower standard of cleanliness and comfort than that which prevails among even the humblest of our own poor, and that they are content to work for wages upon which no industrious Englishman, however much might be said to be sweated by an employer, could attempt to live ... [The English inhabitants of the East End of London are becoming] more and more impatient of the presence of their unsavoury and unwelcome neighbours, and more and more anxious that the plague of their continual coming should be stayed (p.9).

While Mr Balfour, who had preceded Sir Henry Campbell-Bannerman as Prime Minister, praised the aims of the Bill he emphasized that the Bill sought simply to limit immigration and had nothing to do with the so-called Jewish question. In his concluding remarks he clearly pointed to the main problem:

> I was very much struck by a personal anecdote which the right hon, member for East Fife [Mr Asquith] told the House in the course of his speech this afternoon. He said that he has been to study the operations of the Jewish Shelter Society, a society which, with the splendid generosity of the Jewish community of this country, has set itself to work to deal with immigrants, not always Jews but immigrants who have come in a state of extreme destitution and poverty to our shores. What did the right hon. gentleman tell us? He told us that these people were on their way in many cases to other countries, and he especially mentioned Argentina. He was told that they stayed here one or two months, and gradually, by ones and twos or in larger numbers, the charity of the great Jewish community here

enabled them to go to Argentina or North America. But who is it of these unfortunates who do not go to Argentina? Is it the fit, is it the healthy, is it those whom we should most desire to retain here if we have to receive immigrants as citizens of our country? No, Sir, those are they who go; but those who stay are those who would not be accepted either in America or Argentina, and would not be accepted by the Jewish community, and by the Jewish emigration societies themselves if the statements are true, as I am sure they are true, made by many speakers this afternoon, to the effect that these great Jewish emigration societies have most wisely and properly laid down the rule that only people such as those whom this Bill admits to this country shall be of the class allowed to go to their great settlements in Argentina. Is not that conclusive proof that unless we do something we must remain the sieve in which the useless dregs remain? (*The Times*, 3 May 1905, p.7)

Mr Balfour subsequently backed and gave a most definite fillip to the developing notion of the Zionist state within the Holy Land. Nowhere was this momentum more apparent than in the Balfour Declaration. On 2 November 1917, at the time of the advance into Palestine of the Allied force under General Allenby, Mr Balfour, then British Foreign Secretary, issued the following declaration:

His Majesty's Government view with favour the establishment in Palestine of a National Home for the Jewish people, and will use their best endeavours to facilitate the achievement of that object, it being understood that nothing shall be done which may prejudice the civil and religious rights of existing non-Jewish communities in Palestine, or the rights and political status enjoyed by the Jews in any other country (quoted in Luke and Keith-Roach, 1922, p.26).

In the light of Mr Balfour's earlier remarks upon the Aliens Bill before Parliament in 1905, the Balfour Declaration and the Jewish state set in the Holy Land are a deft example of 'passing the buck', satisfying both the exigency of Jewish migration and British imperial and strategic ambitions within the Middle East and points east.

While the Balfour Declaration recognized and indeed led in time to a formalization of British relations with Zionism, Mandel, considering Arab responses to Jewish immigration and settlement in Palestine prior to 1914, argues that, 'The Balfour Declaration was not so much the starting point of the [Arab-Zionist] conflict as a turning point which greatly aggravated an existing trend' (Mandel, 1976, p.231). The Balfour Declaration was endorsed by the principal Allied powers and incorporated into the unratified Treaty of Sèvres of August 1920, in which Turkey renounced her sovereignty over Palestine. The terms of the Treaty of Sèvres were repeated in the Treaty of Lausanne of

1923, which also provided for the Mandate system of the League of Nations. Under a Mandate of 24 July 1922 Palestine was allocated by the Supreme War Council to 'His Britannic Majesty'. In its preamble this Mandate repeated the key passage of the 'Balfour Declaration' reprinted above (Talal, 1979, p.10). The terms of the Mandate came into force on 29 September 1923.

Palestine, Iraq and Transjordania were mandated to Britain, and the Lebanon and Syria to France as 'A' type mandates, with a clear indication that future autonomy was being prescribed. The task of the 'A' mandatory power was defined as 'the rendering of administrative advice and assistance ... until such time as they [the mandated territories] are able to stand alone ... The wishes of these communities must be a principal consideration in the selection of the Mandatory.'

The 'A' type mandate was a rather special form, for in the 'B' and 'C' class mandates, such as Germany's former African colonies and Pacific islands, no such expectation of autonomy was prescribed.

A prime feature of the development of Jewish Palestine is that it was of external origin and control. Zionism must be viewed, therefore, not only as a movement of world Jewry which sought to colonialize a peripheral society but as a continuation of the colonial zeal experienced by generations of Western pioneers extending their civilization to foreign lands (c.f. Brown, 1972; Adams, 1975). To this end Article 5 of the Mandate for Palestine specified that:

> An appropriate Jewish Agency shall be recognized as a public body for the purpose of advising and cooperating with the Administration of Palestine in such economic, social and other matters as may affect the establishment of the Jewish national home and the interests of the Jewish population in Palestine, and, subject always to the control of the Administration, to assist and take part in the development of the country.

The League of Nations, by admitting the Balfour Declaration into the terms of the British Mandate, thus lent its support to the Zionist cause.

Throughout the mandatory period, with the co-operation of the British, Jewish institutions organized and directed the flow of financial resources and immigrants into Palestine. In 1929 the Jewish Agency for Palestine replaced the World Zionist Organization as the recognized public body. The British had already made contradictory promises, duly recognized by Balfour:

> The contradiction between the letter of the Covenant [the Anglo-French Declaration of 1918 promising the Arabs of former Ottoman colonies that as a reward for supporting the Allies they could have their independence] is even more flagrant in the case of the inde-

pendent nation of Palestine than in that of the independent nation of Syria. For in Palestine we do not propose even to go through the form of consulting the wishes of the present inhabitants of the country, though the American Commission has been going through the forms of asking what they are. The four great powers are committed to Zionism and Zionism, be it right or wrong, good or bad, is rooted in age-long tradition, in present needs, in future hopes, of far profounder import than the desire and prejudices of the 700,000 Arabs who now inhabit that ancient land. In my opinion that is right. (Quoted in Sykes, 1965, p.5).

In this manner the seeds of discord were sown and colonial Zionism was thereby set to enter and grow in the land of Palestine. The callous disregard of native rights by the British, the French and the Zionists, despite the quite precise stipulations of the Mandate, sought to identify the Arabs as backward, undeveloped, inferior orientals and in so doing present a de facto credence to justify the colonial aspirations of dispossession and displacement of the native Arab population.

CHAPTER 2

Zionism and Colonialism
in the Holy Land

Capitalism and colonialism within the Middle East

The integration of the Mashreq into the world capitalist system reflects
the growth of colonialism and capitalism in the Middle East. Al
Mashreq, the Arab East, includes Arabia, Syria (the present states of
Israel, Jordan, Lebanon and Syria) and Iraq, in contrast to Al Magh-
reb, the Arab West, that extends from Libya to the Atlantic; Egypt
and the Sudan occupy the middle of the Arab world. Even during the
latter part of the nineteenth century when the decaying underdevel-
oping Ottoman Empire was experiencing both direct and indirect
colonization by European capital and merchandise, the Ottomans
still managed to preserve some semblance of domination and overall
unity of the Mashreq through to about 1919.

During the pre-colonial era the tributary mode of production was
relatively undeveloped in the Arab world. Imperialism conjoined with
the old ruling class to impose itself upon the pre-capitalist agrarian
structures that were transformed into an agrarian capitalism. However this agrarian bourgeoisie was to become a dependent bourgeoisie,
brought about by drawing this peripheral region into the capitalistic
system. Subsistence economies were transformed into market-orien-
tated economies through the impact of European capitalism:

> Trade, combining export of agricultural produce and import of
> manufactures, determined the drift of major commercial operations
> in the mid-nineteenth century. Developments in foreign trade re-
> sulted in increased dependence of the economies of Syria, Lebanon
> and Palestine on foreign capital. (Smilianska, 1966, p.231)

The export of raw silk through Beirut provides a specific and prime
example of this process. Previously consumed in local industries
throughout the Mashreq, raw silk was exported in its entirety in the
years when world prices were high. Local industry declined and
inferior silk was imported from Turkey.

The provincialism that had characterized the decadent Arab world of the nineteenth century was particularly evident in the commercial role of the cities, being limited to localized hinterlands. Developing competition from European imports, increasing domination of external capital and the great decline in manufacturing industry dramatically changed this position and resulted in the virtual destruction of the local bourgeoisie artisan class (Issawi, 1966, pp.42–5; Amin, 1978, pp.39–40). Deprived of its ability to derive a surplus from its traditional trade with peasants via the urban centres, this artisan class increasingly became feudal and focused its attention upon the countryside through the development of latifundia (Bonné, 1960, p.188). The bourgeoisie sought to derive from the peasants the surplus that no longer came from trade within the urban centres (Hilan, 1969). In this way a new class of agrarian bourgeoisie—latifundiary landlords—was established by imperialism with the integration of agriculture into the capitalistic market, replacing a system of pre-capitalist landed property and feudal landlords who were in receipt of ground rents. Marx, as a matter of interest, emphasized repeatedly the non-capitalist character of such ground rents (Burns, 1935, pp.558–60). This attempt by the bourgeoisie artisan class to seek refuge in the countryside and to develop agricultural production for the capitalist market was short-lived and doomed to failure. With the emergence of Zionism and its rural settlement policies, there occurred a direct infusion of foreign European and North American capital into the rural milieu through the purchase and expropriation of rural lands.

At the time of the conferment on Great Britain of the Mandate for Palestine, a survey typified the country as of traditional, largely subsistence agriculture; the primitive methods of cultivation were matched by the clustered native-peasant Arab villages, dependent upon a perennial water supply. The largest concentrations of rural settlement and the most prosperous agriculture lay to the southeast of Jaffa and along the coastal plain near Mount Carmel and north of Acre. Elsewhere, apart from the Negev south of Be'er Sheva, the rural areas were characterized in the following manner, although changes were becoming increasingly manifest following the intrusion of Western capital and the introduction of better communications:

A sparse population living in economic isolation and employing very primitive methods naturally adopts a farming system based on bare fallowing. Land is cropped without manure until exhausted and then abandoned until a measure of fertility has been recovered. Increasing pressure of population, and the upward trend in the values of agricultural holdings and produce, the partition of common lands, improved communications and the practical demonstrations of better methods by new settlers are, however, having their effect. Manuring and a rotation of crops for the maintenance of fertility are becoming recognized practices, and, based on a system of mixed farming, should solve the problem of closer settlement and financial stability. (Luke and Keith-Roach, 1922, p.188)

Rural settlements have usually been considered by economists, land economists, economic historians and geographers from a viewpoint that has sought to evaluate the patterns, origins and functions of settlements (Clout, 1972). In reality the processes of rural settlement, invasion and colonization, expansion, spread and competition have generally proceeded in hand with political or military conquest and the movement by newcomers into an already occupied area. The modern Jewish colonization of Palestine commenced between 1880 and 1910. This 'return to the Land' was nowhere better expressed than within the national, religious-political and economic-social aspirations of the Jewish migrants into the rural areas of Palestine, particularly within the 'Hibat Zion' movement, the dominant collective structure for developing Jewish rural settlement. The financial instrument organized by world Jewry to aid this colonization and land acquisition developed into the Jewish National Fund, Keren Kayemeth Leyisrael, which was augmented after 1929 by the Foundation Fund, Keren Hayessod.

The Zionist rural settlement process utilized two types of settlement: the kibbutz and the moshav (Karmon, 1971, pp.82–90). The kibbutz is a collective village where property is held in common; from Eastern Europe, it was particularly favoured by Jewish settlers from Czarist Russia towards the end of the first decade of the twentieth century. The moshav, by contrast, is a co-operative village, incorporating features of both private and collective farming. Each family owns its home and works its own agricultural land; the co-operative, however, collectively purchases feed, fodder, livestock and other supplies, collectively maintains all the farm machinery, and markets all produce. Some moshavim have industrial enterprises, again usually on a co-operative basis, while packing houses and plants are organized by regional partnerships of moshavim.

From a far broader and less time specific framework, present day agricultural development and expansion throughout this area of the Middle East can be viewed as part of the sequence of advances and retreats that has for long characterized change at the edge of cultivation. This is the struggle between the desert and the sown, between Abel and Cain, between the livestock-rearing nomad and the sedentary peasant-farmer. The relative location of the outer limits of cultivation has depended upon the strength of government. In periods of strong central government, developed communications and fortifications, agriculture has advanced and extended spatially. Always lurking in the background, however, is the omnipresent nomad who will again seek to thrust into the settled areas, terrorize and exploit rural communities, causing them to quit cultivation and retreat from the area. This is the contest that has raged from the beginning of time and will continue for so long as man occupies the Earth (Lawrence, 1978, p.35; Lewis, 1955; Issawi, 1966, pp.258–9). The entire Mediterranean basin remains unconquerable; rather it conquers and modifies the potential conquerors:

> Le Proche-Orient n'est pas conquis par les Arabes; c'est lui qui les conquient, qui les assimile as sa substance. Qui agit avec eux comme ses fleurs avec les insectes assez imprudents pour se loger en elles: elles se referment et les dévorent (Braudel, 1949, pp.298–9)

On this broader time perspective the present agricultural progress throughout the Mashreq is a consequence of far more profound causes than the Jewish settlement in Palestine.

Mounting Zionist activities and Arab responses

With the formation and implementation of the terms of the Mandate in Palestine, major rioting broke out in 1921 and again in 1929 between Palestinian Arabs and the ever increasing number of Jewish immigrants. The Shaw Commission (1930) sought the causes of these riots and made recommendations (particularly relating to problems of excessive Jewish immigration) to avoid such disorders in the future. However, the rising rate of Jewish immigration into Palestine, in accordance with the terms of the Balfour Declaration that were incorporated into the Mandate, pointed to a worsening confrontation (Sykes, 1965, Ch.13).

Jewish immigration into Palestine declined from 1929 until 1933 when the Nazis came to power in Germany and the rate of immigration increased to more than 30,000 a year as compared to 9,533 in 1932. By 1935 the number of Jewish immigrants had risen to 61,854. A genuine and unbridgeable conflict of interest grew up between Zionists and native Palestinians; the Jewish underground army, the Haganah, was created during this period (Wasserstein, 1978, p.237). The ensuing frictions led to serious disturbances between the Arab and Jewish communities in 1936. The Arab Higher Committee was constituted to orchestrate attempts to protect the Palestinian homeland. The Peel Commission (set up in August 1936) recommended in July 1937 the creation of a Jewish and an Arab state in Palestine with Jerusalem remaining under British control; the recommendations were opposed by both communities.

25

The Arab revolt that began in 1936 lasted three years, starting with a six-month general strike, guerilla activities and effective liberation of large areas of Palestine. This Arab resistance was effectively broken by the British using tanks and aeroplanes. In a White Paper of 1939 Britain backed away from the idea of a Jewish state within a partitioned Palestine as proposed by the Peel Commission, and sought to limit further Jewish immigration into Palestine to 75,000 over a five-year period. By the outbreak of war in 1939 no agreed plan had been produced, yet the Jewish Agency would not accept the White Paper limitation on Jewish immigration. The fall of the Chamberlain government in Britain also saw the departure of Malcolm McDonald, Chamberlain's Colonial Secretary and a firm supporter of the White Paper. Winston Churchill, who became Prime Minister at the head of a coalition Government in May 1940, had been an ardent friend of Zionism from his 1920s period as Colonial Secretary and was clearly anti-White Paper.

In 1939 with the Arab revolt broken, the British played for time and sought Arab neutrality in the 1939–45 war. From the middle of the war, however, two Jewish terrorist organizations, the Stern gang and the Irgun Zvdi Leumi, made a number of attacks on the British security forces in Palestine and on officials abroad; particularly noteworthy was the assassination in Cairo in November 1944 of Lord Moyne, the British Resident Minister in the Middle East. Throughout the war the Jewish Agency undertook extreme measures to secure military recruits in Palestine, ostensibly to serve with the British forces. However such measures should be seen in the context of the longer term logic of Zionist colonization in Palestine and the attempt to create a Jewish military force (Davis, 1979).

In November 1947 the British served notice that they were quitting Palestine by 1 August 1948, and the United Nations proposed the 'Plan for Partition and Economic Union' for the partition of Palestine, supported by both the U.S.A. and the U.S.S.R. The U.N. plan would have resulted in a Jewish state with a population half Jewish and half Arab, a Palestinian state almost entirely Arab in population, and a separate Jerusalem under the U.N. Trusteeship Council. The two proposed states were to have been linked into an economic union. The Jewish Agency accepted the plan with reservations, particularly relating to the status of Jerusalem, while the Arabs rejected it. The British withdrew their Mandate on 14 May 1948.

Events rapidly overtook the recommendations. On the day the British withdrew, the Jewish National Provincial Council at Tel Aviv unilaterally proclaimed the new state of Israel. Fighting broke out immediately between the Arab and Jewish factions. The better armed and organized Jewish forces, with the resources and influence of international Zionism, occupied not only the territory allotted to the Jewish state, as envisaged by the U.N., but also more than half of that earmarked for the proposed Arab state. This Zionist success in retrospect can be seen to be due in part to the massive defeat wreaked upon the Palestinian Arabs by the British occupying forces in 1936–39 and the failure of Britain as the mandatory authority to prepare the local Palestinian population for independence. The opportunist Hashemite-Jordanian and Egyptian forces occupied the remainder of this stillborn Arab political entity. (*See* Fig. 9.) The lack of 'a mass peasant organization capable of waging armed resistance' (Kayyali, 1978, p.229), assured the Zionists of victory (*see also* Porath, 1978).

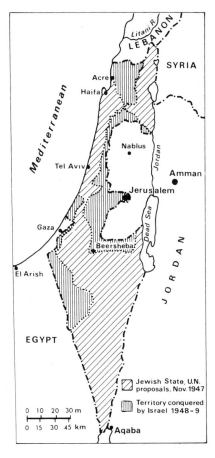

FIGURE 9. The U.N. proposals for the partition of Palestine, November 1947

27

This disorganization and lack of leadership within the native Palestinian Arab movement contrasted with the directed and organizational qualities of Western political Zionists so that 'the road to a General Strike and the Revolt [of 1936] was paved by the growing Jewish immigration and land purchases' (Porath, 1977, p.299). The Arab protests, culminating in the 1936–39 armed revolt, were part of a broad Arab struggle for national independence, complicated in Palestine by the Zionist colonial intrusion and the disparity between the Palestinians' coherence of aims and their political disunity (Carré, 1977, p.41). But 'the failure of the Palestinian Arab national movement to produce the required leadership' (Kayyali, 1978, p.231) must be considered in relative terms, particularly in the failure of the Mandate authorities to develop Palestine and to train up its leaders.

Britain has long prided itself on its practice of and procedures for decolonization, the preparation of former colonial territories for home rule and their introduction to the 'Commonwealth of Nations'. The British presence in Palestine was quite a different affair. Spearheaded by the Balfour Declaration of 1917, the long term British colonial aim was the creation of a civilized, democratic, Western-orientated state in that crucially strategic area—the meeting place of Europe, Asia and Africa, so insightfully termed 'the Crossroads' by George Cressey (1966). Against such imperialistic endeavours the League of Arab States, founded in March 1945 by Egypt, Iraq, the Lebanon, Saudi Arabia, Syria and Transjordan, sought to oust foreign powers from the region, to work towards political federation and to plan for economic and social co-operation. The rivalries and basic differences between the founding members owed much to the pro-imperialist ruling families that had come to power following the 1914–18 war with the support of Britain and/or France.

The colonial Zionists were operating locally in Palestine within a virtual political vacuum and evolved their own quasi-governmental structure under the Mandate. The earliest Zionist institutions were to provide both nationalist disciplines and experience in democratic conflict resolution (Horowitz and Lissak, 1978). The centre was the Jewish Agency and the sub-centres included the various Zionist parties, such as the *Histradut*, the labour confederation of Jewish Palestine and *Landsmanschaften*, associations of Jewish immigrants from specific countries. Despite the terms of the class 'A' Mandate as it referred to Palestine, which clearly suggested a definite expectation that further autonomy was being prescribed, the British ruled Palestine as though it was the most backward of Crown Colonies.

This negative, conservative attitude of the Government of Palestine spilled over into its restrictive monetary and fiscal policy with an almost complete reliance on taxation and an insignificant utilization of loan financing, an inadequate expenditure on economic development and social services, particularly the minuscule expenditures directed to education and health (Nathan, Cass and Creamer, 1946, p.349). Two separate economies developed, the Jewish and the Arab. The Jewish economy became increasingly financed from external funds directed through the Jewish Agency and its related instruments; the Jewish settlers were able to purchase land from, and progressively to dominate, the natives. *See* Porath (1978) for a discussion of the aggressive policy of Jewish land purchase during the period of the Mandate, and for details of the substantial transfers of funds into Palestine by the Jewish institutions, *see* Ulitzur (1939) and Halevi and Klinov-Malul (1968, pp.20, 38). In the interwar years the Jewish Agency itself transferred more than 12 million Palestinian pounds (LP) into the country, an amount representing two-thirds of all transfers made by national institutions (Ulitzur, 1939, pp.240, 271). In total, the Jewish sector raised some LP 80 million between 1920 and 1945 as opposed to government revenue of LP 100 million. In contrast the Palestinian Arab was dependent upon a Government which, even in 1932–5 with budget surpluses accumulating, did not substantially expand expenditures. As a result the Palestinian Arabs in 1948 found themselves not only militarily, but administratively, economically and politically quite unequipped to move towards the challenge of sovereignty.

CHAPTER 3

The British Mandate
and Increasing Jewish Immigration

Jewish immigration into Palestine
and its justifications

In 1922 when the Mandate came into being, 83,000 of the 750,000 living in Palestine were Jewish. This population grew and underwent a radical change during the next fifty years (Fig. 10). Between 1922 and 1948 the total population increased by 246 percent, while the

FIGURE 10. Growth of population in Palestine–Israel, 1922–80. Sources of data: Official census reports, U.N. Demographic Yearbooks and British Admiralty, Naval Intelligence (1943)

Jewish percentage tripled from 11 percent in 1922 to 33 percent in 1947. Despite the changing boundaries the present 85 percent Jewish total is indicative of the marked Jewish immigration and Arab emigration that occurred after the attainment of Israel statehood in 1948.

Jewish immigration into Palestine was well under way by 1923, gaining in momentum after 1924 with the fourth Aliya, or immigration wave (Aliya is literally translated as 'going up' to the homeland):

First Aliya (1882–1903), 20–30,000 Jewish immigrants
Second Aliya (1904–14), 35–40,000 Jewish immigrants
Third Aliya (1919–23), 35,000
Fourth Aliya (1924–31), 82,000
Fifth Aliya (1932–38), 217,000
World War II, 92,000
Post-World War II (1946–May 1948), 61,000
(Source of data: Sicron, 1957, p.21)

Behind such gross data lurk the means by which such changes occurred. The native resistance to the Zionist colonialization was almost
ignored in the West, where the focus of attention was on the Zionists'
claim that Britain was blocking their further entry into Palestine. Yet
even by 1948 Jews owned only about 6 percent of the land and made
up one-third of the population. The Jewish endeavour was thus to:

> Address the world as the aggrieved, with Britain [colonial power]
> as your enemy; ignore the natives, and have nothing said about
> them, so long, *objectively*, as you cannot be seen directly to be
> exploiting them. (Said, 1980, p.23)

This 'epistemological achievement', the blotting out from knowledge
of some one million natives was quite a remarkable and audacious
feat. Chaim Weizmann's 'miraculous cleaning of the land, the miraculous simplication of Israel's task', whereby the native Arab presence
would simply be ignored by Zionism in its international appeals for
assistance (McDonald, 1951, p.176) recalls the biblical text:

> The land, under which ye go to possess it is an unclean land with
> the filthiness of the people of the lands, with their abominations,
> which have filled it from one end to another with their uncleanliness.
> (Ezra 9:11)

The native problem had been recognized in 1895:

> We shall have to spirit the penniless population across the border
> by procuring employment for it in transit countries, while denying
> it any employment in our own country. Both the process of expro-
> priation and the removal of the poor must be carried out discreetly
> and circumspectly. (Herzl, 1960, Vol.1, p.88)

The colonization of the land was to be justified on the international
stage much as Western capitalists had advanced their ideas of imperialism throughout the nineteenth century. The natives were to be
typified as wogs, ignorant and stupid, brutal and savage, while such
Western scholars as the French geographer Paul Leroy Beaulieu saw
colonialization as bringing civilization to the periphery (Murphy,

1948). On a broader scale the entire ethos of the colonial literature of exploration and colonialization can be reconsidered as an extension of capitalism into the periphery that in time resulted in the subordination of such areas to the dominant world trade system.

Ernst Frankenstein, a German born and trained barrister then residing in England, typified the international Zionist sentiments in the dark days of war-torn Europe, 'The Jewish problem of our epoch ... may be summed up in one word: homelessness' (Frankenstein, 1943, p.67). Frankenstein undertook a brief survey of the views of the Arab states to the establishment of a Jewish state. The Syrian attitude was typical, even though the Syrians considered Palestine part of their own land:

> We Syrians have suffered too much from sufferings resembling theirs [Zionists], not to throw open wide to them the doors of Palestine. All those among them who are oppressed in certain retrograde countries are welcome. Let them settle in Palestine but in an autonomous Palestine, connected with Syria by the sale bond of federation. Will not a Palestine enjoying wide internal autonomy be for them a sufficient guarantee? If they form a majority then, they will be rulers. (Frankenstein, 1943, p.132)

But Frankenstein believed that:

> In the last resort the Arab problem, i.e. the antagonism between the Arabic-speaking population and the Jews, is a clash of the dynamic modern civilization with the static and petrified primitivity of 4,000 years ago, a clash between the most progressive democracy and primitive feudalism, a clash between modern tolerance and medieval religious fanaticism. (Frankenstein, 1943, p.139)

Frankenstein was convinced that the clash could not be avoided, and if the Jews had not come to Palestine, others would have had to take their place to try to win over the land and its inhabitants to a better and happier life, perhaps by less peaceful means. The native Arabs were considered primitive, lazy, inferior and exploitable people, to be removed and evicted, their lands to be taken to create a Jewish state. It was inferred that the native Palestinians were little more than a hindrance to progress in the region (Fisher, 1955). Walter Hollstein tells how in 1945 the Zionist leaders actually approached President Roosevelt with the suggestion that the Palestinian Arabs should be transferred en masse to Iraq (Weinstock, 1969, p.22). While the massive movements of Western capital into the region effected certain changes, the attempt was made to show that Palestine needed Jewish care:

> It seems as if God has covered the soil of Palestine with rocks and marshes and sand, so that its beauty can only be brought out by those who love it and will devote their lives to healing its wounds. (Weizmann, 1959, p.371)

Chaim Weizmann suggested that the native Arabs had failed to utilize and develop the natural environment, a condition sufficient for dispossession and settlement by those with the will to 'redeem' the land (Said, 1980, pp.83–92).

A customary justification for the colonization and occupation of the Holy Land by Zionists is in the ostensibly improved levels and increased areal extents of agriculture, the 'making the desert bloom' myth.

> The Jewish agricultural colonies have grown up in the course of the last forty years and show a level of agriculture and scientific development far in advance of anything else of the kind in Palestine. They established themselves in many cases on uncultivated and unpromising land and have transformed it into extensively cultivated and remunerative plantations. They drained swamps, planted eucalyptus and pines, cultivated the vine, and greatly developed the orange trade of Jaffa. (Luke and Keith-Roach, 1922, p.55)

This quotation came from the *Handbook of Palestine*, issued under the authority of the Government of Palestine with an introduction by Sir Herbert Samuel, then High Commissioner for Palestine and a leading Zionist of his day. Israel was seen as 'the creation, out of what was once a wilderness, of a modern welfare state' (Epstein, 1959, p.319). It is not being said that the area was a wilderness immediately before the modern Jewish state although a quick reading would logically impart such a suggestion. Fortunately the historical geography of Palestine is sufficiently well documented to demonstrate the natural fertility and prosperity of the land and to refute categorically such allegations.

Writing in the late tenth century, Istahari and Ibn Hankal described the basic characteristics of the land:

> Filastin is watered by the rains and the dew. Its trees and its ploughed lands do not need artificial irrigation; it is only in Nablus that you find the running waters applied to this purpose. (Le Strange, 1965, p.28)

A somewhat similar justification was made by the Israelite colonists in c.1250 B.C. who also emphasized that even before conquest the area was 'a land flowing with milk and honey'. We question the generality of the 'making the desert bloom' myth, even with the injection of Western capital into a peripheral society.

Even more heinous is the implicit suggestion that advanced capitalist societies have a right to occupy and colonize an area because of supposed superior levels of capital resources and technology, and to oust a population from a land. If this tenet were valid, the English in the Aberdare Mountains of Kenya, the Boers in South Africa and the Chinese in Tibet, due to their 'superiority', would be justified in their securing land from the disadvantaged natives who would, anyway, only misuse or underutilize a valuable natural resource (*see* Hazlewood, 1979).

During the period of the Mandate official immigration policy was based on the economic absorptive capacity of Palestine. This position was clearly expressed in the Churchill White Paper of 1922 and was frequently reiterated (Halevi and Klinov-Malul, 1968, p.38). The Jewish Agency took exception to the specific conclusions of a number of reports on the absorptive capacity, notably that the Mandate government's estimates of cultivable land were much too low. Accordingly, about 40 percent of all expenditures of the Jewish national institutions in 1917–39 were used for land purchases and agricultural settlement in Palestine. At root the attitude adopted by the Jewish national institutions suggested:

> Palestine was not very inviting economically; it was therefore the function of the institutions, as representatives of world Jewry, to create the economic environment for the absorption of immigration—a recognition that much of the investment in land purchase and agricultural settlement would be social, as opposed to private, cost. (Halevi and Klinov-Malul, 1968, p.35)

The Geographical Handbook for *Palestine and Transjordan*, referring to native agriculture, provides a useful benchmark: 'To the great majority of Arab cultivators cereal crops are now the most important agricultural activity' (1943, p.244). Such native agricultural systems varied from a two-year rotation of wheat or barley with winter leguminous crops or with summer crops of durra and sesame, to a three-year rotation in which leguminous crops were normally introduced between these summer crops and the winter cereals. Bare fallow was sometimes introduced between crops to clear the land of weeds. The proportion of arable land, 81 percent of the cultivated area in the early 1940s, was considered to be 'very high for a Mediterannean country' (Geographical Handbook, *Palestine and Transjordan*, p.244). However, dry farming in which cereal crops are grown almost to the exclusion of any other crop was important to the region extending from Morocco in the west through the Middle East and into Afghanistan (Grigg, 1970, pp.170–1).

> Considering the low yields of cereal crops in relation to this dispro-
> portion [arable versus other agricultural uses], it would seem advis-
> able, from the economic standpoint, to replace extensive grain-
> farming by intensive irrigated cropping. Geographical Handbook,
> (*Palestine and Transjordan*, p.239)

Extension of capital and intensive, irrigated cropping, increasingly directed to a non-local market, particularly northwest Europe, was seen as the way to incorporate the area into the capitalist sphere. Imperialism (within the present context, Zionism) was the theory and colonialism was the practice of changing the 'useless and relatively unoccupied' territories into useful, productive extensions of the capitalist realm.

The feature of agricultural land purchase was replacement of Arab by Jew and not extension of agricultural lands alongside the native Arab population. The Shaw Report of 1930 warned of the problems of excess Jewish immigration and the Simpson Report of 1930 emphasized that there was no margin of land available for agricultural settlement of new immigrants. The inquiry by John Hope Simpson concluded that Arab interests demanded a temporary end to Jewish land settlement. Simpson also remarked on the question of Arab unemployment. 'It is wrong', he argued, 'that a Jew from Poland, Lithuania or the Yemen should be admitted to fill an existing vacancy, while in Palestine there are already workmen capable of filling that vacancy.' These views were supported in October 1930 by the White Paper authorized by the then Colonial Secretary, Lord Passfield, the former Sidney Webb (Bethell, 1979, p.24).

Important data that indicated the extent, prosperity and absorptive capacities of agricultural lands in Palestine together with the opportunities for real capital investment were assembled by the Jewish Agency in its mounting campaign to justify increased immigration of Jews into Palestine. The Jewish Agency emphasized that the Mandate government's estimates of cultivable land were far too low, that Jewish purchases of agricultural land from Arabs did not lead to any significant displacement of Arab farmers, and that the absorptive capacity of agricultural land should be estimated on the basis of modern agricultural techniques and not on average yields of *fellah* farms (Halevi and Klinov-Kalul, 1968, pp.33–4). That data on agricultural lands can now also be used against those who argue that it was the Jews who created the basis for the supposed agricultural prosperity of Israel.

Halevi and Klinov-Malul stress that at least until the mid-1950s a concentration of new immigrants was found in agriculture, 'since agriculture was considered the most suitable vocation for settlers in developed areas' (p.134). Significant amounts of funding were directed by the Jewish Agency to settling uneconomic sites: 'remote and arid districts were often settled because of security considerations' (Halevi and Klinov-Malul, p.134). In this manner agriculture was transformed and brought into the capitalist sphere with massive infusions of Western capital. Yet in another context Halevi and Klinov-Malul admit that 'there was a sudden abundance [in 1948–51] of cultivable land previously cultivated by Arabs who fled from Israel during the war' (Halevi and Klinov-Malul, 1968, p.6). Whereas the pragmatist may seek to employ various data in different contexts one must realize that such data can be and must be cited as evidence for the extent of cultivation prior to the creation of Israel.

The direct and brutal colonialization is dealt with in an almost perfunctory manner by Moshe Dayan in his recounting of the 'reconstruction of settlement' in the land:

> We came to this country which was already populated by Arabs, and we are establishing a Hebrew, that is a Jewish state here. In considerable areas of the country [the total area was about 6 percent] we bought the land from the Arabs. Jewish villages were built in the place of Arab villages. You do not even know the names of these Arab villages, and I do not blame you, because these geography books no longer exist; not only do the books not exist, the Arab villages are not there either. Nahalal arose in the place of Mahalul, Gevat—in the place of Jibta, Sarid—in the place of Haneifs and Kefar Yehoshua—in the place of Tell Shaman. There is not one place built in this country that did not have a former Arab population. (Moshe Dayan, 1969, p.3).

Such references concerning the pre-Zionist settlement pattern suggest not an empty, inhospitable land but an area characterized by a native peasant agriculture that was to be repressed by a colonial Zionism and its quite massive infusion of Western capital (Lehn, 1973–4). Dayan's veiled and Orweillian reference to the destruction of 'these geography books' is particularly sinister. Examples do exist of the systematic destruction of pre-Israeli materials, particularly certain land-use maps; however, sufficient material still exists in Western libraries even though tampering has sometimes taken place there as well.

During the period of the British Mandate the Arab peasant 'definitely became a proletariat but, in general, not one that was forced off the land in order to make way for a new socioeconomic regime' (Carmi and Rosenfeld, 1980, p.196). What did occur was that many of these peasants became wage earners, on an ever increasing scale seeking employment outside the village within the 'developing' urban sector.

The urban employers exploited the numerous peasant-proletarians as unprivileged casual labourers, who were now no longer entirely dependent upon the land yet who were not alienated from it, and in fact usually retained a home within the village. 'Not only was transition to the city not easily attainable for a casual labourer, it was not necessarily an attraction for one with a home in the village' (Carmi and Rosenfeld, p.196). While the system of casual labour did not generally afford the necessary wherewithal for a full transition to the city, the possession of a home, family and subsidiary means of livelihood within the village provided a base that turned the peasant-proletarian, casual labourer into a migrant labourer. Carmi and Rosenfeld thus indicate certain of the insidious processes that became increasingly apparent under the Mandate.

With the creation of the new state of Israel two demographic themes emerged as national priorities: the eviction of the native Arab population and the attraction of even more Jewish immigrants to settle in Israel. In 1948 alone some 780,000 Palestinians left, hastened on their way by such massacres as that at Deir Yassin in April 1948 where the Irgun and Stern gangs were active. Menachem Begin, then the leader of Irgun, said later, 'The massacre was not only justified, but there would not have been a state of Israel without the victory at Deir Yassin' (Begin, 1970, p.77). Joseph Weitz, director of the Jewish National Land Fund, was most emphatic in a conversation of 18 May 1948, with Moshe Shertok of the Israeli Ministry on the matter of eviction:

> Transfer—*post factum*; should we do something so as to transform the exodus of the Arabs from the country into a fact, so that they return no more? ... His [Shatok's] answer—he blesses any initiative in this matter. His opinion is also that we must act in such a way as to transform the exodus of the Arabs into an established fact. (Weitz, 1965, Vol.3, p.293).

Edward Said carefully chronicled the methods by which the inconsequential native was translated into an absentee 'refugee' by the supposedly democratic Israeli state (Said, 1980, pp.102–114). Nazzal (1979), for one, examined the Israelization of part of Palestine, provided evidence of the systematic expulsion of the indigenous inhabitants from Galilee and related such actions to the overall plan to establish the Zionist state (*see* Allon, 1970, Vol.2, p.268).

Article 13 of the Universal Declaration of Human Rights (1948) states that:

1. Everyone has a right to freedom of movement and residence within the borders of each state.

2. Everyone has the right to leave any country, including his own, and to return to his country.

Both the United General Assembly (Article 12) and the International Covenant on Civil and Political Rights (1966) further affirm these fundamental rights of individuals. Whether the masses of Palestinians who emigrated did so entirely of their own free will as the Israelis argue or whether they were coerced in some way, the important and crucial point is that the Palestinians have the right to return. On 11 December 1967 the U.N. General Assembly passed Resolution 194—affirming the rights of Palestinians to return to their homes and property—and has passed the same resolution on twenty-eight subsequent occasions. Yet Israel declares that Arab-owned land is absentee property and thus liable for expropriation by the Jewish National Fund which holds land 'for the whole Jewish people'. The conclusion must be that the Palestinian Arabs are not allowed to return to their lands (Rowley, 1977).

The following report was presented to Prime Minister Yitzhak Rabin in 1976 by Israel Koenig, the Northern District Commissioner (Galilee):

a. The reception criteria for Arab university students should be the same as for Jewish students and this must also apply to the granting of scholarships. A meticulous implementation of these rules will produce a natural selection and will considerably reduce the number of Arab students. Accordingly, the number of low-standard graduates will also decrease, a fact that will facilitate their absorption in work after studies.

b. Encourage the channeling of students into technical professions, the physical and natural sciences. These studies leave less time for dabbling in nationalism and the drop-out rate is higher.

c. Make trips abroad for studies easier, while making the return and employment more difficult—this policy is apt to encourage their emigration.

d. Adopt tougher measures at all levels against various agitators among college and university students.

e. Prepare absorption possibilities in advance for the better part of the graduates, according to their qualifications. This policy can be implemented thanks to the time available in which the authorities may plan their steps. (Koenig, 1976)

The racist policy recommendations encapsulated within the Koenig plan essentially translate certain of the Weizmann visions into the realities of the modern Zionist state.

Some pro-Zionists have used the Nazi Holocaust as justification for

the taking over of Palestine, whereas the development of the anti-Arab
sentiment among the Zionist settlers with their *chosen people* ideology
bears some resemblance to the anti-Jewish dogma of the Nazis and
their creed for the *master race*.

Elie Cohen wrote of human behaviour in a German concentration
camp during the Second World War:

> It must now be explained how it is possible for the super-ego with
> acknowledged non-criminal standards of adults or adolescents to be
> replaced by a criminal super-ego ... which made it possible for the
> SS to murder Jews, Poles, Russians etc. It can even be said that this
> was a necessity for the SS, for these people, according to Nazi
> ideology, were noxious creatures. To destroy them was as necessary
> for the SS as the extinction of Colorado potato beetles was for the
> Netherlands. (Cohen, 1954, pp.233-4, 237)

David Hacohen, chairman of the Knesset Foreign Affairs Committee
in July 1967 is reported to have said to a British Parliamentary
delegation on the subject of the Palestinian refugees, 'But they are not
human beings, they are not people, they are Arabs' (Gilmour, 1980,
p.94).

In an intriguing paper R.P. Stevens has related certain of the
affinities between the emergence of Boer South Africa and Zionist
Israel. The relationship between Jan Smuts and Chaim Weizmann is
significant:

> The importance of this little publicised relationship ... helps to
> throw into perspective both the contradictions of western liberalism
> and the psychological climate which rationalised the dominant
> position of a white minority in South Africa on the one hand and of
> a new European settlement in Palestine on the other. (Stevens,
> 1973-4, p.35)

Stevens also sheds some light on the intrigues surrounding the Jewish
National Home issue and of Smuts' part particularly, naming
Smuts 'as one of those who is responsible for the Balfour Declaration'
(Stevens, 1973-4, p.41). Earlier H. Tingsten had written:

> The Boers believed that they were God's own people and compared
> their long wandering with the Exodus of the Jews from Egypt to
> Canaan. The blacks were to them the children of Ham, regarded as
> inferior by God and created to be the servant of the whites. (Ting-
> sten, 1955, p.12)

What justifications are valid for ejecting the Palestinians from the
land of Israel? Not making the desert to bloom, not the superiority of
the civilized Israelis over the primitive Arabs, and certainly not the

treatment of the Jews during World War II when Zionist colonial activity existed in Palestine prior to the rise of National Socialism in Germany. Perhaps Ernst Frankenstein's 'homelessness' justifies Israel, but why cannot room be found for the native Palestinians as well?

The fight to gain Jewish immigrants from foreign lands

As well as gaining the expulsion of the native population it was crucial to attract even more Jewish immigrants into this Promised Land. There is evidence to suggest that many Jews, particularly those from elsewhere in the Middle East, were reticent to quit their established homes to settle in Israel.

M. Gilbert (1975), in considering the spatial distributions of Jews by various geographical areas such as 'Iraq 600 B.C.-1900 A.D.' and 'Tunisia 1800-1975', implied that anti-Jewish feelings led to the removal of large established Jewish communities throughout Islam from the 1930s onward. However, the question remains whether such Jews were eventually pushed from their lands by vitriolic, intolerant host communities or were in some way pulled to Israel. S.D. Goiten has written of the harmony that characterized relationships between Arabs and Jews until the advent of Zionism (Goiten, 1967). From the late nineteenth century the colonial ambitions of ardent Zionists appear to have soured this accord and, particularly after the imposition of the British Mandate in 1917, sought to increase dramatically Jewish immigration into the Holy Land. M.M. Mardor (1967) related that Iraqi and Persian Jews had been isolated 'from all contact with Palestine and the Zionist movement' for many years; it was therefore more difficult to coerce these Jews into emigrating because 'they suffered from a kind of inertia' (p.85). In addition, the Iraqi Jews were 'shocked by the idea of doing work that might soil their hands. It took immense effort to bring them to some understanding of the Zionist ideal of labour' (Mardor, 1964, p.92). Bracha Habas (1963, p.186) also noted that the Zionist ideology would not have been accepted in many, if not most, Jewish circles.

Again the aim was clear; attainment of the Zionist political conception required, indeed demanded, a sizeable Jewish migration to Palestine. Shlomo Hillel travelled to Iraq on three occasions 'to serve the immigration effort', but grew increasingly bitter and distressed by the lack of co-operation from Jewish communities within Iraq (Habas, 1963, pp.228-9). Ruth Klieger met with a similar response in Egypt which she visited in order to set up an organization 'for illegal immigration to Palestine' and 'to try to raise funds for this purpose from the rich Jewish community in the country' (Kimche and Kimche,

1954, p.64). An enraged Katani Pasha, head of the Jewish community in Cairo stated 'that he would set his dogs on her, or any other Palestinian emissary coming to Cairo' (Kimche and Kimche, 1954, p.65). Emissary Munya Mardor related that:

> Our chief concern in Syria and Lebanon was, as I have said, to persuade the youth to settle in Palestine. For the most part, the middle-aged and older Jews had become reconciled to their lot, and it was next to impossible to wean them from the attitudes and habits of generations, and to fire them with zest for a new life in the land of their fathers. . . . We usually had to accept that attitude, but not the assumption that the young people were satisfied with their lot and with the prospect of going on in their parents' immutable ways. We were determined to get them to Palestine and to a life of freedom, and of work in the service of their natural homeland. (Mardor, 1964, pp.89–90).

A similar position existed in the Yemen where Jews were firmly established in the settled, commercial fabric (Kafih, 1961, pp.227–9). The emigration of Yemeni Jews to Palestine commenced in 1882 and increased after 1909; following the creation of the state of Israel, all the Yemeni Jews, some 50,000, moved to Israel.

The vision and determination of the fervent young men and women of the Jewish Bureau, fired with the Zionist spirit, prevailed; they gained an inflow of Jewish stock which led in time to statehood and the attainment of population thresholds necessary to retain a demographic viability for the future. This immigration was hardly a spontaneous and spirited movement of visionaries, but more often than not of folk who needed special inducements.

Emissaries from the Jewish Bureau were particularly active in Syria and Lebanon between the two world wars, yet further immigration was the imperative, over-riding consideration:

> The search for new bases for the illegal immigration effort was an unending one; step by step, the young men of the Bureau combed every Jewish centre of population that was accessible to them by land. As a result, in the thick of the second World War, they hit on the idea of expanding the effort to include North Africa. . . . It was to this unknown and distant Jewry that the Bureau turned in 1943 in its search for new bases of operation. . . . However ominous shadows soon fell across their path. The activities of the emissaries in Tunisia had aroused hostility in certain Jewish circles (Habas, 1963, pp.237–8)

Indeed, the Tunisian Jews wrote to the authorities, 'informing upon them. . . . The emissaries were ordered to leave Tunisia and they returned to Palestine' (Habas, 1963, pp.260, 295). Even after the short-lived anti-Jewish pogroms in Iraq in 1941, 'Jews were in no hurry to go to Palestine' (Habas, 1963, p.186). As soon as the pogrom died down Jews 'began to sink roots anew in the hostile country. Jews invested large sums of money in the construction of the new Baghdad; they erected a Jewish neighbourhood which became the centre of the capital. Within two years Jewish capital had created an entire city' (Habas, 1963, p.186).

Such outrageous developments angered those fired with the Zionist spirit. Indeed the emissaries from the Jewish Bureau were not slow to realize that, 'Zionist ideology would not be accepted in many, if not most, Jewish circles. ... One emissary endeavoured to win converts among the intelligentsia but failed.' (Habas, 1963, p.187). The 1941 pogrom did, however, cause some Iraqi Jews to move to Palestine, although 'when the tumult died down, many of them returned to Baghdad'. In fact when the first Zionist emissaries from Palestine arrived in Baghdad in the summer in 1947, 'the Jewish population was very fearful, and the emissaries realised that they would first have to educate the people' (Habas, 1963, p.187).

Because Iraqi Jews were most reluctant to uproot themselves, emissaries arranged for the massive smuggling of arms and incendiary devices into Iraq (Mardor, 1964, pp.45–9). Vigal Allon, writing to an emissary in Iraq in 1947, suggested that disturbances were likely to occur and promised to do his utmost to increase the Zionist arms caches (Allon, 1970, pp.133–5).

> It was no coincidence that two of the last emissaries to serve in Iraq ... were elected to the Knesset. The people were very grateful towards the young men and women whose dedicated efforts had contributed so much to the creation of a Jewish State. (Habas, 1963, p.226)

The education or persuasion of the Iraqi Jewish population took a number of forms. Yehuda Tagar of the Israeli Foreign Ministry and formerly a secret Zionist envoy in Iraq related how, through the actions of Zionist 'agent provocateurs' and their bombing of Jewish targets in Baghdad during 1950 and early 1951, over 90 percent of Iraq's most ancient and flourishing Jewish community of 130,000 suddenly emigrated to Israel (Special Correspondent, *Middle East International*, 1973, pp.18–19).

What is more, the oriental or Sephardic Jews, essentially non-European Jewry, held serious misgivings in moving to the fledgling Zionist state. Many found the modern, secular, capitalistic, industrialized state to be a stark contrast to their earlier, undeveloped, pious environments. Upon arrival in Israel the Sephardic Jews were often forcibly directed to the inhospitable, hard, undeveloped and ill-equipped settlements in the Negev and the Galilee or to the abysmal slums about the periphery of Tel Aviv and the notorious Katamon district in Jerusalem and its Shmuel Hanevi neighbourhood; these latter two areas 'proved to be almost instant slums' (Greenberg and Nadler, 1977, p.77). Even in the 1980s, prejudice and lack of opportunities often characterize relationships between the Sephardic community, some 55 percent of the population, and the dominant Ashkenazim or European Jewry.

One may suggest that it was the creation of Zionist Israel (cause) which served to set Arab against Jew (effect) and generate the need for migration (effect), rather than a Zionist Israel (effect) emerging as a spontaneous flow of individuals from the Arab lands (cause).

European Jewry was asked not only to contribute finance but manpower to the Zionist settlement of the Holy Land. Perhaps the most absurd attempt to attain Jewish immigration into Palestine from Europe was made by Vladimir Jabotinsky, one of the most militant of the early Zionists; with Mussolini's backing he established a Zionist naval college at Civitavecchia in 1934 and dared to proclaim, 'We want a Jewish Empire. Just like there is an Italian or French on the Mediterranean, we want a Jewish Empire' (Gessner, 1935, p.11). With Mussolini's lurch toward Hitler Jabotinsky and his New Sionist Organization (Revisionists) sought out another patron for their policy of immigration to Palestine. Surprisingly they found one in the anti-Semitic government of Poland which wished to divest itself of its Jewish population and, to this end, trained the 'Irgun' Zionist commandos in the Carpathian Mountains for future service in Palestine. The Revisionists, in turn, abetted the anti-Semites by requesting that Poland:

> Ask Britain to turn over the Mandate for Palestine to you and make it in effect a Polish colony. You could then move all your unwanted Polish Jews into Palestine. (Briscoe, 1959, p.268)

Menachem Begin was then the Revisionist youth leader in Poland and openly collaborated with avowed anti-Semites in such fantasies in the hope of gaining Jewish migration into Palestine. Clearly the Zionist strategy was to utilize anti-Semitism for its own ends.

Zionists also collaborated with the Nazis in Germany to 'free Germany of its Jews'. In August 1933 the so-called Ha'avara agreement was signed between Germany and the Jewish Agency. The agreement gave Jews emigrating to Palestine a special right to transfer their capital to Palestine and led to special economic relations between the Jewish community in Palestine and Nazi Germany (Hilberg, 1967, p.95). The effort of anti-racist Jews to boycott Nazi products was undermined by the Ha'avara agreement and the refusal of the 18th Zionist Congress to participate in the boycott. Blumenfeld, writing on behalf of the Zionist Federation to Nazi official Bülow-Schwante on 11 June 1934, emphasized that, 'The propaganda which calls for boycotting Germany, in the manner it is frequently conducted today, is by its very essence completely un-Zionist' (*see* Schleunes, 1970, p.198). Following the Anschluss with Austria in 1938 Pino Ginsberg and Moshe Bar-Gilad were sent to, respectively, Berlin and Vienna to complete further agreements. Ginsberg was enabled to pick young Jewish pioneers for emigration to Palestine, even from those who had been despatched to concentration camps, and set up special training camps for selected immigrants. Bar-Gilad met with Captain Adolf Eichmann, head of the Central Bureau for Jewish Emigration, to arrange for the creation of pioneer training camps for selected young Jewish emigrants (Kimche and Kimche, 1954 pp.15, 17–19). Applications for migration of German Jews to Palestine flooded the Hechalutz, the Zionist pioneering movement (Kimche and Kimche, 1954, pp.31–32). Such Nazi-Zionist co-operation continued until 1941 when the Nazis suspended the accords, claiming that military requirements on the Russian front made it impossible for them to provide trains to transport Zionist pioneers on their way to Palestine. It was then, apparently that the Nazis finally opted for their barbaric 'final solution' in earnest.

The overall conclusion from such readings as outlined here and from Lenni Brenner (1982), who has now codified and reviewed the means by which Zionists accommodated and sometimes even collaborated with the Fascist regimes of Europe in the 1930s, is that throughout this tragic period the Zionists were primarily interested in the creation of the Zionist state and not with the ghastly plight of the millions of Jews who perished during the Nazi Holocaust. Indeed the unanimity of the Eastern and Western blocks in later supporting and making possible the statehood of Israel might be said to have been rooted in the horror of the Holocaust.

CHAPTER 4

The Emergence of Israel, 1948–67

The geopolitical context of the Middle East

The position of the Middle East in the Heartland-Rimland thesis, derived from the initial work of Sir Halford Mackinder, sometime Reader in Geography within the University of Oxford and later Director of the London School of Economics and Political Science, is relevant to this discussion. Despite subsequent modifications and developments of the thesis, particularly relating to advances in air transport, Mackinder in 1904 saw Russia as occupying a pivotal strategic position on 'the world island' that could, in time, lead to her emergence as a potentially dominant world power. Mackinder was attempting to provide an overall global structure and somewhat broader context for 'the Eastern Question', a subject so beloved of nineteenth-century European history course lecturers. The Eastern Question essentially derived from the weakening of Turkish rule within the Balkans, the Russian pressure southward, the Russian endeavour to become protector and champion of the various Balkan Slav nationalities against the Turks, and the resultant effect on the lines of communication between Britain and its eastern interests in India and beyond. Further south in Palestine one of the innumerable quarrels between the Christian communities, on this occasion around supposedly trivial rights in the Church of the Nativity in Bethlehem, was a direct cause of the Crimean War (1854–6), France championing her Latin protégés and Russia the Orthodox Church. The Crimean War may thus be viewed as yet another confrontation in a long sequence of Russo-Turkish wars from 1768, reflecting the persistent pressure imposed upon Turkey by a Russian desire to extend its influence to the Balkans and the Mediterranean.

Mackinder's definition of the pivotal area in 1904 was subsequently developed into a 'heartland' concept by James Fairgreave (Fairgreave, 1915, p.332) and further advanced by Mackinder in 1919:

Who rules East Europe commands the Heartland:
Who rules the Heartland commands the World-Island:
Who rules the World-Island commands the World.
(Mackinder, 1942, p.150)

Mackinder, with his essentially European, turn-of-the-century perspective, saw the middle tier of German and Slavic states, from Estonia to Bulgaria, as the key to world domination. By contrast the American N.J. Spykman believed that Mackinder had overemphasized the potentialities of the Heartland; he felt that Mackinder's Inner or Marginal Crescent, which he termed 'the Rimland', of greater importance. Adopting a more worldwide view than that of the European Mackinder, facilitated no doubt by his mid-twentieth century position, Spykman saw the Rimland as extending in a crescentic formation from Scandinavia in the northwest, southwards through Europe to embrace the Middle East, on eastwards through southern and eastern Asia and north to the Sea of Okhotsk in the northeast (Fig. 11). Spykman proposed a counter theory:

> Who controls the Rimland rules Eurasia:
> Who rules Eurasia controls the destinies of the world.
> (Spykman, 1944, p.43)

The U.S. foreign policy of containment in the post-war era was an attempt to lessen the dominant effect of the Russian-controlled Heartland over the World Island and hence the world (Cohen, 1963, p.40). In 1956 Meinig introduced an updated version of the Heartland (*see* Fig. 11). The essential point is that Korea, Vietnam and South-East Asia in general, Eastern Europe and the Middle East are all within the Rimland.

In a report dated 26 November 1940 (during the period of the German-Russian pact), the German Ambassador to Moscow, Herr Schulenburg, reported that Molotov, the Soviet Foreign Minister, was prepared to accept the draft of a proposed four-power pact between Germany, Italy, Japan and the Soviet Union, subject to certain conditions. One of the conditions simply 'Provided that the area south of Batum and Baku in the general direction of the Persian Gulf is recognized as the center of the aspirations of the Soviet Union' (Air University, 1954, p.693). Cutting through eastern Turkey and Iraq and western Iran towards the Gulf and Saudi Arabia this triangle, with Batum and Baku in the north and the Gulf to the South, is the very heart of the Middle East. It effectively divides the globe between East and West. Soviet aspirations within the region are not limited to a piece of territory but should be considered against the backcloth of geostrategic relationships and conquests envisaged by Czarist and Soviet imperialists alike. There is every indication that this general area, both for its oil and strategic location, remains a centre for Russian expansionary pressure, while the Western policy of containment seeks to prevent 'extensions of Soviet control in the Rimland' (Jones, 1955, p.497).

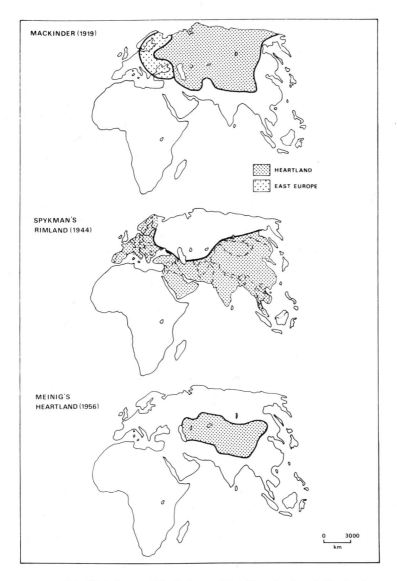

FIGURE 11. Global geopolitical views of the Heartland and Rimland
(after de Blij, 1967)

The 'Truman Doctrine' and its associated theory of containment endeavoured to construct a shield across the northern border of the general area of the Middle East eastwards from Greece and Turkey, substituting American for British power. President Truman also decided to sponsor the state of Israel as a bastion of democracy against Soviet expansion and Arab radicalism, against the advice of his Secretary of Defence, James Forrestal. Forrestal foresaw that the creation of a Jewish State would hamper the twin strategic tasks of keeping the Russians at bay and maintaining peace in the oilfields and shipping lanes. K.R. Bain (1969, p.200) has shown that the fate of Palestine always came second to more basic goals in the region; far more significant was Truman's concern about the general stability in both Europe and the Near East. A U.S.-backed and western-oriented Zionist state accorded with such a policy. The U.S. position towards Israel thus fits into the broader format of U.S. power politics in the Middle East–Mediterranean basin which itself can again be viewed as a modern manifestation of the age-old 'Eastern Question' and the containment of Russian expansionary efforts within the region.

Emerging political structures

It can now be appreciated that not only Israel but the Arab States themselves were creations, extensions of, and inextricably bound up with an external imperialism (Hussein, 1975). For example, from 1920 to 1948 in Egypt, Iraq and Syria, the national latifundist bourgeoisies gained in wealth and quite willingly accepted their provincial, tributary roles. The petty bourgeoisies became transformed into state bourgeoisies that never seriously attempted to promote Arab unity. In 1948, following the declaration of Israel statehood, Abdallah of Transjordan quickly moved to negotiate the annexation of the West Bank while King Farouk of Egypt acquiesced in Egypt's occupation of the Gaza Strip. The non-realization of a Palestinian state in the aftermath of World War II, in a period that was supposed to have witnessed the decolonization of the area, is somewhat reminiscent of the partitions of Poland by Austria, Prussia and Russia in the last quarter of the eighteenth century that resulted in Poland's disappearance from the map of Europe until 1918.

In the period following World War II emerged a new *status quo* in which the two super powers, the U.S. and the U.S.S.R., while apparently in competition, worked towards a policy of peaceful coexistence and sought to prevent any fundamental social change within the region. The U.S. became firmly entrenched in the oil-rich Arabian peninsula while the U.S.S.R. furthered it's influence in Egypt, Syria and Iraq, and quite readily accepted the partition of Palestine, perhaps seeing it as of only minor importance or, alternatively, as a potential gain for the Soviets because of its ostensibly leftist initial public utterances. A further aspect of this emerging equilibrium was the Arab-Israel *modus vivendi* whereby Israel was to refrain from aggression against its Arab neighbours who would, in turn, dampen any Palestinian attempts to challenge the existence of Israel.

Ths mounting nationalist pressure in Egypt threatened to break this state of equipoise. A revolt of the Egyptian army in 1952 succeeded in ousting the monarchy, leading in 1954 to the emergence of Nasser. In 1954 Egypt reached an agreement with the United Kingdom whereby the British occupying forces would quit the Suez Canal Zone by 1956. In that year, however, the Suez Canal Company was nationalized by Egypt in response to the withdrawal by the U.S. of its offer to finance the Aswan High Dam.

A particular situation was also developing in Israel where, upon his return to power in 1955, David Ben-Gurion emphasized that he would only undertake to form a Cabinet on condition that strenuous efforts be made for an Israeli expansion to the south. In the Suez fiasco of 1956 Britain hoped to return to the Middle East after being ousted by the U.S., and Israel attempted to annex the Sinai with Anglo-French backing. The French at this time were also involved in their Algerian war. The Suez venture by Anglo-French and Israeli forces was firmly opposed by the U.S.; a U.S.-U.S.S.R. agreement and demand by the U.N. Assembly led to the withdrawal of the allied forces while the U.S. enforced an Israeli withdrawal from Arab territory seized during the crisis. The two great powers would brook no rivals (Carlton, 1981; Neff, 1981).

Ben-Gurion's stress on the importance of territorial expansion of Israel owes much to Eretz Yisrael, a concept that continues to effect Israeli notions of national territory. This spatial concept, particularly its areal extents derived from an inherited cognition, is fervently advocated by the important and influential leaders of Israel. Outsiders may well wonder about the depth of such feelings. Fundamental to an appreciation of the subsequent development of Israel after the attainment of independence in 1948 is this idea of 'the Promised Land for a Chosen People' (Herzl). The Promised Land has fired the imagination of Jews through the centuries, but especially in recent years has inspired activists within the Jewish Bureau, most of whom became established in influential positions within the new, yet still fledgling, state.

After the need for continuing Jewish immigration into Israel, as discussed in Chapter 2, the further and immediate priority was for the realization of a state that would encompass the specific area of Eretz Yisrael. The Old Testament is generally less precise concerning the specific boundaries of this homeland. One of the earliest references concerning the earlier covenant with Abram, relates that:

> In the same day the Lord made a covenant with Abram, saying, Unto thy seed have I given this land, from the river of Egypt unto the great river, the river Euphrates. (Genesis 15:18)

The river of Egypt referred to is probably not the Nile but rather the Wadi el Arish in Sinai (Rowley, 1977). Other passages are equally expansive. Moses, according to Numbers 34:3–12, inherited a land that included much of present-day Israel and parts of Egypt, Iraq, Jordan, Lebanon and Syria. A fundamental point is that the Promised Land has always included Samaria and Judea, the present so-called West Bank, including Jerusalem, the areas being firmly embedded in the twelfth-century B.C. lands of the Twelve Tribes with Israel reaching its maximum extent during the reign of King Solomon in the tenth century B.C. (Fig. 12). The generally accepted territorial extent of Eretz Yisrael now appears to be the Jordan valley to the east, the present Israeli-Lebanese border to the north, and a line from the Wadi el Arish in the south-west across to a point to the south of Eilat on the Gulf of Aqaba in the south.

The particular importance of Jerusalem to Israel, both ancient and modern, cannot be overemphasized. Since the time of David it has been the Jewish ambition to lay particular claim to this single symbolic place, 'because the Temple and the City are inextricable in Judaism ... and serve as the quintessence of the land' (Davies, 1974, p.194). The prophet Zechariah looked towards the restoration of Jerusalem:

> Thus said the Lord of hosts; Behold, I
> will save my people from the east
> country, and from the west country:
> And I will bring them, and they shall
> dwell in the midst of Jerusalem: and
> they shall be my people, and I will be
> their God, in truth and in righteousness. (Zechariah, 8:7–8)

The words of Ben-Gurion in 1949 still represent the prevailing Israeli sentiment concerning the Holy City and the symbolic attachment to land as place with meaning and soul:

> [Jerusalem] is an integral part of Israeli
> history in her faith and in the depths of
> her soul. Jerusalem is the 'heart of hearts'
> of Israel. ... A Nation which over 2,500
> years has always maintained the pledge vowed
> by the banished people on the rivers of

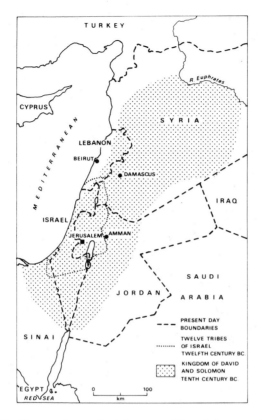

FIGURE 12. The varying territorial extents of Israel. Sources of data: I Chronicles 18:5–14 and Isaac (1976)

Babylon not to forget Jerusalem—this nation will
never sanction its separation. [Moreover]
Jewish Jerusalem will never accept foreign
rule after thousands of her sons and
daughters have freed, for the third time,
their historic homeland and delivered
Jerusalem from destruction. (Divrei Ha-Knesset, 1949, p.221)

The specific agenda was clear; for Israel to attain its 'birth-right' it would have to seek to incorporate those areas of Eretz Yisrael oustide Israel into the developing state, such a spatial expansion being referred to in Israeli parlance as 'the redemption of the land'.

51

Arab counter-offensives and the war of 1967

The inexorable build-up to the war of 1967 began in 1963: continuing yet ominously lower rates of Jewish immigration, mounting conflicts and Israeli diversions of the Jordan waters, disturbances between Ashkenazi and Sephardic communities within Israel, the real possibility of President Nasser of Egypt breaking ranks and about-turning on the *status quo*.

Somewhat ironically the war of 1967 which had been fought by Israel to confirm, maintain and reinforce the *status quo* had quite an opposite effect: it provided a particular and direct fillip to the development of serious Palestinian liberation movements, largely unshackled from and unhindered by Jordanian and Egyptian bureaucratic controls. Certain of the liberation groups were to become progressively revolutionary in their outlook.

The Palestine Liberation Organization (P.L.O.) was founded in 1964 to co-ordinate the separate groups working for a national homeland for Palestinians. The two most important factions of the P.L.O. are El Fatah and the Popular Front for the Liberation of Palestine (P.F.L.P.).

P.F.L.P., developed from the Baath in Syria, is dominantly a Marxist-Leninist group that came into being after the war of 1967 when the old Movement of Arab Nationalists reconstructed itself as a guerilla organization. Committed not only to the Palestinian homeland but also to Marxism and the class struggle, the Popular Front for the Liberation of Palestine is fervently anti-imperialist and anti-monarchist.

El Fatah has been the dominant voice in the P.L.O. since 1969. Initiated in January 1959, the Fatah group was founded in 1961, having grown out of one part of the fundamentalist Muslim Brotherhood that began in Cairo in 1928. Its name means 'victory' and is an acronym from the Arabic initials of the words 'Palestine Liberation Movement' read backwards. Its military wing is El Assifa. Yasser Arafat joined the fervently Pan-Arab nationalist Muslim Brotherhood while an engineering student at the University of Cairo.

El Fatah commenced its guerilla operations in Israel in 1965 (Smith and Andrews, 1977), but it was only after the 1967 war when El Fatah assumed P.L.O. leadership that the largely inconsequential P.L.O. became the major adversary to Israeli colonialism. The Muslim Brotherhood was fused with the Arab nationalism envisaged by Gamal Abdel Nasser to create an independent Palestinian political entity.

CHAPTER 5

The Aftermath of the 1967 War and the Occupied Territories

The initial section of this chapter considers the relationships that developed between the Palestinians and neighbouring Arab states following the war of 1967 as related to Israeli occupation of the West Bank, East Jerusalem and the Gaza Strip. The remainder of the chapter examines the spatial–land policies of Israel in the occupied territories from 1967: the second and third sections focus direct attention upon the progressive Israeli settlement of the West Bank and the particular importance of the 'Judaization' of East Jerusalem; the final part considers Israeli acquisition of Arab lands within the West Bank, giving a detailed documentation of the Israeli policy of land sequestration in this crucial area of the occupied territories.

The Arab states

Following the Six-Day War of June 1967 a victorious Israel occupied the West Bank, East Jerusalem, the Gaza Strip and the Golan Heights, thereby increasing the number of Arabs under Israeli control from 300,000 to more than 1.3 million. Moreover, in the aftermath of the war the status quo within the region that had existed for some twenty years was disrupted. In this new climate El Fatah gradually assumed leadership of the Palestine liberation struggle.

Clashes in the Lebanon between Palestinian fedayeen (guerillas) and Lebanese government forces occurred until the truce of October 1969; the Palestinian-Jordanian conflict broke out in January 1970. Hussein of Jordan, who had become increasingly apprehensive over the mounting Palestinian power base, particularly that of the Marxist P.F.L.P. within his country, brought the matter to a head. In September 1970, 'Black September', Bedouin troops of the Royal Jordanian Army attacked Palestinian refugee encampments, including those in 'the Battle of Amman', killing 2,600 fedayeen commandos and Palestinian civilians. In Syria in 1970 the right wing of the Baath came to power following a coup. President Assad moved swiftly to arrest the left wing of the Baath movement and effectively put an end to the revolutionary Palestinian activities in Syria.

In Egypt, following Nasser's death in September 1970, the most repressive of Nasser's socialist state policies were quickly overturned and the core of the Nasserite ruling group removed from power. The manifold problems confronting the deteriorating Egyptian economy demanded attention. By May 1971 Sadat had terminated the Egyptian alliance with the U.S.S.R., had visited the U.S. and received President Nixon in Cairo and had openly abandoned the crusade for Arab solidarity in favour of a more nationalistic concern for Egypt's welfare. These developments confirmed Egypt's reintegration into the West and were intended to help Sadat, whose eyes were steadfastly set on the level of U.S. funds directed towards Israel, obtain a massive inflow of both U.S. aid and Arab capital to bolster his ailing economy.

By 1973 Israel and Iran, supported by their special relationships with the U.S., were emerging as the dominant centres of sub-imperialism within the Middle East. The Iranian seizure of the Arabian (Persian) Gulf islands of Tanb, also claimed by Ra's al Khaymah, and Abu Musa in late 1971 had particularly worried the affluent Saudis and the Gulf States. The close co-operation between Sadat and the reactionary Feisal at this time was significant to the 1973 war that sought to redress the balance of power within the Middle East. The Palestinians mattered little in such circumstances. The Egyptian-Syrian alliance in the war of 1973 materialized from such a base:

> The aims of the war were thus clearly defined: to re-establish Arab dignity, to obtain the restitution of Sinai and the Golan Heights through negotiation, to establish a little Palestine independent of King Hussein, to recognize definitely in exchange a State of Israel reduced to its just proportions, and thus to improve the Arab bourgeoisie as the main voice in the dialogue with the United States and to put an end to Israel and Iran's ambition to become the main sub-imperialisms. (Amin, 1978, p.70)

In essence, Egypt was competing with Israel's position as prime recipient of U.S. aid and backing. Sadat was intent upon reinforcing the Washington-Cairo-Riyadh axis; he wanted the Suez Canal to be repaired and he needed an inflow of foreign capital. Yet the hopes of an Israeli retreat from the territories occupied in 1967 did not materialize.

Saudi Arabia, rich yet surprisingly ineffective, was particularly ambivalent, distancing itself from the various entanglements within the region (Lacey, 1981). An ultra-conservative feudal monarchy firmly upheld internally by the National Guard under Prince Sultan, Saudi Arabia was particularly concerned to maintain the status quo and privileges of the ruling Saud family. They privately possessed many reservations about the revolutionary fervour and intensity of the P.L.O. under Yasser Arafat and particularly about such leftist-extremist factions as the P.F.L.P.

The Saudis, nevertheless, consider that they occupy a special position in the Middle East. The Holy Prophet Mohammed was born in the Hejaz, the western region of Saudi Arabia; the holy cities of Mecca and Medina are *the* centres of Islam; and the Hajj, the pilgrimage to Mecca, is attended by pilgrims from throughout Islam (Rowley and Hamdan, 1977). In 1981 alone over two million hajjees (pilgrims) journeyed to Mecca. The Saudis cherish a desire to be not only the centre of spiritual Islam but also to become the centre of the modern Arab world (Ochsenwald, 1981). Partly in response to such an end the Gulf Co-operation Council (G.C.C.) was founded in May 1981, comprised of Saudi Arabia and the five Gulf states of Bahrain, Kuwait, Oman, Qatar and the United Arab Emirates.

There is little doubt that both Israel and the Arab states of Egypt, Jordan, Lebanon, Saudi Arabia and Syria have serious misgivings about the continuing development of the P.L.O., about its becoming a Pan-Arab political organization which would look beyond the confines of both Palestine and Israel. But, U.N. Resolution 3236 of 22 November 1974 guarantees the international right of the P.L.O. to press for self-determination and to be the Palestinians' sole legitimate representative.

The Palestinian position has been nowhere more complex than within the Lebanon. Indeed, it is there that the lingering internecine quarrels of the Arab states emerge in some detail. The continuing Lebanese conflict can be traced back to April 1975, ushered in by a mounting Lebanese resentment at the increasing independence of Palestinians who appeared to be operating as a state within a state. The point of ignition occurred when the Phalange, the right wing Lebanese Christian party, ambushed a bus-party of Palestinian fedayeen at Ain Al-Rummaneh, a Christian suburb of Beirut. The specific details of and causes for the ambush are shrouded in mystery, although Israeli involvement seems certain. Bitter fighting broke out between the Phalangists backed by Israel and the Palestinians who were supported by left wing and mainly Muslim Lebanese.

Following Syrian intervention in February 1976 reforms were initiated in an attempt to improve the conditions of Muslims within the Lebanon. A semblance of peace was restored, but hostilities soon broke out again. The Syrians under President Assad, who had become particularly alarmed at the possibility of a leftist-controlled Lebanon on his border, switched support from the leftist Palestinians to the rightist Christians. A full Arab summit was called at Riyadh in October 1976 where an Egyptian-Syrian agreement was concluded that endorsed the ceasefire. The Palestinians had suffered a dramatic defeat from the concerted actions of the conservative Arab states, particularly of Syria, Jordan and Saudi Arabia. While intermittent fighting was to continue, the Palestinian effort within the Lebanon had been seriously set back by collusions among those who opposed the Palestinian aim for the creation of a political entity and/or those who viewed with concern the development of left wing, anti-imperial policies.

In 1978 Israel occupied the Lebanon south of the Litani River for several months. Upon Israeli withdrawal two U.N. zones were established to the south and southeast of the Litani River policed by the U.N. Interim Force in Lebanon (U.N.I.F.I.L.). The area between the U.N. zones and Israel, the so-called 'Haddadland', was controlled by Major Sa'ad Haddad's Christian militia which works closely with the Israelis. The Palestinians became firmly entrenched in their enclave around the coastal cities of Tyre and Sidon, sometimes referred to as Fatahland (Fig. 13).

Following the end of the Lebanese Civil War of 1976 a reorientation and acculturation of much of the southern Lebanese population to-

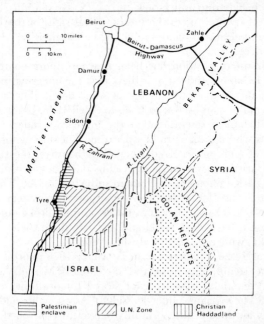

FIGURE 13. Southern Lebanon—showing the Israeli occupied ('annexed') Golan Heights, the U.N. zones, the Palestinian enclave and 'Haddadland' prior to June 1982

wards Israel was achieved through the implementation of what has been termed the 'Good Fence' policy. This policy was instituted by Israel 'as a humanitarian assistance program for residents of south Lebanon (who as a result of the civil war, had been cut off from the supply and administration of food, fuel, medical treatment, etc.) regardless of race or creed' (Israeli Defence Spokesman, 1981, p.31). Under the Good Fence arrangement the inhabitants of the southern Lebanon are able to obtain five basic services at the Lebanese-Israeli border. They can receive medical aid, participate in trade and commerce, send and collect mail via the regular Israeli postal service, visit relatives in Israel and seek employment within Israel. Medical clinics were established along the Lebanese-Israeli border at Metulla, Dovev and Hanita and serious cases are transformed to Israeli hospitals. Between June 1976 and October 1981, 190,600 Lebanese received medical care: 78,500 were Christians, 106,400 Muslims and the remainder Druzes. Lebanese have been permitted to cross the border to work in Israel, returning to the Lebanon each evening. Wages are paid in Israeli currency, enabling workers to purchase goods in Israel, although they may convert up to 50 percent of their wages into Lebanese currency.

A state of relative equipoise was thus achieved in the southern Lebanon through the concerted operations of U.N.I.F.I.L., Haddadland and the Good Fence policy, with the Palestinian base to the west along the coast. Although Israeli-Palestinian confrontations flared up intermittently after 1978—the Israelis responded to Palestinian offensives, for example, by bombing densely populated parts of Beirut and Tyre—generally, and particularly between July 1981 and June 1982, a relative calm existed. It was within the Lebanon that the problems of Arab solidarity with the Palestinians needed to be worked out if concerted backing for or suppression of the Palestinians was to have emerged. However, the personal interests and fears of the separate Arab states made and make such a Pan-Arabist rapprochement most unlikely.

The occupied territories
and advancing Israeli settlement

The West Bank, an area of 2,270 square miles, was the home of 650,000 Palestinians at the time of the Six Day War in 1967. Following the occupation of the West Bank, Israel embarked upon a policy of colonial settlement within the area. The three main types of Israeli colonial settlements in the West Bank are the outpost or nahal villages, religious settlements and residential suburbs, although with time the rural settlements obtain an agricultural base.

Outpost villages are a sub-variety of the communal kibbutz and occur when settlement is seen as the best way to 'improve the security situation but when farming can become profitable only after years of thorough reclamation work' (Orni, 1963, p.178). In the outpost villages nahal units, the Pioneer Settlement Corps of the Israeli army, undertake site preparations, construct the villages, sink wells and provide mobile power supplies and power cables, sanitation and sewerage facilities. Certain soldiers, whose demobilization is imminent, are posted in as permanent settlers, often to remain after their demobilization. The nahal settlement form has been the prime settlement type introduced to colonize the West Bank. The years of 'thorough reclamation work' both in the physical and human sense prior to agricultural profitability includes sequestration and purchase of lands and consolidation of holdings into viable economic units. Such settlement is considered by many to be in direct violation of the Geneva Convention of 1949, which categorically states that 'an occupying power shall not deport or transfer parts of its own civilian population into the territory it occupies' (United Nations, 1976, paras.1–2). The counterclaim by Israel is that Samaria (Shomeron) and Judea (Yehuda)—that is, the entire West Bank including Jerusalem as traditionally within Eretz Yisrael—are an integral part of the modern state. What is more, as the Israeli government is not strictly posting 'in parts of its own civilian population', Israel may be said to be adhering to the word if not the spirit of the Geneva Convention.

Two examples will demonstrate some of the impact of the colonial settlement upon the established order. The dunum referred to in the example equals 0.25 acre or 0.101 hectare. Mehola (3 on Fig. 14a), established in February 1968 on a strategic site covering the road to Tubas, was the first nahal in the Jordan valley; 1,689 dunums of land were expropriated from Bardala village together with further lands from Ain al Beida. The Mehola well had seriously depleted the water supply in the two proximate Arab villages by December 1978 when Mehola had a population of 137 persons with an established commercial agricultural economy, including field crops, grapefruit, and turkeys, and a small metal-fabrication plant. Salit Nahal (53 on Fig. 14c), established in September 1977 between Tulkarm and Kaddum, expropriated 1,268 dunums of land from Kufr Sahr village, and, with additional lands earmarked, was to become a moshav by December 1979. By December 1978, seventeen houses had been completed and the village contained a residential population of forty-six.

The second major type of Israeli rural settlement is the religious village, particularly for Gush Emunim, Group of the Faithful. An initial settlement is established by the group, and in various ways lands are assembled to facilitate the transition from the initial colonial

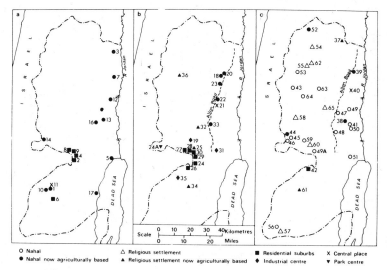

O Nahal
● Nahal now agriculturally based
△ Religious settlement
▲ Religious settlement now agriculturally based
■ Residential suburbs
◆ Industrial centre
X Central place
▼ Park centre

FIGURE 14. The progression of Israel: settlements in Judea and Samaria, 1967–78: a. 1967–70; b. 1971–75; c. 1976–78. Source: Rowley (1981)

settlement form to an integrated village community with related rural-farming structures. Within the initial stages such settlements are often 'illegal' in the sense that they are not recognized by the Israeli government for allocations of various fundings for health, education, welfare, social services, etc., although external funding is obtained from, such organizations as the Jewish National Fund, Youth Aliyah and Keren Hayesod.

As of February 1979 all of those settlements established in the West Bank prior to December 1978 had been 'regularized', that is legalized, recognized, and accepted by the Israeli Government. Since the conservative Likud government attained power in 1977 to December 1978, seventeen colonial settlements were established in the West Bank, eight of these being founded by religious groups. Ofra (32 on Fig. 14b), east of Ramallah, on the east-west road to Jericho, was established by Gush Emunim in May 1975 and 'regularized' in July 1977. The village site was formerly a Jordanian army base with 180 and 250 dunums of land having been expropriated from, respectively, Ain Yabrud and Silwad. As of December 1978 Ofra had 360 dunums of agricultural lands with additional pastures and plans for further major land acquisitions, a population of 302, and possessed several workshops in addition to the agricultural enterprises. During the later stages of development both the military and religious rural settlements are comparable, and may develop as either kibbutz or moshav although moshavin are now by far the dominant type.

The third general type of Israeli settlement, the residential suburb is usually established directly by the Israeli government. Such settlements have been located particularly along the northern and eastern edges of Jerusalem as well as adjacent to smaller urban centres such as Bethlehem and Hebron. Qiryat Arba (6 on Fig. 14a), begun as an 'illegal' settlement in April 1968 and recognized by the Israeli government in February 1970, is a large urban settlement for religious Jews adjacent to Hebron in Judea. 1,620 dunums of agricultural land were expropriated from individuals in Hebron and Halhal, and by 1979 the population was estimated to be 1,677 with factories, fabrication units, and various services in operation and some individuals commuting to work in Jerusalem. The initial Israeli settlements in the West Bank, following the occupation during the war of 1967 and mainly agricultural and service centres, were established along the eastern slopes of the Samarian Mountains, the Jordan Rift Valley and about the Jerusalem-Latrun salient (Fig. 14a). Between 1971 and 1975 further settlements were developed along the eastern slopes of the Jordan Valley but to the west of the earlier settlements, in a concentration to the north and east of Jerusalem, to the west of Jericho and about Bethlehem (Rowley, 1981, p.457). The Jordan Rift area settlements have now been linked by the new Allon road, a modern rapid-transit military highway (Fig. 15).

The continuing Israeli colonization of Samaria is of particular importance. Physically different from Judea, Samaria is composed of a group of isolated mountain blocks with intervening fault basins. While the Samaritan rendzina soils developed on chalk and soft limestones are somewhat less fertile than the Judean terra-rossa type soils developed on dolomites and limestones, they are deeper, less rocky, and consequently easier to work. Therefore, together with its greater rainfall, Samaria has traditionally possessed a denser population than Judea and can generally be characterized as a prosperous agricultural area centering upon Nablus (Karmon, 1971, pp.316-17). Whereas the initial Israeli settlements along and overlooking the Jordan Rift Valley could have been considered military outposts, the direct colonization of the Samarian and Judean agricultural heartlands about Nablus and Hebron pointed to longer term Israeli objectives. Figure 16 demonstrates the developing pattern of colonial settlement and the increasing extent of Israeli land holdings within the West Bank reached by December 1978.

W.W. Harris (1980) suggests that between 1967 and 1977 'official government settlement programmes' were restricted, apart from East Jerusalem, to relatively empty areas. It was, Harris asserts, only after 1977 with the new Likud government under Begin that official settlement began to spread into the densely populated core of the West

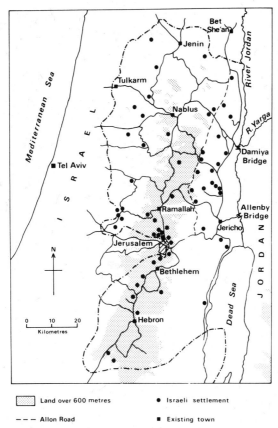

Land over 600 metres   ● Israeli settlement

– – – Allon Road   ■ Existing town

FIGURE 15. The West Bank, Samaria and Judea, showing Israeli settlements and the Allon road, 1980. Source: Rowley (1981)

Bank. Prime exception is taken to Harris's ideas on two grounds: the earlier settlement during the first ten years of Israeli occupation of the West Bank was not in 'relatively empty areas', and his suggestion that a major shift occurred in Israeli land policy between the Labour government and the new Likud government elected in 1977 is misplaced. The first exception will be documented in the final section of this chapter. As to the second, the eventual spread of Israeli settlement into the West Bank heartland could be discerned and inferred from emerging patterns of Israeli settlements, land sequestrations and attitudes developing prior to 1977. An evolving pattern could be seen to be leading directly to the colonization of the West Bank agricultural core, which would have taken place even without the election of the conservative Likud government.

61

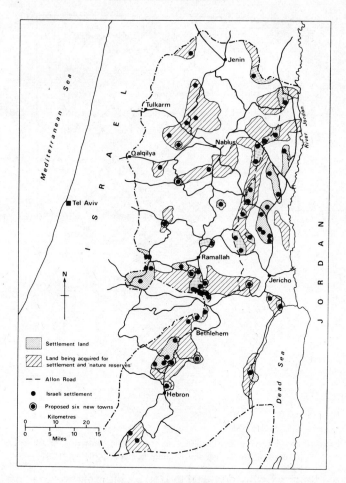

FIGURE 16. Israel. Settlements and landholdings within the West Bank, December 1978. Source: Rowley (1981)

Upon his appointment as head both of the Jewish Agency's land settlement department and the rural settlement department of the World Zionist Organization in 1978, Matityahu Drobles began formally to consider the development of a consolidated and general master plan for the Israeli colonization and settlement of Judea and Samaria. The resulting *Master Plan for the Development of Settlement in Judea and Samaria*, issued in October 1978, hereinafter referred to as the Drobles plan, was to cover the five-year period between January 1979 and December 1983 (Drobles, 1978).

The Drobles plan for the future disposition and extension of Jewish settlement in the West Bank emphasizes that the surveys underway when the plan was issued may lead to suggestions for further settlements. The plan has now been accepted as policy by the Likud government, indeed as the specific agenda for colonization of the West Bank. Fund raising activities worldwide by the Jewish Agency, and especially by the World Zionist Organization, are underwriting much of the financial costs of the entire programme.

Five pages of text within the twelve-page Drobles plan itemize the specific details relating to the planned 'Disposition of Settlements'. The following passage sets forth the recommendations for the Adumin block:

> *Adumin Block.* The temporary settlement of Maaleh Adumin already exists here, along with its adjacent industrial zone. The permanent urban settlement is now under construction at a site near Aizariyah, just outside Jerusalem, and where an additional 300 families would take up residence in the first year and 1,500 within five years. Also in the area is the settlement of Mitzpeh Jericho, for which an additional 100 families is proposed in the first year of the plan and 300 after five years. In addition to these two settlements it is proposed to establish a series of three new settlements which will form a territorial continuity with the Beit-El Block settlements to the north: Pe'era (Maaleh Adumin B, near Ain Farah), which is to be a large community settlement based mainly on tourism and holidaying, to be inhabited by 150 families in the first year and 400 families five years later; Maaleh Adumin C, north of Pe'era; and still further north Maaleh Adumin C—the latter two being community settlements meant to be inhabited by 300 families each within five years.

Table 1 is abstracted from the text of the second section of the Drobles plan relating to the twenty-one blocks, including the Adumin block example quoted above. These settlement blocks, together with existing settlements where enlargement is planned and proposed new settlements, are located in Figure 17. The map also shows that apart from settlement along the West Bank Highlands the Israeli colonization is located within the so-called settlement blocks. The blocks are defined on Figure 17 while the identification numbers relate to the block numbers in Table 1.

TABLE 1. Planned development of existing and projected settlement in Judea and Samaria, 1979–83

The village names are preceded by an *E* for an existing settlement or a *P* for planned settlement. The settlement type refers to the specific functional type give in the plan; see the text for fuller definitions of individual items. The planned numbe of families in new settlements and the additional number of families in existin settlements is that envisaged at the end of the plan period (1983).
Source of data: *Master Plan for the Development of Settlement in Judea and Samar* (Jerusalem, 1978), pp.3–7.

Settlement block	Village name	Location	Settlement type	Planne number of families
1. Adorayim	*P.* Adorayim	Dorah junction, E. of Sikha village	Community	300
	P. Eiton	Nr. Tel Eiton	Agricultural	100
2. Adumin	*E.* Maaleh Adumin		Urban	1,500
	P. Mitzpeh Jericho		Community	300
	P. Pe'era (Maaleh Adumin B)	Nr. Ain Farah	Large community/ Tourism	400
	P. Maaleh Adumin C	N. of Pe'era	Community	300
	P. Maaleh Adumin D	N. of C.	Community	300
3. Amos	*P.* Amos + further village envisaged?	Rujm-a-Nahah N.E. of Hebron	Large community	400
4. Ariel	*E.* Ariel (Haris)	Samaria, transverse road	Urban	1,500
	P. Ariel B	Hirbet a-Shelal	Community	300
5. Beit-El	*E.* Beit-El		Community	400
	E. Rimon		Community	300
	E. Kohav HaShahar		Community	300
	E. Ofra		Community	300
	P. Kohav HaShahar B.	E. of K.H.	Community	300
6. Dotan	*P.* Dotan	Mirka junction overlooking Dotan valley	Large community	500
7. Elon Moreh	*P.* Elon Moreh	S.E. of Nablus on Jabl Rujaib	Large community	400
8. Ephraim	*E.* Gitit	Jordan rift continuity		
	E. Maaleh Ephraim			
	E. Mevoh Shiloh			
	P. Mevoh Shiloh B		Community	300
9. Givon	*E.* Beit Horon		Community	200
	E. Givon		Community	150

Settlement block	Village name	Location	Settlement type	Planned number of families
	P. Givon B	Hill N. of Givon	Urban	3,000
	P. Givon C	W. of Givon B	Community	300
10. Gush Etzion	*E.* Rosh Tzurim		Community	30
	E. Elon Shvut		Rural Centre	100
	E. Kfar Etzion		Kibbutz	20
	E. Elazar		Moshav	15
	E. Migdal Oz		Kibbutz	70
	E. Tekoah		Now proposed: Urban	800
	P. Haforit		Agriculture/ Industry	100
	P. Efrat	S. of Bethlehem	Community	300
	P. Etzion B	Beit Fajr Forest	Community	300
	P. Etzion C	Givat Hamukhtar	Community	300
	P. Elazar B	Sheikh Abdallah Ibrahim	Community	300
	P. Nahalim	W. of Nahalin village	Community	300
11. Karnei Shomron	*E.* Karnei Shomron		Urban	800
	E. Elkana		Urban	800
	P. Karnei Shomron B	S. of K-S	Community	300
	P. Karnei Shomron C	E. of K-S	Community	300
	P. Karnei Shomron D	S.E. of K-S C	Community	300
	P. Karnei Shomron E	E. of K-S C	Community	300
12. Kedumin	*E.* Kedumin			200
	P. Kedumin B	Imam Ali	Industry/Intensive Agriculture	300
	P. Kedumin C	Ras-a-Bayyad	Industry/Intensive Agriculture	300
	P. Kedumin	A-Ras S. of Tal village		300
13. Maarav (each located on border of 'Green Line')	*P.* Maarav A	S.E. of Kafin village	Agricultural	100
	P. Maarav B	S.E. of Baka-al-Gharbiyeh	Agricultural	100
	P. Maarav C	E. of Kibbutz Bahan	Agricultural	100
	P. Maarav D	E. of Tulkarm	Agricultural	100
14. Modiin	*E.* Shilat		Community	80
	E. Kfar Ruth		Community	80
	E. Mevoh Modiim		Community	80
	E. Mevoh Horon		Community	150
	P. Matityahu		Community	300
	P. Matityahu B	W. of Bilin village (hill 386)	Community	300
15. Nahal Tirzah	*P.* Tirzah	Jabl Thayour	Large Agricultural	400
16. Neveh-Zuf	*E.* Neveh-Zuf		Community	200

65

Settlement block	Village name	Location	Settlement type	Planned number of families
	P. Neveh-Zuf B	Hirbet Rushniyeh (S.W. of N-Z)	Community	300
	P. Neveh-Zuf C	Nr. Kafr	Community	300
	P. Neveh-Zuf D	Ayin	Community	300
17. Reihan	E. Reihan A			100
	P. Reihan B	W. of Arakah village		100
	P. Mei-Ami			80
	P. Mei-Ami B		Moshavim	100
	P. Barkai B			100
18. Shiloh	E. Shiloh		Community	300
	E. Tapuah		Community	300
	P. Shiioh B	Batan Hiluah (W. of S.)	Community	300
	P. Shiloh C	Jabl Batan (N.W. of S.)	Community	300
	P. Shiloh D	Jabal Rawat (N.E. of S.)	Community	300
19. Shomron	E. Sanour		Community	200
	E. Shomron		Community	200
	P. Maaleh Nahal	N. of Bourkah village	Community	300
	P. Maaleh Nahal	Jabl Yazzid (E. of M.N.)	Community	300
20. Tarkumya	P. Tirat-Horesh	E. of Tarkumya	Community	400
21. Yatir	E. Yatir			300
	E. Lutsifer			300
	P. Kramin			100
	P. Raveh	N.E. of Kramin		300
	P. Yatir B	N.E. of Yatir	Community (Agriculture, Industry, Tourism)	300
	P. Yatir C	N.E. of Yatir	Same as Yatir B	300
	P. Yatir D	N.E. of Yatir	Same as Yatir B	300
	P. Susiya	N.S. of Samua		300

The master plan specifies the nature of the various settlement types. Within *urban settlements* some 60 percent of the families will be employed in industry, handicrafts, and tourism and the remainder in services and work outside the settlement. In the towns in proximity to Jerusalem the proportion of those employed in outside work will be greater. In the *community settlements* the economic basis in the development stage will see about 50 percent of the families earning their living from industry and handicrafts, about 12 percent from capital-based

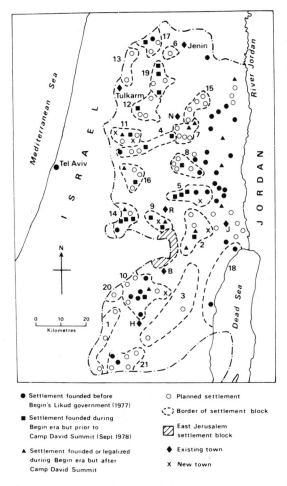

FIGURE 17. The Drobles plan for the development of settlement in
Judea and Samaria, 1978–83

intensive agriculture, about 25 percent from outside work and some
13 percent from local services. The *agricultural* and the *combined settlements* will be based on agricultural branches, mainly intensive, depending on the means for production in the area, as well as on
industry, handicrafts and tourism. Some of the settlers will be engaged
in local and regional services.

The community settlement, Yishur Kehillati, used in the colonization of the West Bank is a small private enterprise rural settlement.
Although the settlers have certain communal obligations, such as

participation in the settlement co-operative union which has responsibilities for community services and, in an advisory capacity, for economic matters, the settlers are not constrained by the collective decision-making strategies of the settlement and can work in other centres if they so wish. Commuting occurs from Yishav Kehillati to the larger places in Israel, such as Jerusalem and Tel Aviv–Yafo.

The Drobles plan emphasizes that the settlement 'throughout the entire land of Israel is for security and by right and that settlements within the West Bank have been determined following a thorough examination of the various sites with respect to their being suitable and amenable to settlement, taking into account topographical conditions, land-preparation possibilities etc.' (Drobles, 1978, p.2). The cost basis for the implementation of the plan is as presented within Drobles' plan: 'The calculation for investment is based on the additional families which, by the plan, would take up residence in Judea and Samaria—27,000 in the five years.' The average investment for settling one family totals 2 million Israeli pounds; the following breakdown from Drobles (1978, p.9) is at 1978 prices:

Infrastructure (road, electricity, sewerage, etc.) I£	150,000
Temporary housing	150,000
Permanent housing (including public buildings)	600,000
Water sources	100,000
Means of production	900,000
Miscellaneous	100,000
Total investment per family	I£2,000,000

Although the above is for the average investment per family in all settlements, the investment for a rural settlement is higher than that for an urban settlement. Drobles proposes forty-six new settlements to be established with 5,000 new families after one year and 16,000 after five years, and with an investment of 10 billion Israeli pounds after one year and I£32 billion after five years. Further he proposes the thickening of thirty-eight existing or under-construction settlements with 3,000 new families after one year and 11,000 after five years, and with I£6 billion invested after one year and I£22 billion after five years. Thus the overall investment for executing the five-year plan has been estimated at I£54 billion of which I£16 billion would be required in the first year to activate the plan and I£9.5 billion in each of the four ensuing years.

Addition of the tabulated proposals within Table 1 presents a grand total of 26,855 families, about 100,000 individuals, for settlement in Judea and Samaria by 1983, some 9,700 families from the enlargement of existing settlements and those that were under construction in 1978 and over 17,000 families within new settlements. Multiplying this grand total of 26,855 by the average family investment of I£2 million, gives the total of I£54 billion. Onto this total envisaged cost must be added a significant amount to cover inflation and devaluations since 1978, and the cost of further settlements that will doubtlessly be recommended after ongoing surveys are completed. At July 1981 the I£54 million equalled some £235 million or $70 million for the five-year West Bank settlement plan. Our conservative but realistic estimate in 1983 is at least £600 million or $900 million. The Jewish Agency, restructured in 1971 to include the World Zionist Organization and all Jewish fund raising bodies, is underwriting and maintaining the financial solvency of the entire settlement plan. The United Jewish Appeal in the United States and Keren Hayesod in sixty-nine other countries are now contributing some two-thirds and one-third, respectively, to the costs of the West Bank settlement programme.

Whereas the estimates may vary, the important conclusion is that such a considerable investment indicates not only a real commitment and firm resolve by Israel to settle the West Bank but also the intention to incorporate Judea and Samaria, when the time is right, into the state of Israel. Indeed, relating to the investment required to finance the continuing settlement of the West Bank, 'This investment is absolutely essential and is a condition for the execution of a paramount national mission' (Drobles, 1978, p.3). The intention for permanent settlement is all too clear: the incorporation of Judea and Samaria into Israel is a realization of national mission, the unity and integrity of Eretz Yisrael. Also the Israeli settlement policy of the West Bank is serving, in the words of Mardechii Nisan, to 'create political facts' regarding Israel's future boundaries in any final agreement with the Arabs (Nisan, 1978, p.97). 'Establishing "new facts" also includes greatly extending the road network, setting up numerous military bases and outposts, and organizing Israeli businesses and commercial operations in the occupied areas' (Peretz, 1970, p.39). While the Israeli policy is to implant agricultural and industrial settlement between existing Palestinian villages the policy includes *mitzpim* settlements, 'observation posts' that 'are intended to be the nuclei of future settlements and are sited in quasi-military fashion in the mountains above the largest Arab villages' (Jerusalem Post International Edition, 18–25 November, 1979, p.13). The Drobles Plan also includes details of seven planned new towns in the West Bank (Table 2).

One apparent setback to the overall Israeli settlement plans in the West Bank occurred 22 October 1979, when the Supreme Court of Israel ruled for the first time that an Israeli settlement on the occupied West Bank, Elon Moreh, established by the Government a few months

TABLE 2. Seven planned new towns in the West Bank, 1978–83

Source of data: Drobles, 1978. Note: Qiryat Arba is listed as a new urban centre b Drobles (p.11) but is not included within his earlier itemization as set out in Tabl 1 nor in Figure 17.

Town	Settlement block	1978 status	Population 1979	Envisaged population 1983
Ariel	Ariel	Established 1978	+260	+1,500
Elkana	Karnei-Shomron	Established 1978	+200	+ 800
Givon	Givon		500	3,000
Karnei-Shomron	Karnei-Shomron	Established	+200	+ 800
Qiryat Arba	Beit-El	New settlement	+200	+1,000
Maaleh Adumin	Adumin	Construction commenced	+300	1,500
Tekoah	Gush Etzion	New settlement	+200	+ 800

earlier, was illegal. In doing so the Court ruled, in the face of conflict-ing military opinion, that there was no security justification for the settlement which, unlike previous settlements, was established in the north of the West Bank, densely populated by Arabs. For many right-wing Israelis and particularly for the Gush Emunim group that settled Elon Moreh, the judgement is an intolerable precedent; it suggests that Israeli settlements in the West Bank might be dismantled and their land returned to their former Arab occupants.

The Israeli government is firmly committed to the settlement of the West Bank, the area referred to by Prime Minister Menachem Begin as Judea and Samaria and an integral part of historic Israel, and to populating it with Israelis in an attempt to change its demographic composition. While it is possible that legislation may be introduced in the Knesset to overcome the threat to continuing Israeli settlement in the occupied territories, the judgement provides fine insights into certain of the settlement procedures, justifications and overall aims and is considered as important enough to warrant inclusion as an appendix. Despite this, since the time of the judgement in October 1979, Israeli settlement has proceeded throughout the occupied ter-ritories unabated.

Ths 'Judaization' of Jerusalem

It does seem somewhat paradoxical that it is Jerusalem, the Holy City for Jews, Christians and Muslims, that poses one of the greatest barriers to a lasting peace in this area of the Middle East. Following the cessation of fighting between Jews and Arabs in 1949, West Jerusalem came under Israeli control while East Jerusalem, largely the Old City and its environs, was under Arab-Jordanian control. The western and eastern sections were separated by an armistice line, the so-termed 'Green Line'. The city remained thus divided until 1967 when the Israelis entered and captured the Old City, exercising full and exclusive control of the unified city to the present time. By contrast the special significance of Jerusalem and the international status accorded to the city was provided for in the United Nations General Assembly Resolution 181, and also by specific assurances and under-takings regarding the *corpus separatum* of the Holy City, entered into by Israel upon its admittance to the United Nations in May 1949 (Hirst, 1973-4). Israeli attempts to set Jerusalem up as its national capital, a status not recognized by other countries who, apart from certain Latin American countries, maintain their embassies in Tel Aviv, has to be considered against the backcloth of the Mandate and the subsequent U.N. proposals regarding the *corpus separatum* of the Holy City. It would appear that neither Israel nor Jordan acquired sovereignty over any part of Jerusalem by 1950, nor by the outbreak of further hostilities in June 1967 (Talal, 1979, pp.25-7). Rather, between 1949 and 1967 Israel and Jordan could be considered to be in effective control of West and East Jerusalem respectively as military occupants with an armistice line, the Green Line, separating them. The admin-istrative reality, however, is that following the Six-Day War in 1967, Jerusalem became united under Israeli control and the Israelization of East Jerusalem has proceeded apace.

Historically the Old City of Jerusalem has been divided into quite specific Jewish, Armenian, Christian and Muslim quarters (Fig. 18). Since 1967 the Israelis have proceeded to expel Arabs from certain residential districts and to increase Jewish settlement, a twin process that can be related to the overall Israelization of the Holy City. The new Jerusalem plan for the 'Judaization' of the city incorporates the following recommendations:

1. The Israeli expropriation of 116 dunums in the Old City of Jeru-salem. The plan called for the expulsion of 10,000 Arabs on the pretext of congestion and inferior housing conditions, while at the same time it planned to accommodate 5,000 Jews in the extended Jewish Quarter (Arieh, 1973, p.117).
2. The removal of the Arab Moghrabi Quarter adjacent to the Wail-ing Wall.
3. The Arab areas outside the Old City walls have been classified in three categories:
    a. Archaeological sites where building is not allowed.
    b. Green Areas where no construction is permitted.

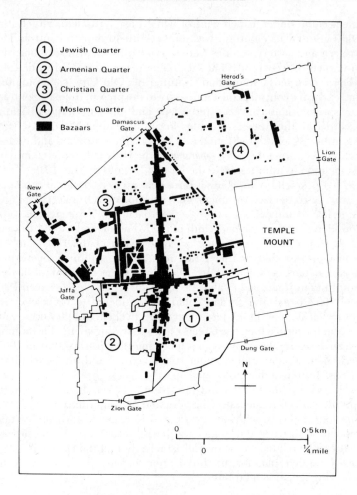

FIGURE 18. The Old City of Jerusalem and its quarters

   c. Special Areas subject to specific regulations which limit building activity.

Most of the land, some 20,000 dunums, left outside the zones has been expropriated by the Israelis and used in its entirety as sites for the construction of new Jewish neighbourhoods and satellite centres such as:

1. Ramot Eshkol on 600 dunums, comprising 2,200 dwellings and associated services.

2. Maalot Dafna on 270 dunums, with 1,400 dwellings and related services.

3. Ramot on 2,500 dunums, having 8,000 dwellings and 38,000 inhabitants with further major developments envisaged.

4. Newé Ya'aqov on 820 dunums with 4,000 dwellings, associated services and 18,000 inhabitants.

5. Gillo on 4,000 dunums with 10,000 dwellings and 35,000 inhabitants is earmarked for further and accelerated development.

6. East Talpiyyot on 2,700 dunums with 5,000 dwellings and 15,000 inhabitants.

These details are derived from Kroyanker (1975, pp.191–202) and planning notes. These several expropriations and wholesale removals and clearances of population, buildings and property appear to run foul of Article 53 of the Geneva (Fourth) Convention, to which Israel is a signatory. This article states that 'Any destruction by the Occupying Power of real . . . property belonging to private persons or to the state, or to other public authorities or to social or co-operative organizations, is prohibited except when such destruction is rendered absolutely necessary by military operations'. The compulsory acquisitions considered here can in no way be construed as strictly necessary for military purposes. Rather, the Israeli demand for housing and settlement in East Jerusalem proceeds in order to reverse the demographic balance between Jewish and Arab populations.

Kutcher (1975), from a conservationalist's viewpoint, is also concerned by the wholesale destruction of the Old City, noting that 'redevelopment' in the name of both fast profit and short-sightedness should be resisted. However, Kutcher fails to recognize or adequately to consider that this redevelopment is part of the systematic process by which the Israelis are attempting to de-Arabize East Jerusalem.

While the precise details of the future plans for the rest of the Arab lands in both the city of Jerusalem and its environs are unknown, information compiled from local press reports reveals the following:

1. The land use on 70,000 dunums to the east of Jerusalem was to be reclassified by military order as restricted areas. It was on this land that the Ma'le Adumin (Al-Khan Al-Ahmar) centre was established.

2. New Jewish suburban developments about the city of Jerusalem have been suggested by the Israeli planner Shaked. Three of these settlements and four villages are earmarked to accommodate between 75,000 and 150,000 inhabitants and a further five satellite centres are to accommodate 25,000 inhabitants. The location of these settlements is suggested to be to the north and northwest of Ramallah and Al-Khan Al-Ahmar, mentioned above.

3. Other suburban settlements are envisaged to the northwest of

Ramallah and in the Ras to the north and northwest of Beit Jala (Ash-Sha'ab, 1975, p.3).

4. A scheme incorporating 10,000 dwellings between Newé Ya'aqov and French Hill is also being considered.

5. Extension and development of the Hebrew University's Mount Scopus Campus is underway; further land sequestration to the east of the campus will be necessitated for accommmdations.

6. It has been reported that a further 10,000 dwellings are to be built between Ramot (Nabi Samuel) and Newé Ya'aqov by 1982–3 (Rabinovich, 1974).

7. By 1982 there should be approximately 40,000 Jewish families living beyond the former armistice line in Jerusalem (Rabinovich, 1974).

The planning and re-development of the so-called Special Zone also reveals the Israeli longer-term settlement policies in the Holy City (Sharon, 1973, p.139). The area covered by the outline scheme of the Special Zone within the master plan for Jerusalem is approximately 10,500 dunums (10.5 square kilometres), that is about 10 percent of the 100,000 dunums (100 sq. km.) of the Greater Jerusalem town planning area. The Special Zone is peripheral to and largely to the east of the Old City (Fig. 19). The development of residential areas is now proceeding at Abu-Tor, North Talpiyyot, Wadi el Joz and A-Tur on the Mount of Olives, on the slopes of the Mount of Offence and on the northeastern slopes of Government House Hill.

In January 1982 four quite massive developments in East Jerusalem appeared to be of prime importance (Fig. 20): Newé Ya'aqov is to the north-northeast of the Old City, Gillo to the south, Ramot to the northwest and Talpiyyot to the southeast. Each of these developments are eastwards of the former Green Line and the enormity of the structures give the overall impression of great bastions against any Arab counter-offensive from the east. The Gillo complex, for example, dominates the hills to the south of the city, is constructed of massively reinforced Jerusalem limestone and is built to resist ground attacks from and mount offensives towards Bethlehem and Beit Jala. These settlements establish a firm Jewish hold on the eastern approaches. In 1967 the population in the twenty-eight square miles of East Jerusalem was 65,000 Arabs, but by 1982 the 186,000 total was comprised of 115,000 Arabs and 71,000 Jews. The overall purpose of the continuing massive Israeli construction activity is to increase the Jewish population so that Israeli possession of the united city becomes irreversible. By 1982 the Greater Jerusalem metropolitan area had attained a population estimated at 350,000.

A specific intention of Israeli planning policy, as it relates to Jeru-

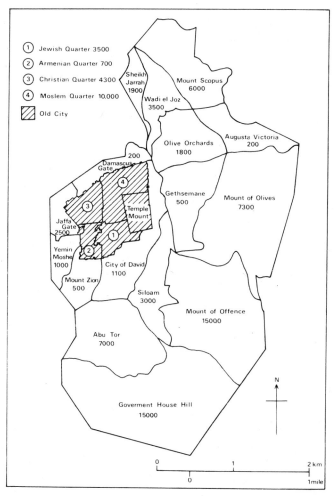

FIGURE 19. Proposed population of the Special Zone in Jerusalem. These totals are now being exceeded. Source of data: Sharon (1973)

salem, is to limit the Arab population in Jerusalem to a one-third minority (Kroyanker, 1975, p.20). Professor Nathaniel Litchfield, then Chief Planner to the Jerusalem municipality declared in his comments before the Jerusalem Committee in 1973 that this proportion had been dictated by the Prime Minister of Israel (Jerusalem Committee Proceedings 11, 1973, p.53). This one-third Arab to two-thirds Jewish policy logically called for a related proportion of con-structional activity for the two groups—a proportion never been

75

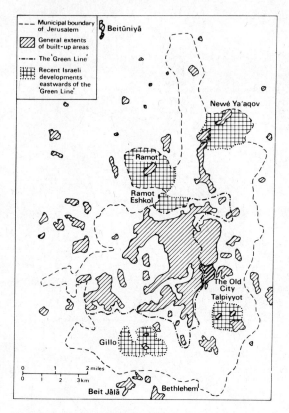

FIGURE 20. Jerusalem, showing recent Israeli developments eastwards of the so-called 'green line', the armistice line between 1948 and 1967

followed by the Israeli administration. The Israeli plan required building 68,000 extra rooms for the Arabs by the year 1985 and 250,000 for the Jews, based on an occupancy rate of 1.2 persons per room for the Jews and 1.6 persons per room for the Arabs (Jerusalem Master Plan, 1968, p.6). If the 68,000 Arab rooms are converted to housing units, 7,400 units should have been constructed by 1976; however, during that time only 1,000 residential units were completed for Arab housing, either in the form of simple units or as additions to existing housing (Kroyanker, 1975, p.44). The Arab component of the housing programme, as envisaged by the planning authority, lagged by more than 6,000 units. On the other hand, many residential units in the Jewish neighbourhoods constructed on expropriated Arab lands find no Jews to occupy them. These apparent speculative developments are often left as accommodation for potential newcomers to Israel or sometimes as second-homes for U.S. Jews. This Jewish colonization of East Jerusalem is now seeking to attract more overseas Jewish capital to certain speculative residential developments. The two advertisements for real estate taken from *Stay Kosher in Israel* (1982), a publication for Torah-true orthodox Jews visiting Israel, is indicative of the process (Fig. 21). One of the advertisements, at least,

FIGURE 21. Real estate advertisements directed to the North American Jewish market. From *Stay Kosher in Israel* (1981)

seems to be directed to the holiday home or second-home market, emphasizing the specific Jewishness of the developments, with the one price apparent being in U.S. dollars, while another advertisement refers to its international business dealings exceeding $1 million.

Israeli researchers adopt a somewhat singular perspective to the problems deriving from the development and growth of Jerusalem.

Shilhav (1982), for example, considers the spatial location and spread of ultra-orthodox Jewish neighbourhoods in Jerusalem, until 1967 centred to the northwest of the Old City, bounded on the north and east by the former armistice line that divided Jerusalem between 1948 and 1967 and to the southwest by the central business district which lies just to the northwest of the New Gate to the Old City. Shilhav refers to the extension of Israeli suburbs beyond the former Green Line, recalling that it was 'The decision ... by the Israeli government to extend Israeli suburbs and neighbourhoods beyond the former armistice line' (Shilhav, 1982, pp.7–8). For Shilhav the problem of Israeli suburban development, in this instance at Ramot to the north, is viewed from an Israeli perspective whereby the ultra-orthodox Jewish territorial niche became converted into an enclave bounded on all sides by the secular (Jewish) system (Shilhav, 1982, p.8). Indeed the construction of new access roads to Ramot through the ultra-orthodox areas has given rise to confrontations between the ultra-orthodox and the non-orthodox Jewish populations. This conflict is of prime concern to Shilhav; he ignores the problems of Arab land sequestrations and related evictions.

In a somewhat similar vein Miron Grindea (1982) describes the terrible high-rise apartment structures that, for strategic reasons, now ring Jerusalem as 'the seal of modernity, energy and optimism' (Grindea, 1982, p.81), failing lamentably to recognize both the 'politics of the jarring sects' and the developments as hard Le Corbusier-type architectural styles that are impinging and impressing themselves upon the Holy City.

The continuing and concerted Israeli drive towards giving the Old City a dominant Jewish character has touched upon some extra-sensitive points, particularly within the Haram al-Sharif, Jerusalem's ancient Temple Mount. The Haram, which has for long been fought over by Jews, Christians and Muslims, is located in the southeast of the Old City. The Haram platform has been artificially prolonged towards the east and the south partly on substructures referred to as Solomon's Stables. In the centre of the Haram area is an outcrop of bare rock now surmounted by the beautiful mosque, the octagonal Dome of the Rock (Qubbet al-Sakhra). This rock has probably a greater continuity of religious tradition than any other spot in the world and many traditions, Muslim and Talmudic, are associated with the rock. Jew, Christian and Muslim revere the Haram as the place of Abram's attempted sacrifice of his son Isaac, the site of King Solomon's resplendent Temple demolished by Nebuchadnezzar in 586 B.C. and rebuilt by Herod five hundred years later, or the place from which the Holy Prophet Mohammad began his journey to heaven on the back of al-Buraq, the magic steed of the human face. At the southern end of the Haram rises the celebrated Mosque al-Aksa, the 'far distant' shrine to which God conveyed the Prophet in a single night (Surah, 17:1), and is now Islam's most holy sanctuary outside of the Hejaz region of Saudi Arabia.

Since 1967 Muslims have feared that the Israelis would move to seize the Haram and destroy certain Islamic sanctuaries. Although this allegation has been repeatedly denied by Israeli authorities, a number of Jewish writers, scholars and visionaries have given substance to such suspicions by their recommendations to 'retrieve' certain sites (Zander, 1971, p.2). In June 1967, within hours of the conquest of the Old City, the Chief Rabbi of the Israeli army, Brigadier Shlomo Goren, later to become a leader of the orthodox conservative Gush Emunim, entered the Haram to conduct prayers, suggesting that a synagogue should be erected on the esplanade of the Aksa mosque. In addition, on 17 August 1969, four days before the fire in the Aksa mosque, a group of the Jewish National Youth-Betah, despite the protests of Muslim officials, held a ceremonial parade on the Haram adjacent to the Dome of the Rock where their leader in his address complained that the Temple Mount was still 'held by aliens' and called for the rebuilding of a third Temple (Zander, 1971, p.2). In September 1967, the Israeli Defence Minister confiscated the keys of the Moghrabi Gate, thus depriving the Muslims of their long established right to the sole control of the entrances and areas of the Haram. A deepening concern and fear that the Haram would be desecrated has developed within the Arab population. Such feelings were reinforced by the fire in al-Aksa mosque on 21 August 1969. Israeli authorities demonstrated that the fire was started by an Australian Christian Michael Rohun, who was subsequently committed to a mental asylum for an indefinite period. However, the investigation committee, comprised of engineers, set up by the Muslim Council subsequently reported that the fire had been started in more than one place at the same time; this finding implied that more than one person was involved and suggested a deal of organization in the arson.

The appeal by thirteen Jews to the Israeli High Court of Justice for an order nisi against the Minister of Police on 13 April 1969, four months before the fire in the mosque, was considered a prelude to Israeli moves against the Haram al-Sharif (Benevenisti, 1976, p.293). This order nisi asked the Minister to give cause why he should not ensure that suitable protection be given by the Israeli police to prevent the applicants' prayers on the Temple Mount from being disturbed, and also to show reason why instruction should not be given to Israeli police personnel to refrain from interfering with the applicants' prayers (Benevenisti, 1976, pp.293-4). The rejection of this request by the High Court was based on the remarks of the Israeli Attorney General that agreed *inter alia* with the views expressed by the Minister of Religious Affairs in the Knesset which stated that:

'There is nothing in the law which forbids a *minyan* (a gathering of ten Jews) from visiting the Temple Mount and praying there . . . however, the implementation of this right depends on the maintenance of public order, and this was within the jurisdiction of the Minister of Police' (Benevenisti, 1976, p.294).

The Attorney General, on his part, assessed the problem as political and not judicial.

These decisions had the effect of appearing to legalize the Jewish claim to the property of the Haram and the right of Jews to pray on it in contravention to the status quo agreement driving from the U.K. Royal Commission on the Holy Places issued in 1930 (see Talal, 1979, pp.44-6). In fact, in the following press interview the Israeli Minister of Religious Affairs stressed that the Temple Mount, the Haram al-Sharif, and the Tomb of the Patriarchs in Hebron, the Ibrahimi mosque, were Jewish property because they were purchased with blood and money (Benevenisti, 1976, pp.288-9).

Further Israeli activities in Jerusalem which have caused and are causing particular concern to the Arabs are the archaeological excavations conducted around the Haram al-Sharif. From 1971, Unesco has continued to express its concern for the preservation of religious sites in the Old City. In 1972, for example, the General Conference of Unesco adopted a resolution in which it 'Urgently calls upon Israel: a) to take the necessary measures for the scrupulous preservation of all sites, buildings and other cultural properties, especially in the Old City of Jerusalem . . . (b) to desist from any archaeological excavations . . . the transfer of cultural properties, and any alterations of their features, and historical character, particularly with regard to Christian and Islamic religious sites.'

Israel has ignored this resolution, rejecting all proposals for 'internationalizing' Jerusalem and has proceeded to undertake two large archaeological digs. One is under the supervision of Benjamin Mazar of the Hebrew University in Jerusalem while the other is sponsored by the Israeli Ministry of Religious Affairs. The Mazar dig commenced in 1969 and continues, although somewhat intermittently, covering the area to the south and southwest of the Haram. The excavation undertaken by the Israeli Ministry of Religious Affairs has taken the form of tunneling under Islamic buildings of great historical importance, being supervised by Rabbi Perla who lacked both knowledge and insight relating to the Islamic areas above the tunnel. The sole concern of this dig appeared to be in exposing the Herodian Temple wall. Although more professional than the excavation undertaken by the Ministry of Religious Affairs, the Mazar dig nevertheless constitutes a most real threat to the future of the Haram and the surrounding area. Chief Rabbi Nissin, in a memorandum to the Israeli Ministerial Committee for the Holy Places, asserted that the four walls of the Haram area are sanctified and emphasized that it is the praying at the Wailing Wall which is the prime concern for Jews while other activities are incidental. Nissin requested that the entire length of the western wall of the Haram be cleared of all buildings adjacent to it and that it be made available for Jewish worship. It is feared that this attitude of the religious authority, reinforced by the discoveries of the Mazar excavation from the Herodian period, would result in the entire area surrounding the Haram being designated a Jewish praying area, and that this would ultimately result in transforming the entire Islamic historic area in general and the Haram in particular into a Jewish domain. Thus a continuing and fundamental problem relates to the future prospects for the Haram and the rights of the Muslims. Perhaps a pointer is provided by Hebron where Israeli authorities have given permission to Jews to pray in the Ibrahimi mosque— considered by many Muslims as a prelude to the Israelis taking ever increasing control of the Haram in Jerusalem.

Intermittent disturbances and outbreaks of violence between the Israeli occupying forces and the Arabs continue about the Haram. The attack on Easter morning, 11 April 1982, supposedly by Allen Goodman, an American-born Israeli soldier, resulted in the death of two Palestinians, injuries to many more and desecration and damage to the Dome of the Rock, its coloured glass windows and its brilliant coloured tiles.

The application of Israeli law in Jerusalem has also brought more problems to the Jerusalem Arabs. For example, 'The officials of the Israeli Ministry of Religious Affairs wanted to impose all the Israeli laws and procedures on the Sharia (religious) legal system of East Jerusalem ... the Ministry ... also wanted to take over control of the Waqf (Muslim endowment) property' (Benevenisti, 1976, p.282). The Israelis considered that the Sharia in Israel was not identical with the one applied in Jordan. What is more, the Qadis (judges) did not renounce their citizenship and would not swear allegiance to the President of Israel. The reactions of the Muslim leadership came in the form of a *Fatwa*, that is a binding religious opinion which strongly objected to the Israeli interference in Muslim religious affairs. The *Fatwa* stated *inter alia*, 'since the principle of Islamic law requires Muslims to take upon themselves, under conditions such as those now reigning, all responsibility for matters of their religion, it is prohibited for non-Muslims to be in charge of Muslim religious affairs.' The *Fatwa*, as such, presented the Islamic legal background to resist the

Israeli interference in Islamic affairs and it also provided a real incentive to those who cared to resist the annexation of Jerusalem and the general occupation on political grounds. Depending on this *Fatwa* the Sharia Courts now work independently of the Israeli authorities and are based upon the willingness of the people to accept their rulings.

Some of the worst fears of the Arab population in Jerusalem are now being realized with proceeding developments and 'urban renewal' programmes. *The Architects' Journal* of 29 November 1978, for example, enthuses over the Safdie-Lansky proposals, named after two prominent Jewish architects, for building a 'new Jerusalem'. Two major aspects are in train; relating to the first of these:

> Since 1967, the Israelis have been at work on the Old City, reaffirming its Jewishness. Before the Western Wall, the site of the Temple Mount that is Judaism's most holy place, a great square has been cleared to accommodate the thousands who congregate to pray on holy days. (*Architects' Journal*, 1978, p.1016)

The architectural qualities of the redevelopment are considered, emphasizing that the redevelopment area 'with its tight little alleys and courtyards, had greatly run down under Jordanian rule. Now the architects are renovating and re-building the housing and reinjecting shops, store-rooms and workshops into the tower storeys' (*Architects' Journal*, 1978, p.1017). The words 'run down' and 'rebuilding' are the operative words here with no mention of the removal of real people from real homes. The architects are, we are informed, at home in 'this wonderfully rich geometry'.

The second major Safdie-Lansky project is the complex at Mamilla immediately outside the Jaffa Gate, the main entrance to the Walled City, on both sides of the upper end of the part that borders the Old City. This development, the first stage of which is budgeted in excess of £100 million, includes two hotels, offices, shops, 350 apartments, underground fall-out shelters and parking for 2,400 cars. Furthermore, 'Astragal' of *The Architects' Journal*, in referring to the architecture of Zionist colonial settlements at Ramot, built on confiscated Arab lands to the northwest of Jerusalem, confined his attention to the so-called architectural qualities of housing schemes: 'it has real dignity and it shares the vigour that has made Israel what it is' (Astragal, 1978, p.1020). Later Astragal considers a scheme as aesthetically unsatisfactory in that 'it divorces people from the ground' (p.1021), which is precisely what each of the Israeli settlement policies has done to the native Palestinian Arabs. The enormity, complexity and cost of the Safdie-Lansky proposals reinforces the view that the Israelis see their control of the city as permanent.

Israeli segregation policies and acquisition of Arab lands

Zionists have characterized Israel from its establishment in 1948 as a Jewish state based upon Zionist segregationist ideology (Weinstock, 1969, p.244). The Arab presence was simply to be ignored in the foundation and development of the state. Although three-quarters of a million Arabs lost their homes and quitted that area of Palestine delimited as Israel in 1948, 140,000 remained in Israel and 650,000 more came under Israeli jurisdiction in 1967.

The suppression of the native, and now minority, population by the Israelis has been proved (for a more detailed examination of human rights violations by the Israeli authorities, *see* Gilmour, 1980, Ch.5: Lustick, 1980; and Ott, 1980, pp.42–60). Ann Lesch (1979) has carefully documented the cases of individual Palestinian deportations from the West Bank and the Gaza Strip for 'security reasons', although international law classifies such deportations as a war crime (Ott, 1980, p.42). Alternatively the Law of Return, a very fundamental of Zionism, passed by the Knesset in 1950, grants every Jew the automatic right to become a citizen as soon as he or she sets foot on Israeli soil (Mallison, 1980). In a chapter for *Population of the Middle East and North Africa, a Geographical Appraisal*, Blake (1972) has outlined the numerical aspects of 'immigration and dispersal of the population' in Israel. It is quite ludicrous for Blake to have considered immigration into Israel without focussing at least some attention upon certain of the enactments of the Israeli government relating specifically to state immigration policies of two basic types: the 'positive' Law of Return and the 'negative' Law of Nationality that essentially deprives the Palestinian Arab residing outside Israel of his right to return, if he so desires.

The U.S. State Department's annual human rights reports note the continuing, systematic torture of Palestinian Arabs by the Israeli authorities, while many examples of Jewish civilian vigilantism, military brutality and collective punishments towards Palestinian Arabs have been recorded (Ott, 1980, pp.44–60). Gilmour (1980) has discussed the discriminatory practices in job opportunities, housing and, particularly, education. The poor state of Arab education in Israel is considered by Jiryis (1979) who provides data, for example, upon the marked variations in local government grants and the resources directed to educational services between the Jewish and Arab sections. In 1974–5 such grants were 4–10 lires per person in the Arab sector and 70–125 lires in the Jewish sector. Furthermore repeated closures of Bir Zeit university and other institutions of higher education in the West Bank under Israeli security measures indicate the range and pervasiveness of what the Israelis refer to as 'the struggle against terror, subversion and violence' within the West Bank.

Yet at the end of the day such details almost appear to possess an air of unreality, being dependent upon differing values, positions and interpretations, with the need painstakingly to evaluate and sift through formidable bodies of evidence and various hearsay reports. For this reason and writing as a human geographer, my attention has been directed to land as a most tangible and real resource. We will look at the Israeli land policies and expropriations within the West Bank, and link them to Israel's historic and ever continuing relationship to land.

Of fundamental importance in the on-going Israeli colonization of the West Bank is the ownership of land. The Drobles plan specifies that settlements will be established on state-owned land and 'not on private Arab-owned land which is duly registered' (Drobles, 1978, p.1). The significant words are 'duly registered', raising doubts about Israeli procedures for the registration of land by Arabs and the overall legality of expropriating lands from Arab owners. Israeli officialdom may for various reasons refuse to register land or not recognize the validity of registration of various Arab-owned lands. Even cultivated, productive land may be considered 'uncultivated' if it falls within the category of 'absentee property' (Ott, 1980, p.21).

In relating it to international law, Gerson calls the Israeli occupation of the West Bank the 'unofficial Israeli policy of creeping annexation' (Gerson, 1978, p.172), particularly the progressive development of civilian settlements on the West Bank as contrary to the spirit of both the Hague Regulations and the Geneva Convention. Gerson also quite wrongly suggests that 'settlement and land acquisitions (in the West Bank) were more in the nature of incipient *ad hoc* populist trends than the outgrowth of established government policies' (Gerson, 1978, pp.173-4). Although there may be a grain of truth in such a careful assertion, the relationship between such national institutions as the Jewish Agency and the World Zionist Organization and the state of Israel is such that those Jewish institutions are usually considered 'as part of general government. The rationale for considering the national institutions as part of general government is that they were set up in order to undertake many government functions' (Halevi and Klinov-Malul, 1968, p.43). In addition, the Drobles plan illustrates that planned developments within the West Bank are not piecemeal and unrelated: the co-ordinated efforts of the Jewish Agency's land settlement department and the rural settlement department of the World Zionist Organization are of particular relevance.

Specific features of the Drobles plan fit into the overall recommendations of the Begin plan on administrative autonomy for the West Bank and the Gaza Strip presented to the Knesset in December 1977, together with supplementary amendments of May 1979, discussed by international lawyer David Ott (1980, Ch.2–3). The Begin Plan envisaged the granting of 'administrative autonomy' to the Arab population of the West Bank and the Gaza Strip, although Israeli authorities would continue to be responsible for 'security and public order'; and Israeli residents would be permitted to acquire land and settle in the occupied territories. But Ott demurs: 'For not to decide on independence for dependent territories is in effect to decide that they should not be independent' (Ott, 1980, p.8). Relating to the Begin plan in general Ott concludes:

> In general, then, the Plan's land provisions, in the light of their specific legal effect, can be seen to abrogate to the Israeli occupation regime authority far beyond that permitted by international law to a belligerent occupant. Indeed, the Plan's attacks on Palestinian proprietary rights recall the Israeli government's assault on Arab land ownership in Israel after 1948, and one may reasonably conclude that the Plan aims to enable Israel to achieve in the occupied territories similar massive transfers of Palestinian property into Israeli hands once 'autonomy' is instituted. (Ott, 1980, pp.23–4)

Massive disruptions and pressures of the occupation are now producing a further movement of Palestinians out of indigenous agricultural activities into subordinate positions within the Israeli construction industry and other unskilled labour sectors.

Field surveys have been undertaken within the West Bank to provide specific and categorical data on the locations, the amount and type of land expropriated by Israeli government or quasi-government organizations. Updated to March 1980, and matching information from the Drobles progress reports (Drobles, 1980), the surveys show the total land area controlled at that time by Israeli authorities to be approximately one-third of the West Bank; two years later, however, it appears to have passed 40 percent.

The acquisition of lands is detailed in Table 3 within three main geographical areas: the Jordan valley settlements divided between the valley itself and the foothills to the west, the West Bank Highlands and East Jerusalem. The data reveal that as of March–April 1980 some 84 km² (c.51 square miles) in the Jordan valley and its foothills were controlled by Israeli settlements. Of this area about 76 percent was under private ownership, including 40 percent owned by absentees. In the West Bank Highlands an area of about 63 km² (c.38 square miles) was controlled by Israeli settlements including the 20 km² tract at the sites of Yalu, Beit Nuba and Amwas. Of this, 97 percent was privately owned, but six settlements in the sector used no privately owned land; it appears that new Israeli settlements or the expansion of existing settlements would necessitate the requisition of additional private property.

> Israel will have to take possession of large tracts of Arab-owned land in the West Bank if plans for Jewish settlement are to be implemented there, the *Post* was told yesterday. (*The Jerusalem Post*, 23 May 1978, p.2)

In East Jerusalem, where the municipal boundaries were extended and annexed to Israel in June 1967, some 14 km^2 (*c.*5.4 square miles) were controlled by settlements in East Jerusalem. Of this, about 97 percent was Arab-owned private property and the rest was Jewish or state owned. The data indicate that overall within the West Bank about 162 km^2 (101 square miles) of land were directly controlled by Israeli settlements, about 86.5 percent of this land being privately owned and 13.5 percent state land. A prime assertion of the Drobles master plan was that:

> We should ensure that there is no need for the expropriation of private plots from the members of the minorities [sic]. This is the chief and outstanding innovation of this master plan: *all* the areas proposed below as sites for the establishment of new settlements have been meticulously examined, their location precisely determined, and all of them are without any doubt State-owned—this according to the preliminary findings of the fundamental and comprehensive land survey now being carried out' (Drobles, 1978, pp.1–2).

But, as we have seen, Arab lands have been, are being and will continue to be expropriated by the Israeli occupying force.

The procedure whereby Arab-owned land is expropriated and taken into Israeli ownership is twofold: road development followed by land (settlement site) acquisition. A prime requirement in the Israeli colonization process is the development of a network of purpose-built, adequate, all-weather roads. Thus colonization methods, commencing with the identification of 'public need', enable roads and trackways to be constructed by the military government in the West Bank. Land required for these roads is expropriated and compensation offered to owners with no right of appeal against confiscation or amount of payment offered. The acquisition procedures for land earmarked for the new Jewish settlement itself may progress in one of several ways. In the case of *official* settlements, the military government informs Arab village elders, mukhtars, that a certain land area located in the vicinity of their village is to be 'developed' and is thus declared 'state land', i.e. expropriated by the military government. Any individual Arab landowner is allowed twenty-one days to present a case to a military appeals committee against such seizure. Shortly after the Arab community has been informed of the intended expropriation and prior to any hearing before a military appeals committee, work commences upon the construction of access roads. A good example is the sequential development in the Samarian hills about the small town of Anabta. Early in 1981 the site of the new colonial village and its lands, Shavei-Shomron B, sited amongst Arab fields planted with almond and olive trees, occupied some 400 acres and was planned to house thirty-five or more Jewish colonial families by June 1981 and 200 families by 1983.

Israeli authorities can also take lands from the indigenous population on all-embracing 'security grounds', although the term remains undefined and is therefore open to many interpretations and qualifications by Israeli authorities. For example, the Israeli settlements at Mechora and Beka'ot in the Jordan valley foothills were established on lands seized from, respectively, Beit Furik and Tamun residents. A number of these land sequestration cases have been fought unsuccessfully right through to the Israeli High Court by Arab villagers seeking to determine the nature and definition of 'security grounds'. The repeated failures of such legal actions by the villagers have meant that Israeli settlement has proceeded unabated at, for example, Nahal Ro'i, Beit El, Matityahu and Haris in the West Bank Highlands (*see* Table 3).

Whereas the official sequestration of Arab lands is guided by a semblance of legal procedure, the so-called unofficial Israeli settlements, for example those being developed by such religious groups as Gush Emunin, do not abide by such impeding 'legal' niceties. Yet the Gush Emunin sites appear to accord with the strictures and overall strategy of the Drobles plan, particularly as it relates to the identification of specific settlement sites: sites settled by Gush Emunin have been earmarked as potential settlement sites in the Drobles plan. It has been in the rate of settlement rather than in the actual settlement procedures where differences have arisen between official and unofficial settlement agencies.

Ths threshold relationships between an Arab village and its agricultural and other land holdings is such that seizure of even part of such holdings or diversion or reallocation of certain of its water will have direct and immediate ramifications for flock and herd totals and agricultural outputs, and will therefore modify the population carrying capacity. Population displacement can thus be obtained. The procedures and sheer volume of land expropriations and related evictions set forth in Table 3 reveal the harshness and iniquity of the continuing Israeli colonial policies.

Colonization of the West Bank progresses, almost as a geography of

the soul, to fulfil the Zionist commitment to settle the land of Israel—
an irredentist policy that seeks to expand the boundaries of the modern
Israeli state to incorporate the specific territory claimed on the basis
of historical attachment and association.

TABLE 3. Israeli land acquisitions in the West Bank at March 1980

All areas are given in dunums: 1 dunum = .247 acre or 0.101 hectares and
1,000 dunums = 1 km² or .386 square miles.

The total area estimates include only those areas visible in the control of
West Bank settlements, and should not be mistaken for estimates of land areas
under the control of the Israeli occupation authorities as a whole. Military
reserves, state land not allocated for settlement and absentee land not allocated for settlement are not included. In March 1980 the total land area
controlled by Israeli authorities amounted to between 25 and 35 percent of
the West Bank. The total area of the West Bank is 2,200 km² or 900 square
miles.

The previous status of the land, and usually the village from which it was
seized, are given immediately beneath each entry.

Source of data: field surveys, March–April 1980.

JORDAN VALLEY SETTLEMENTS

Settlement	Total area	State land	Private land
1. Almog	500	500	

Site of pre-1967 horse-racing track. Irrigated by newly bored wells near
Jericho.

2. Argaman	8,600	8,600[1]	

Previously cultivated and irrigated by six wells seized with land. Owned
by residents of Zbeidat, Marj Naje, Nablus and the village of Makhrouq,
which was destroyed in 1967.

3. Fassa'el Block	24,000		24,000[1]

(Fassa'el, Tomar, Netiv Hagdud, Na'aran, Gilgal)
Previously cultivated and partially irrigated by Fasa'el spring. Owners
from Fasa'el, Akraba, and settled bedouin.

4. Massu'a	4,300		4,300[1]

Located on site of al Ajajre, destroyed in 1967. Previously cultivated and
irrigated by wells and Fara canal. Village of Jiftlik also destroyed in area
in 1967.

5. Mehola	4,500		4,500[2]

Entire area previously cultivated und irrigated by Bardala and Ain El
Beida farmers. IDF (Israeli Defence Forces) used defoliants on Ain El
Beida lands in 1969. Wells and springs in areas are depleted by new
deep-bore wells for settlements. Lost water partly replaced by Israeli
pipeline.

6. Mizpe Shalem	100	100	

Not previously cultivated.

Settlement	Total area	State land	Private land

7. Nu'emi
Recently established as Nahal (1979).

8. Qalya   1,500   1,500
Not previously cultivated.

9. Shelah
Recently established as Nahal (1979).

10. Yafit   500   500
Not previously cultivated. Under construction in 1979.

11. Yitav (old site of
    Na'aran)   3,000   3,000
Previously cultivated and irrigated by former residents of al Auja Foqa and El Auja Tahta. High percentage of absentees (i.e. 1967 refugees) in this area. Houses of 10,000 refugees destroyed in 1967. Banana and citrus groves dried up in 1979 for an estimated loss of I£3 million as a result of failure of village spring apparently depleted by two Israeli deep-bore wells.

JORDAN VALLEY FOOTHILL SETTLEMENTS

Settlement	Total area	State land	Private land

1. Beka'ot   3,000   3,000
Previously cultivated and owned by residents of Tamun village. Seized for security reasons in 1970 and field crops destroyed.

2. Gitit   3,800   3,000
                1,200   1,200
Owned and previously cultivated by Aqraba residents. IDF defoliated 1,800 dunum area in 1972. Wheat fields ploughed under in 1979. A further 1,200 dunums seized in 1979.

3. Hamra   4,500   4,500[1]
Previously cultivated and partially irrigated. Several houses destroyed on site in 1970. Owners from Beit Dajan village. More land seized in 1975. Tomato plants destroyed.

4. Kochav Ha Sha'ar   100   100
Deir el Jerir land. Seized for security reasons in 1976.

5. Ma'ale Adumin   5,000[3]   5,000[4]
Largely wasteland, except valley floors cultivated previously by Issawiyya and El Azzariyya residents.

6. Ma'ale Adumin B   7,000   7,000
Common grazing land owned by the village of Anata. Seized in 1979.

7. Ma'ale Efrayim   5,000[5]   3,700   1,300
1,300 dunums seized for security reasons in 1979. Wheat fields ploughed under for Trans-Samarian Highway.

Settlement	Total area	State land	Private land
8. Mechora	4,800[6]		4,800

Owned and previously cultivated by Beit Furik residents. Crops uprooted in March 1978. Land seized on security grounds in 1979.

| 9. Mevo Shilo | 1,200 | | 1,200 |

Previously owned and cultivated by Abu Falah, Mughayer and Turmos Ayya residents. Land seized for security reasons.

| 10. Mitzpe Jericho | 50 | 50 | |

Former Jordanian army camp. Settlement constructed while negotiations at Camp David were in progress, September 1978.

| 11. Hamra | 400 | | 400 |

Absentee plot. Previously cultivated.

| Hamra | 400 | | 400 |

Absentee citrus grove.

| Hamra | 150 | | 150 |

Absentee land. Previously cultivated.

| 12. Ramonim | 300 | | 300 |

Previously cultivated and owned by Taibe residents. Seized in 1977 for security reasons.

Jordan Valey

| Sub-total | 83,900 | 19,950 | 63,950 |

Settlement	Total area	State land	Private land
1. Beit El	600		600

Owned by El Bireh and Ramallah residents. Subdivided for residential building sites. Adjacent to Beit El army camp on site of former Jordanian base. Owners lost case in High Court in 1978 on security grounds.

| 2. Beit Horon | 50 | 50 | |

Former Jordanian army camp. Settlers threatening to seize private land around camp.

| 3. Dahariyya | 20 | 20 | |

Inside former British and Jordanian police post.

| 4. Efrat | 2,000 | | 2,000 |

Partially cultivated with grapevines and owned by farmers from El Khadr. Seized in 1979 for security reasons.

| 5. Elazar | 350 | | 350 |

Owned and cultivated by Khadr residents, some grapevines uprooted in 1973.

| 6. Elkana | 150 | 50 | 100 |

Former British and Jordanian police post. In 1976, an additional 100 dunums of olive orchards fenced in, owned by farmers from the village of Masha.

Settlement	Total area	State land	Private land
7. Elon Moreh			

New site at Jebel Kalur. Forest pine trees cut down in 1980.

8. Etzion Block	3,000	1,000	2,000

(Alon Shvut, Kefar Etzion, Rosh Tzurim)
1,000 dunums site of pre-1948 Jewish settlement. Additional 2,000 dunums requisitioned from Artas and Nahalin villages. Several houses destroyed in 1968. Vineyards uprooted.

9. Givon	100	100	

Former Jordanian army camp. Settlers threatening to seize private land around the camp.

10. Haris (Ariel)	500		500[7]

Some cultivation. Thirty-six olive trees uprooted at site. Land from Kufr Haris and Salfit villages. Additional 3,200 dunums seized in 1979 for expansion of Ariel from the farmers of Salfit. Lost case in High Court.

11. Har Gilo	600	400	200

Former Jordanian army base; area extended by requisition from Beit Jala owners.

12. Kaddummim	300		300

Owned by Kaddum villagers. Some thirty olive trees uprooted. Site adjacent to army camp.

13. Karnal Shomron	110	100	10

Original site of forest. Pine trees cut down. Additional ten dunums seized in 1979, thirty olive trees cut down, owned by farmers from Kufr Lagef.

14. Shayalet & Kefar Ruth			

In no-man's land and Israeli territory, outside West Bank.

15. Ma'ale Adumin	30,000		30,000

Owned by El Azzariyya and Abu Dis residents. Partly subdivided for building lots. One house destroyed on site belonging to Greek Orthodox Church. Construction began in August 1979.

16. Maeleh Karnai Shomron	50		50

Site of forest. Pine trees cut down. Thirty olive and almond trees for Azzum farmers cut down in 1979 to make road for site.

17. Matityshu	500		500

Land seized from village of Niilin in 1979. Villagers lost High Court case on security grounds.

18. Mevo Horon & Canada Park	20,000		20,000

Largely owned by farmers expelled from the three villages of Yalu, Beit Nuba and Amwas, destroyed in 1967. Almond and olive tree orchards seized with the land.

19. Migdal Oz	300[8]		300

Owned and cultivated by Beit Omar residents. Plum trees and vineyards uprooted in 1977.

Settlement	Total area	State land	Private land
20. Nabi Salah	110	40	70

Forty dunums site of British and Jordanian post.

21. Nahal Ma'ale	300		300

Owned by Silat Ed Dahr residents. Some twenty trees and an uninhabited house destroyed on site in 1977.

22. Nahal Reihan			

Unknown.

23. Ofra	250[9]	50	200

Former Jordanian base. Additional 200 dunums seized by settlers in 1977. Fig trees fenced in and other fruit trees uprooted.

24. Qiryat Arba	1,200		1,200

Some 700 dunums requisitioned initially, and 500 later. Grapevines uprooted, houses destroyed. Owned and cultivated by Hebron residents.

25. Sal'it	500		500

Communal grazing land of Kufr Sur.

26. Sanur (Dotan)	50	50	

Former British police post.

27. Shilo 'dig'	80		80

Owned and cultivated by Quaryut villagers. Fifteen almond trees cut down by settlers in 1977. Olive trees uprooted for new road to settlement in 1979.

28. Shomron	100	100	

Former army camp.

29. Tapuah	150		150

Partially cultivated. Seized from Yasuf villagers in 1978.

30. Tekos	2,000		2,000

Previously owned and cultivated by Rafida residents. Seized in 1975.

West Bank Highlands

Subtotal	63,370	2,010	61,360

EAST JERUSALEM

Settlement	Total area	State land	Private land
1. Atarot	1,500		1,500

Owned by Jerusalem area residents.

2. East Talpiot	2,000	500	1,500

500 dunums from former U.N. zone. Remainder from Suc Bahir and Sheikh Saed.

3. French Hill &			
Ramot Eshkol	3,600		3,600

Seized from landowners from Lifta, Issawiyeh, Anata and Jerusalem.

Settlement	Total area	State land	Private land

House destroyed on site in 1972. Attempt to destroy several houses in area resisted by landowners.

4. Gilo	4,000		4,000

Owned by Sharafat, Beit Jala, Jerusalem and Beit Safafa residents. Vineyards and other fruit trees uprooted. Some houses destroyed in 1976.

5. Jewish Quarter	20	6	14

Pre-1948, some Jewish population, but two-thirds Arab-owned. Post-1967, 6,500 Arab residents evicted.

6. Neve Ya'acov	1,500		1,500

Owned by Jerusalem area residents. Pre-1958 Jewish settlement site is today an Israeli army base. Present housing block is adjacent.

7. Ramot	2,000		2,000

Owned by Beit Iksa and Beit Hanina residents. Nearby village of Nabi Samuel consisting of fifty houses destroyed in 1970. 350 villages forcibly evicted from their homes.

East Jerusalem Subtotal	14,620	506	14,114
West Bank Total	161,890	22,446	139,424

1. These are the so-called 'jiftlik' or 'mudawwara' lands which in the nineteenth century were nominally under the title of the Sultan. The British and Jordanian governments subsequently recognized the residents' rights of ownership to those lands, though registration in the names of individual owners has not been completed in some cases.

2. It appears that 40 percent of the lands under settlement in the Jordan Valley are absentee lands, which implicitly suggests that they are private property. Yisrael Nedivi, of the Jordan Rift Settlement Committee, has said that water shortages and land disputes would follow West Bank autonomy. On 2 November 1978, *The Jerusalem Post* reported that 'Nedivi said that 40 percent of the land in the Jordan Rift belongs to absentee landlords who will claim their property once they are allowed to return.'

3. This does not include 70,000 dunums reportedly closed, most of which would be state owned. Future use and exact locations are uncertain.

4. Land of the mawat, or wasteland class, is generally held to be government property. However, isolated patches of cultivated land in the valleys might be successfully claimed as private property.

5. Perhaps another 5,000 dunums were closed, but future use is uncertain.

6. This excludes an area of 10,000 dunums reportedly closed. Location and intended use are at present uncertain.

7. This is mostly uncultivated land. It is probably private property, but villagers' claims are much weaker in this type of case.

ISRAEL INTO PALESTINE

8. Larger closures have been reported in the area. Location und future use remain uncertain.
9. An additional 150 dunums have reportedly been closed. Whether this area is simply forbidden to Arab building or has actually been seized is uncertain.

94

CHAPTER 6

The Present and the Future

This penultimate chapter will focus attention upon the particular importance of U.N. Security Council Resolution 242 of 1967 which remains the U.N. blueprint for a settlement of the Arab–Israeli conflict, Israeli and Arab responses to the resolution, the importance of the U.S. in effecting any real and lasting settlement, and the likelihood of such concerted action by the U.S. The attempt to bypass the Palestinians to proceed to the Israeli-Egyptian accord will be discussed and attention will be directed to the lingering plight of the Palestinian refugees and the possibility for the creation of an independent Palestinian political entity. The position of the occupied territories, particularly Jerusalem, will be considered and an assessment of the potential for further conflict will conclude the chapter.

U.N. Resolution 242 and hopes of settlement

The U.N. Security Council adopted Resolution 242 on 22 November 1967:

> Emphasizing the inadmissability of the acquisition of territory by war. . . . Affirms . . . the establishment of a just and lasting peace in the Middle East should include the application of both the following principles:
> (i) Withdrawal of Israeli armed forces from territories occupied in the recent conflict.
> (ii) Termination of all claims of states of belligerency and respect for and acknowledgement of the sovereignty, territorial integrity and political independence of every state in the area and their right to live in peace.

It should be remembered that Resolution 242 conceded the status quo within the armistice lines of 1948.

The Israeli and Arab positions towards Resolution 242 reveal certain of the impediments to any significant accord and progress in deliberations. The Israelis have repeatedly said that Article (ii) amounts to an Arab recognition of Israel's right to exist and the Arabs

95

interpret Article (i) to mean that Israel must withdraw from the territories occupied in 1967.

Further controversy has raged over the specific interpretation of Article (i), the withdrawal clause. Perry (1977) has shown that the Arabs and their supporters interpret the word 'territories' to include 'all of the territories' while Israel points to the omission of the definite article 'the' in the English version and argues that the resolution calls for withdrawal from 'some, but not necessarily all' of the occupied territories. Perry concludes, however, that:

> The rules of international law applicable to the interpretation of treaties—and, by analogy, other documents—heavily confirm that the phrase 'withdrawal from territories' cannot be considered as meaning other than the 'withdrawal from all territories occupied' in 1967. (Perry, 1977, p.431)

While the 'termination of . . . states of belligerency', under Article (ii) of the resolution, is not the same as 'true peace', the Arabs emphasize that ending belligerency is the most that they can exchange at present for an Israeli withdrawal to 'secure and recognized borders', and that a complete normalization of relations will take time. By contrast the Israelis fear that this is only a tactical manœuvre from which the Arabs would move on to destroy Israel.

The Palestinians have now apparently come round to considering a *de facto* acceptance of the state of Israel and the creation of the Palestinian state centred on the West Bank, including East Jerusalem, and Gaza. This compromise is a major shift from their earlier position that demanded a general liberation of the entire area of Palestine. The P.L.O. National Council restated in 1974 and again in 1977 its readiness to proceed to discussions on the basis of such proposals towards peaceful co-existence. Shortly after President Carter came to office in 1977, for example, the Palestinians emphasized their willingness to recognize Israel in a general settlement which would include the realization of a Palestinian political entity. The U.S. categorically refused to talk about a Palestinian state, confining itself to 'the refugee problem' and, furthermore, would not recognize the P.L.O. as a partner in such discussions. Again in November 1978 Yasser Arafat stated:

> The P.L.O. will accept an independent Palestinian state consisting of the West Bank and Gaza, with connecting corridor, and in that circumstance will renounce all violent means to enlarge the territory of that state. I would reserve the right, of course, to use non-violent means, that is to say diplomatic and democratic means to bring about the eventual unification of all Palestine. (Quoted in Ott, 1980, p.145)

Responding to this statement made in his presence U.S. Congressman Paul Findley sought further clarification from Arafat who answered categorically, 'We will give *de facto* recognition to the State of Israel ... we would live in peace with all our neighbours'. Findley concluded that 'Israel can no longer say the P.L.O. is pledged to destroy Israel with force.'

The formation of an independent Palestinian state, comprised of the West Bank and the Gaza Strip is viewed by Israel as a mortal danger to its very existence. Moshe Ma'oz (1978), for example, sees the changed P.L.O. attitude to acceptance of 'the mini-state in the West Bank and the Gaza Strip' as a result of the loss of its last outpost with relative freedom of action in the Lebanon, but whose aim would be to work 'to undermine the status quo of Israel's legitimate existence within the 1949 boundaries' (Ma'oz, 1978, p.551). Furthermore, the West Bank, Judea and Samaria, would be the core area of such a Palestinian state; but the Zionists consider both an integral part of Israel, contributing to the security of the Israeli state.

Apart from a further eruption into large-scale open warfare, initiated either by the Arabs to recover territories occupied in the war of 1967 or by Israel taking pre-emptive action against certain of its Arab neighbours, there can be little doubt that the best forum for developing and considering any negotiated general settlement between the Israelis and the Arabs would include the reconvening of the U.N.-sponsored Middle East peace conference at Geneva.

To have any hope of success a Palestinian presence would be crucial at Geneva. But why should the Israelis want such a conference to take place, let alone succeed? The Israelis possess the territory which Ben-Gurion dared to envisage, Jerusalem is united under Israeli control, the U.S. continues to bankroll the Israeli economy and provide it with advanced weapon systems. Israel sees such a conference as offering little beyond dubious promises and worthless agreements from the Arabs. With Menachem Begin Premier of Israel since May 1977 and re-elected in July 1981 with strong support from right-wing conservative religious groups, any possibility of a Palestinian presence at Geneva with Israel in attendance has receded. But who could represent the Palestinians in their absence? Certainly not the parvenu Hashemite dynasty in Jordan, installed by Western imperialists, that has repeatedly moved against P.L.O. activists within Jordan; not Egypt which became ostracized in the Arab world following the Israeli–Egyptian peace treaty; not the feudal monarchist Saudi Arabia; not even the fanatical Libya or Ba'athist Syria. Whereas the impasse that exists between Israel and the Arabs in general could be overcome with dynamic and concerted leadership from the U.S., it is extremely doubtful whether the U.S. has the will to persevere.

The position of the U.S.
and the Israeli–Egyptian peace treaty

A fundamental key to any lasting peace settlement within the Middle East is the position of the U.S., yet the U.S. is apparently unwilling or unable to develop an overall Middle East policy based on a compromise between the Israelis and the Arabs. Approximately six million Jews reside within the U.S., representing 2.7 percent of the U.S. population and about 40 percent of world Jewry; many are more conservative and orthodox, that is Torah-true, than their fellow Jews in Israel. The political importance of U.S. Jewry, both due to particular concentrations in certain geographic areas—notably 1.25 million residing in New York City—and certain professional areas such as the legal professions and media, enables them to exercise a far more telling influence in high places than simple numerical population totals would suggest. Kenen (1981) traces from its emergence in 1951 the rise of the more formalized lobby for Israel, known as the American Israel Public Affairs Committee (A.I.O.A.C.) since 1959. Kenen reiterates the view that Israel is the vanguard of democracy in the Middle East, standing against Nazism, Fascism and Communism, and is thankful that successive U.S. Administrations, including the Reagan Administration, have been led to recognize that Israel is a strategic asset—the strongest anti-Communist regime within the Middle East (Kenen, 1981, p.332). But Mathias's (1982) evaluation of the role of ethnicity, including Jewish 'ethnic politics', in the complex process of shaping U.S. foreign policy brings to mind Ambrose Bierce's definition of politics as 'a strife of interests masquerading as a contest of principles'.

Lilienthal (1978) has provided insightful information on the Zionist lobby of both the U.S. Congress and Senate that has effectively counterbalanced the effect of Arab manipulations of certain international commodity markets, most notably oil. The U.S. assistance to Israel falls under three major headings: financial, military, and political.

Since the creation of the state of Israel in 1948 the U.S. has consistently assisted the fledgling state through technical assistance and cultural grants, important Export-Import Bank loans and direct economic aid: 'Economic assistance from the United States government has taken many forms—grants, soft currency loans, hard currency loans, and technical assistance' (Halevi and Klinov-Malul, 1968, p.162).

The extent of Israeli reliance upon U.S. financial and military backing can be seen in a brief itemization of certain facts. In 1976 for example the Israeli balance of payments deficit amounted to $3,810 million:

Donations from world Jewry, German compensation payments, sales of state bonds overseas and transfer of funds by new immigrants helped to cover two-thirds of Israel's balance of payments deficit, the remainder being met by United States loans. (Blake, 1978, p.313)

Israeli G.N.P. is almost static, recording a mere 9 percent rise in 1980. Foreign debt stands at $17,500 million, representing 83 percent of the G.N.P., $4,500 for every person in Israel. While Israeli exports have risen from $1,400 million in 1973 to $10,200 million in 1981 the 1980 import bill amounted to $13,900 million, fuelled in part by a massive $2,200 million energy bill. In 1980 military security cost Israel $5,400 million, coming to represent nearly one-third of the $17,700 million budget. In 1981 defence expenditure had risen to $7,340 million although rapid inflation makes strict comparison somewhat unreliable. Onto this defence expenditure must be added an additional $1,400 million in U.S. military aid to offset losses from the Israeli–Egyptian peace treaty. The entire economy of Israel can be said to rely on U.S. backing and money transfers from Jews within the U.S. In the fiscal year 1981 direct U.S. aid to Israel amounted to $2,200 million. Between 1948 and 1982 Israel has received $14,900 million in U.S. military aid, one third in direct grants and the remainder in thirty-year repayable loans. In addition the U.S. has given Israel economic aid grants totalling $7,150 million, including $806 million in the 1982 financial year. These economic aid grants are now used almost in their entirety to 'repay' the U.S. for outstanding debts on the military aid loans, thus providing a novel dimension to the term 'never-never' repayment. In the 1982 financial year U.S. military aid to Israel reached $1,400 million, some $850 million (39.3 percent) in loans; this military aid is now estimated to rise by 21.4 percent to $1,700 million in 1983, $1,200 million (41.7 percent) in loans. Although the 1983 U.S. economic aid programme to Israel is scheduled to total $785 million, with some $260 million of this total repayable at 14 percent, massive lobbying is proceeding to obtain increases to match the real 1982 level, adjusted to accommodate inflation. A final $887.7 million package, with a further and sizeable special grant to cover replacements of losses incurred in the 1982 summer incursion into the Lebanon might result for 1983. In early December 1982 the U.S. Senate Appropriations Committee increased the proposed total economic and military aid to Israel to $2,500 million, some $475 million more than President Reagan had requested, representing 21.74 percent, over one-fifth of the proposed total U.S. foreign aid of $11,500 million.

The political backing of Israel by the U.S. is repeatedly epitomized within the United Nations. For example in 1976 the P.L.O., strengthened by U.N. Resolution 3236 of November 1974 guaranteeing its international right to press for self-determination and to be the Palestinians' sole legitimate representative, openly supported a Security Council resolution on Palestine that restated that 'the Palestinian people should be enabled to exercise its inalienable right to self-determination, including the right to establish an independent state in Palestine in accordance with the Charter of the United Nations.' The resolution went on to record explicitly that all states in the region possessed fundamental rights to live in peace, to territorial integrity and independence, thus unambiguously agreeing with Israel's right to exist (Said, 1980, p.225–6). The U.S. vetoed the resolution.

Successive U.S. presidents have had to bow before the power of the Jewish lobby. Certain episodes will demonstrate the usual chain of events and the inability of three U.S. administrations to deal effectively with the crises.

In December 1969 the U.S. made proposals towards effecting separate peace plans between the United Arab Republic (U.A.R.) of Egypt and Israel and between Jordan and Israel. No mention was made of the Palestinians over and above that of the refugees. The ten-point peace plans submitted to Egypt by the U.S. as a basis for a U.A.R.–Israeli peace settlement saw a final settlement as including secure and recognized borders and security arrangements that could also include demilitarized zones. Similarly, the U.S. set forth proposals for a Jordanian–Israeli peace settlement, to be agreed under the auspices of Gunnar Jarring, the U.N. special representative. Included within these proposals were provisions for Israeli withdrawal that allowed 'for alterations based on practical security requirements'; for agreement on Jerusalem, 'recognizing that the city should be unified with free traffic through all parts of it and with both countries sharing in civic government'; for a Jordanian affirmation that the Straits of Tiran and the Suez Canal were international waterways; and for the establishment of an international commission by Gunnar Jarring 'to determine the choice of each refugee on returning to Israel' (New York Times, 23 December 1969).

By 21 January 1970 U.S. Deputy Assistant Secretary of State Rodger Davis was saying publicly, 'if we can get the Arabs to accept the obligation of peace, then we can get the Israelis to accept territorial adjustments.'

Moshe Dayan mounted a particularly vehement attack on the two sets of proposals, asserting for example in January 1970 that because Egypt wanted neither peace nor a return to the ceasefire lines, 'all of Egypt is the battlefield'. Under the auspices of the Israeli–U.S. friendship groups and American Jewish organizations, special meetings were held with U.S. officials throughout December 1969 and January 1970. The Nixon administration's plans slowly subsided and died a death in face of heated Congressional lobbying, particularly that of fourteen U.S. Jewish organizations to the then Secretary of State, William Rogers. By late January a plaintive President Nixon had sent a message to the Jewish Conference emphasizing that the U.S. was 'prepared to supply military equipment necessary to support the efforts of friendly governments, like Israel, to defend the safety of their people.' The U.S. initiative had come to nothing.

A similar verdict could be passed upon the theatrical shuttle-diplomacy of the Kissinger years. Dr. Kissinger, initially as President Nixon's Special Advisor and subsequently as Secretary of State to presidents Nixon and Ford, attained no just or lasting settlement. But perhaps that was not the objective; Mazlish suggests that Kissinger's 'central message—that the United States was dedicated to the preservation of Israel but not its territorial conquests, and that it wished to help in bringing peace to the area as honest broker (and, implicitly, thereby to avoid being dragged into war with the Soviet Union over a local conflict)—was unvaried' (Mazlish, 1976, p.249). Exception is taken to Mazlish's use of the term 'local conflict' and to the apparent suggestion of an unvarying U.S. position in face of what is an ever evolving situation. This unchanging position of both Kissinger and the U.S. is seen to effect in September 1975 at the time of the Second Sinai disengagement between Israel and Egypt. As a precondition for their acceptance of this further disengagement the Israelis stipulated that the U.S. must agree and pledge never to participate in direct contacts with the P.L.O. unless or until that organization fully and unconditionally accepted Israel's right to exist. The U.S. acquiescence was indeed a triumph for Israel.

In October 1977 the Carter administration launched a joint U.S.-U.S.S.R. Middle East peace initiative. This unique declaration, presented by President Carter before the U.N. General Assembly, called for a comprehensive Middle East settlement, to include Israel's withdrawal from territory occupied in the 1967 war, termination of a state of war and the 'resolution of the Palestinian question'. The U.S. was apparently agreeing formally that the Palestinians had 'legitimate rights' in any settlement and President Carter indicated that if the P.L.O. accepted U.N. Security Council Resolution 242 of 1967 the U.S. would then be able to enter into direct negotiations with that organization.

The full power of the Jewish lobby and the large and powerful pro-Israel bloc in Congress, including Henry (Scoop) Jackson denounced the initiative while Congressman Edward Koch, then in the midst of what was to prove his successful campaign for the mayoralty of New York City, expressed his 'outrage' in a letter dramatically delivered to President Carter in New York before a host of attendant cameramen. Senators Daniel Patrick Moynihan and Clifford Case held a press conference to denounce President Carter's initiative and Moshe Dayan, then Israel's Foreign Minister, met with Alexander Schindler, chairman of the Conference of Presidents of Major American Jewish organizations and Jewish leaders in Atlanta, Chicago and Los Angeles to lobby against this apparent shift in U.S. policy, to raise money for the United Jewish Appeal (U.J.A.) and to mobilize support for Israel in its confrontation with the U.S., emphatically stressing to U.J.A. audiences:

> We are told ... that if we want peace we must accept the Arab terms—we must give up the Golan Heights, the Sinai and the West Bank. Maybe there will be peace if we do that—but there will be no Israel. We are not going to accept this.

Within a matter of days a recalcitrant President Carter was insisting that, 'I'd rather commit political suicide than hurt Israel'. President Carter further emphasized that he would uphold U.S. commitments to Israel and that the U.S.-U.S.S.R. declaration was aimed not toward the Arabs but simply towards Geneva. Mr Carter, the President of the U.S.A., had met his match and this specific Middle East peace initiative would be modified and diluted.

The failure to develop a realistic and successful Middle East initiative, which included a specific reference to the Palestinians, was particularly disappointing since the Carter administration contained Zbig Brzezinski, in the important position of National Security Adviser and William Quandt as the special adviser on the Middle East within the National Security Council. In 1976 Brzezinski and Quandt, then professors of political science at, respectively, Columbia University and the University of Pennyslvania, were among the authors of a Brookings Institution publication entitled *Toward Peace in the Middle East*, later referred to simply as 'the purple pamphlet'. This report called for an independent Palestinian state or entity as a possible solution. Despite their removal from the ivory towers of academia to the corridors of power within the Carter administration, the learned professors' insights and overtures came to nought, at least in terms of the original and comprehensive efforts of the initiative of October 1977.

A somewhat similar chain of events followed the destruction of the Iraqi nuclear reactor on 7 June 1981 and the subsequent air attack on residential districts in Beirut that killed 300 people. The forthcoming Israeli general election for the faltering Begin government may have been critical here; nevertheless certainly the decisive Israeli attacks contributed to Begin's retention of power, although with a reduced majority in a coalition supported by and dependent upon ultra-orthodox Jewish factions with religious nationalists imbued with mysticism and a fanatical commitment to the notion of Eretz Yisrael.

The U.S. registered its displeasure over the bombing of both the Tammuz reactor and urban populations in Beirut by imposing an arms embargo on Israel for having committed substantive violations of an agreement with the U.S., which stipulates that American arms shall only be employed for defensive and not offensive purposes. The U.S. voted for the U.N. resolution censuring Israel for the bombing raid on the Tammuz nuclear reactor, yet resisted pressures that called for the imposition of U.N. sanctions against Israel, making it perfectly clear that it would use its veto if sanctions were mentioned.

With the imposition of the arms embargo an enquiry was instigated by U.S. Secretary of State Alexander Haig. The enquiry failed to determine whether Israel had committed a substantial violation of the U.S.–Israel arms agreement, and concluded that such terms as 'offensive' and 'defensive' were quite meaningless and impossible to differentiate in such circumstances. Yet such terms had been incorporated into the U.S.–Israel arms agreement.

These inconclusive findings mattered little. Just ten weeks after the imposition of the U.S. arms embargo President Reagan, having gone through the form of registering U.S. displeasure, acquiesced to the intensive and constant White House lobbying and rescinded what appeared, in retrospect at least, to be merely a symbolic embargo order, immediately releasing the sixteen U.S.-built jet fighters, fourteen F-16s and two F-15s, for immediate delivery to Israel prior to the visit of the Israeli Prime Minister Menachem Begin to Washington in September 1981.

A conclusion of these events is that the U.S. is hamstrung and quite unable to develop a coherent and positive policy towards the broader aspects of a settlement which would incorporate the rights of the Palestinians and a Palestinian political entity without being taunted by the Jewish lobby as appeasers. The developments following the imposition of the embargo suggest that the U.S. is also quite unable to act in any positive manner against the Israelis due to the presence of the intensive Jewish lobbying within the U.S. and the special relationship that exists between the U.S. and Israel (Knapp, 1980).

The difficulties encountered by the Reagan Administration in completing the sale of five Airborne Warning and Control System (AWACS) jets to Saudi Arabia in October 1981 again indicate the power of the Israeli lobby, here aided by the Republican Senator for Minnesota, Rudy Boschwitz. The sophisticated AWACS radar planes are essentially for defensive-surveillance purposes while the advanced fighter 'planes and bombers provided to Israel can and do have major offensive roles, although it should be recognized that the $8,500 million Saudi package also included 1,177 Sidewinder air-to-air missiles and further equipment to enhance the range and performance of the sixty F-15 fighters the Saudis had on order from the U.S. at the time. The entire package is due for final delivery in 1985. In the meantime the U.S. will continue to operate their AWACS out of Jeddah, Riyadh and Dharan. It is likely that, even following the delivery of the AWACS in 1985, U.S. military personnel will be in operational control of their use. But for the time being at least the dynastic, traditional, yet affluent Saudis require U.S. backing.

The long prepared invasion of the Lebanon that began in early June 1982 saw a direct Israeli movement against P.L.O. positions, particularly about Tyre, Sidon and west Beirut. Whereas the implications of this Israeli advancement into the Lebanon will be considered in some detail in the next chapter it is the lack of a firm U.S. response that should be noted. Indeed by vetoing the Spanish resolution in the United Nations Security Council of 9 June 1982, which sought to condemn Israel for refusing to withdraw its forces from the Lebanon, the U.S. could be seen as condoning the massive Israeli invasion. The full U.N. motion reads:

> The Security Council, recalling its resolutions 508 (1982) and 509 (1982), taking note of the report of the Secretary-General of 7 June 1982, also taking note of the two positive replies to the Secretary-General of the Government of Lebanon and the Palestine Liberation Organization contained in document S 15178.
> 1. Condemns the non-compliance with resolutions 508 (1982) and 509 (1982) by Israel;
> 2. Urges the parties to comply strictly with the regulations attached to The Hague Convention of 1907;
> 3. Reiterates its demand that Israel withdraw all its military forces forthwith and unconditionally to the internationally recognized boundaries of Lebanon;
> 4. Reiterates also its demand that all parties observe strictly the terms of paragraph 1 of resolution 508 (1982) which called on them to cease immediately and simultaneously all military activities within Lebanon and across the Lebanese–Israeli border;
> 5. Demands that within six hours all hostilities must be stopped in compliance with Security Council resolutions 508 (1982) and 509 (1982) and decides, in the event of non-compliance, to meet again to consider practical ways and means in accordance with the Charter of the United Nations.

There does appear to be a certain and overall basic permanence of U.S. feeling between successive administrations. Outlining the 'Carter

Doctrine' on the Middle East in 1980 the then U.S. Defence Secretary, Harold Brown, said that,

> Our interests can be stated quite simply:
> (1) to ensure access to adequate oil supplies;
> (2) to resist Soviet expansion;
> (3) to promote stability in the region; and
> (4) to advance the Middle East peace process, while ensuring (and indeed to order to help to ensure) the continued security of the State of Israel.

Successive U.S. administrations have not differed in any real respect from these policy guidelines, which relate to our evaluation of the Middle East in its geopolitical context in Chapter 4.

One crucial feature of U.S. policy has been its acquiescence to Israel in by-passing the position of the Palestinians, latterly in bringing Israel and Egypt to the Camp David meetings of September 1978 that led on to the Egyptian–Israeli peace treaty of 26 March 1979. This treaty effectively neutralized Egypt and gave Israel a certain sense for safety to the immediate south and might have been a prelude to an Israeli–Jordanian 'accord'. The Egyptian–Israeli treaty pledges that:

> The permanent boundary between Egypt and Israel is the recognized boundary between Egypt and the former mandated territory of Palestine, as shown on the map at Annex 11, without prejudice to the issue of the status of the Gaza Strip. The Parties recognize the boundary as inviolable. Each will respect the territorial integrity of the other, including their territorial waters and airspace (Article 11).

The treaty reached agreement for Israeli withdrawal from Sinai by April 1982, that is three years after ratification, but gave no real attention to either the Palestinians or the West Bank.

Following the publication of the Egyptian–Israeli peace treaty of March 1979, a meeting of member states of the Arab League and the P.L.O. was called in Baghdad. Egypt was not invited. The Baghdad Conference adopted resolutions calling for the immediate withdrawal of each state's ambassador from Egypt, complete severance of diplomatic ties within one month, suspension of Egypt from membership in the Arab League and transferral of Arab League headquarters from Cairo to Tunisia. Throughout April 1979 Islamic countries severed diplomatic relations with Egypt and on 18 April 1979 Egypt was suspended from the Arab Monetary Fund. In retrospect the Israeli–Egyptian agreement represents a final retreat from the pan-Arabism of Nasser and matches with the activities of Egypt in 1948, for it was

Egypt with Jordan that occupied the part of the Palestine homeland not taken by Israel.

The Egyptian–Israeli treaty thus led to the isolation of Egypt within the Arab world, removing the traditional Egyptian pretension to pan-Arab leadership and cutting off important financial support from Saudi Arabia. Despite receiving large amounts of U.S. aid, $15,000 million between 1978–81, Sadat had failed to bring the wider Arab world and Israel any closer together, although immediately prior to his assassination on 6 October 1981 the U.S. had been earnestly and patiently working to effect an Israeli–Jordanian accord. This, particularly since 1967 with a dynamic P.L.O. presence within Jordan, was proving difficult but not impossible. Only time will tell but Sadat's passing has not only set back the Israeli–Jordanian accord but may have adversely affected the Egyptian–Israeli treaty as well.

The Palestinians

Perhaps one of the two most intractable problems facing any lasting peace settlement within the Middle East relates to the Palestinians (the other is territory).

The Israelis appeared to have conceded one point within the Camp David Framework for Peace in the Middle East of September 1978 by accepting that by the end of a five-year transition period on the West Bank and Gaza, the parties were to reach agreement on 'the legitimate rights of the Palestinian people and their just requirements', with the Palestinians being enabled to 'participate in the determination of their own future' through the various mechanisms accepted in the Framework. Within days of the publication of the Framework the Israelis were affirming that 'the expressions "Palestinians" or "Palestinian people" are being and will be construed and understood ... [by Israel] as "Palestinian Arabs"'. The import of such seeming legalistic niceties is that the Israelis continue to refuse to recognize the status of the Palestinian people, essentially the viewpoint adopted in the colonization of the Holy Land by Zionists. Moreover this problem of interpretation persists within the Egyptian–Israeli peace treaty of 26 March 1979, the preamble to which simply reaffirmed the Camp David Framework for Peace in the Middle East; it did not attempt to clarify the position of the Palestinians, although the Framework did commit Egypt and Israel to a search for peace based upon such considerations as U.N. Security Council Resolution 242 and the U.N. Charter. In essence, the Framework left two major issues unresolved; the mechanism to be employed in working towards full self-determination for the Palestinians, and the solution of the refugee issue. Yet if the Framework had attempted to incorporate such

106

requirements it is considered highly unlikely that there would have been a Framework—perhaps that would have been for the best. The matter of Palestinian recognition and self-determination still represents a seemingly insurmountable problem.

It is of interest to recall the evolution of Zionist attitudes towards the Arab occupants of Palestine. Initially it was that there simply were no natives, they did not exist, neatly summed up in a Zionist slogan of the day, 'A land without people for a people without land' (Peretz, 1971, p.251). Later again a gradual change emerged and the viewpoint developed that, although there were some local Arab inhabitants, they were misusing and/or under-utilizing the land in a most wasteful manner. Therefore Zionists, with their superior levels of capital and technology, would be quite justified in ousting these Palestinians. Even later a further attitude has gained momentum, one of benevolent despotism. This viewpoint suggests that the Israelis will manage the Palestinian population in the best interests of the Palestinian Arab population: Arabs will be employed in Israeli industry and commerce, thereby gaining greater material wealth, higher standards of living and better health care than they have ever had before. Such basic differences in and a lack of clarification of fundamental definitions within the Egyptian–Israeli peace treaty did not augur well for a just and durable peace. Not only cannot the Palestinians be ignored, but any lasting peace settlement within the Middle East must recognize the legitimate rights of the Palestinian Arabs, their right to self-determination, their right to decide upon their own form of government without external interference.

The total number of Palestinian Arabs is estimated at nearly 4.5 million. The following data are taken from the Palestinian Statistical Abstract (1979, Table 19, p.262) and U.N.R.W.A. (1981, Table 3, p.70):

Egypt	46,878
Europe	40,000
Gaza Strip	415,924
Iraq	19,184
Jordan	1,250,000
Kuwait	259,408
Lebanon	336,288
Libya	19,226
Palestine (including Jerusalem)	610,545
Saudi Arabia	180,000
Syria	208,538
U.S.A.	100,000
West Bank	722,072

United Arab Emirates, Qatar and other	
Arab countries	114,629
Other	90,000
Total	4,412,692

Of this total some 1.75 million reside inside Israel, the West Bank and the Gaza Strip, and by now the total is probably nearing 5 million.

While all Palestinian Arabs residing outside 'Palestine' may be considered refugees, the term 'Palestinian refugee' as used in this book refers to those persons registered as Palestinian refugees with the United Nations Relief and Works Agency for Palestine Refugees in the Near East (U.N.R.W.A.). In July 1974 the total of such refugees stood at 1,583,646, increasing to 1,757,269 by July 1978 and to 1,884,896 by July 1981; the rate of growth was 2.26 percent per annum in 1974–8 and 3.12 percent per annum in 1978–81.

U.N.R.W.A. defines a Palestinian refugee for operational purposes as those persons or their descendents whose normal residence was

TABLE 4. Distribution of registered refugee population, 1974, 1978 and 1981

Sources of data: U.N.R.W.A., 1974, 1978 and 1981

	1974	1978	1981
Total registered refugees			
Jordan (east)	599,571	682,561	732,615
West Bank	291,977	314,257	334,410
Gaza Strip	322,133	350,114	370,269
Lebanon	191,698	211,902	232,455
Syrian Arab Republic	178,267	198,435	215,147
	1,583,646	1,757,269	1,884,896
Total persons in camps			
Jordan (east)	155,280 (25.90%)	178,489 (26.15%)	189,309 (25.84%)
West Bank	73,850 (25.29%)	80,528 (25.62%)	84,838 (25.37%)
Gaza Strip	193,895 (60.19%)	199,050 (56.85%)	205,445 (55.49%)
Lebanon	97,111 (50.66%)	99,544 (46.98%)	119,868 (51.57%)
Syrian Arab Republic	50,179 (28.15%)	56,462 (28.45%)	63,721 (29.62%)
	570,315 (36.01%)	614,073 (34.95%)	663,181 (35.18%)

Palestine for a minimum period of two years preceding the Arab–Israeli conflict of 1948 and who, as a result of that conflict, lost both home and means of livelihood (Rowley, 1977). To be eligible for U.N.R.W.A. assistance, refugees and descendants born after 14 May 1948 must be registered with U.N.R.W.A., living within the area of U.N.W.R.A. operations and in need by specified definitions (U.N.R.W.A., 1981, p.35). In addition there were 32,252 'displaced refugees', persons who were displaced as a result of the renewal of hostilities of June 1967 and subsequent fighting in the Jordan valley in early 1968.

A continuing fallacy has been that Palestinian refugees have been completely ostracized by containment in camps, separated from the local native populations. In fact, camps accommodate only about 35 percent of the registered refugee population, although they vary from 55.49 percent in the Gaza Strip, to 25.37 percent in the West Bank (*see* Table 4). The specific locations of the Palestinian refugee clusters by city are indicated in Figure 22. The refugees are located in or in camps adjacent to twenty-two major urban centres within the Gaza Strip, Jordan, Lebanon, Syria and the West Bank.

The General Assembly of the U.N. has repeatedly reaffirmed its commitment to Resolution 242, and in 1975 established a permament *Committee on the Exercise of the Inalienable Rights of the Palestinian People* (U.N. 1978), while paragraphs 1 and 2 of the General Assembly Resolution 3236 (XXIX) read as follows that the General Assembly:

1. *Reaffirms* the inalienable rights of the Palestinian people in Palestine including:
    (a) The right to self-determination without external interference;
    (b) The right to national independence and sovereignty;
2. *Reaffirms also* the inalienable right of the Palestinians to return to their homes and property from which they have been displaced and uprooted, and calls for their return.

While specifically alluding to the Palestinian refugee problem the Israelis continue to maintain their position expressed in 1956 which suggests that as '... Israel is a Jewish state' (Hebrew University of Jerusalem, 1956, p.173), the 'Arab Refugee Problem' can be considered through '... resettlement (in other Arab lands); and not repatriation to Israel, as the only practical solution to the refugee problem' (Hebrew University of Jerusalem, 1956, p.177).

Following what may be called the empirical facts of the Palestinian refugee problem it is important to note the economic and social difficulties experienced by a significant proportion of the refugees. For example, the various publications of U.N.R.W.A. demonstrate the

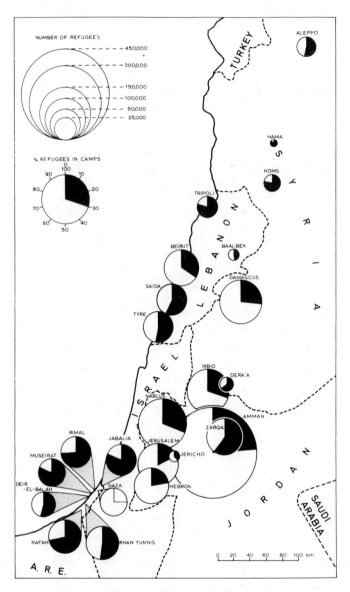

FIGURE 22. The location of Palestinian refugee clusters in July 1981.
Source of data: U.N.R.W.A. (1981)

problems deriving from its strict budgetary constraints and continuing responsibilities to provide basic educational services, health services and relief service to registered refugees (*see* Table 5). The first priority of the Agency has for many years been its educational programme; when budget savings have had to be implemented they have invariably been made in other services. In the first year of operations, 1950–51, just over $300,000 of U.N.R.W.A.'s $35.8 million budget went to education with most of the remainder going to relief and medical services. In 1981, education accounted for 54,1% of the $238.6 million total expenditure; health services were only 15.7 percent, relief services about 23.6 percent and 6.6 percent for other costs. Because of a shortage of funds, the Agency had to cut the basic ration in 1979 and now distributes only food received as contributions in kind from governments and the European Economic Community. As a result of natural increase the number of refugees registered with U.N.R.W.A. is now 1.88 million, with half under the age of twenty. Although the General Assembly of the U.N. renewed the mandate of U.N.R.W.A. for a further three years from 1 July 1981, the growing budgetary deficit prompted the Commissioner General for U.N.R.W.A., Olof Rydbeck, to affirm that:

> Unless the international community is prepared to reform U.N.R.W.A.'S financing by putting it on a new basis, the General Assembly should consider what functions the Agency should perform in its next mandate period, which will begin at the end of June 1981. While United Nations Members have renewed the mandate without proposing any change to the programmes, they have made no provision for the financing of those programmes. Abandonment of the school programme in one or more fields will call into question the purpose which the international community wishes U.N.R.W.A. to serve, with respect both to the geographical distribution of the services to the Palestine refugees and to the nature of those services. The future of U.N.R.W.A. must be resolved in the course of 1981 if the Agency is not to be tossed into 1982 on the tide of unpredictable financial fortune (U.N.R.W.A., 1981, p.6)

In Chapter 4 we discussed the emergence from the 1967 war of certain of the important factions that make up the Palestine liberation movement; Rosemary Sayigh, however, suggests that the roots of 'the Revolution' may be traced back to the first announced Fatah military operation inside Israel in January 1965 (Sayigh, 1979, p.147). Sayigh repeatedly uses the term 'the Revolution' (her widely acclaimed book is entitled *Palestinians: From Peasants to Revolutionaries*), implying rather more than a national liberation movement even though her own

TABLE 5. U.N.R.W.A. Budget: Total costs, 1981 and 1982

Source: U.N.R.W.A. (1981, Table C, p.58)

Specified Service	1982 proposed budget	1981 revised budget
	$000	$000
Part I. Education Services		
General Education	121,034	103,299
Vocational and professional training	15,470	13,394
Share of common costs from Part IV	14,351	12,370
Total Part I	150,855	129,063
Part II. Health Services		
Medical services	16,780	14,860
Supplementary feeding	10,337	9,095
Environmental sanitation	7,157	6,309
Share of common costs from Part IV	8,231	7,094
Total Part II	42,505	37,358
Part III. Relief Services		
Basic rations	40,485	40,928
Shelter	1,351	991
Special hardship assistance	6,464	3,312
Share of common costs from Part IV	13,029	11,211
Total Part III	61,329	56,442
Part IV. Common Costs		
Supply and transport services	12,582	10,770
Other internal services	16,840	14,417
General administration	6,189	5,488
Total Part IV	35,611	30,675
	(35,611)	(30,675)
Part V. Other Costs		
Adjustment in provision for local staff separation costs necessitated by increased remuneration	7,485	12,592
Adjustment in provision for termination indemnities for local staff in event of closure of the Agency	3,000	3,000
Adjustment in provision for repatriation of local staff	400	200
Local disturbances	—	12
Total Part V	10,885	15,804
Grand Total	265,575	238,667

consideration of this dichotomy is somewhat inconclusive (Sayigh, 1979, pp.146, 181).

Two basic aspects of its [the Palestinian Resistance Movements'] revolutionary character were that it substituted mass struggle for passivity and speech-making, and that it brought back the Palestinians to the heart of the Arab/Israeli conflict. (Sayigh, 1979, p.146)

This development more appropriately might be seen as an upsurge in the liberation movement rather than the development of 'the Revolution'.

The various factions that comprise the P.L.O. are united in their fidelity to the land, by their hope for eventual return to that land and through their armed struggle. The development of a revolutionary spirit on the other hand would, in part at least, seek to re-evaluate the fundamental nature and structure of society, both as it exists and in its potential for change, and to consider social and capital re-formations.

The romantic view whereby the downtrodden 'seethe with revolt' and move to a revolutionary posture is largely dismissed by Davies (1962) in his discussion of the conditions likely to lead to revolution: he suggests that often such folk are overwhelmingly pre-occupied with just staying alive or working towards a real, immediate, tangible goal. For the Palestinians this objective is a national homeland, not necessarily a commitment to revolutionary ideology. However, a particular feature of the Palestinian problem is that in time, without achieving a solution generally acceptable to the Palestinian people, a socialist-revolutionary approach could increasingly become attractive. Such a development towards a Palestinian revolutionary spirit would undoubtedly affect the entire Arab world. Even now the attempt by certain elements of the P.L.O. to transform their problem into an Arab-wide struggle working towards some type of Arab national goal causes much concern among the conservative Arab states.

The dispersal of the Palestinian refugee population into host states adjacent to Israel does extend the problem far beyond the confines of Palestine, sharply broadening its political implications. For the political scientist G.A. Almond, the political system is composed of a set of roles, structures and subsystems, whose interactions are affected by the psychological attributes and propensities of the actors involved (Almond and Powell, 1966). In relation to its environment, the entire range of interactions consist of either *inputs* from the environment or from within the political process itself, or the conversion of these *inputs* within the system into *outposts* to the environment (Davies and Lewis, 1971, Ch.4; Duchacek, 1973, Ch.1). The relevance of such a discerned set of interactions to the Palestinians is that there are few outputs to

113

the environment: a Palestinian state simply does not exist. Further, the non-realization of such a real political state-environment would suggest the possibility for mounting and deepening revolutionary inputs.

Barrington Moore (1959), in his appraisal of the evolution of pre-revolutionary Bolshevik ideology and its implementation into Soviet political practices following 1917, provides a classic study of the inter-action between a protest movement and its continuation and applica-tion in practice. The Soviet leaders were increasingly confronted by political responsibility after their successful revolution; the cold, hard, real world led them to deviate from precept and the contrast between promise and fulfilment became increasingly manifest. The gradual emergence and ascendancy of the Party over the working class in turn solidified the forces of revolution. The monolithic structure of the Party assumed an awesome massivity within the state and, combined with the relative absence of mass support for a revolutionary goal and the intellectual's fanatical belief in the desirability of this goal 'pro-duced in official and unofficial Leninist doctrine an attitude of distrust toward the masses' (Moore, 1959, p.61). The burden of government of real territory, the emergent Soviet state, served to detract supposed revolutionaries from revolution.

The Palestinians have no such distraction. The radicalization of mass Palestinian thinking could well proceed on from a national liberation movement to a fundamental re-evaluation of Israel in its imperialistic setting, to a questioning of the order that gave it birth. Indeed, for the development of socialism, 'To travel hopefully is a better thing than to arrive, and the true success is to labour' (R.L. Stevenson, 1881, Ch.6). It is 'environmental pressure', by and large the output function of the state, that literally brings the system down to earth. In contrast the Palestinian stays 'in the air' with an increasing likelihood of a revolutionary effect on the entire Arab 'nation' (*umma*) and ultimately on Israel. Whether a Palestinian state is established or whether a revolutionary spirit develops, fundamental changes will occur throughout the region. The political programme of the Fourth Fatah Conference, May 1980, points toward such an increase in revolutionary fervour (*see* Appendix II).

The marked increases in the size and density of refugee populations with their developing political consciousness will continue the crises within host communities, will mean recurrent outbreaks of violence.

A proper recognition—however limited of the human misery that the [Palestinian] exodus has involved ... has had to wait on the emergence of the resistance movement in the wake of the 1967 war. It is no exaggeration to say that the identity of the Palestinian people has only been reasserted with the rise of the Palestinian guerilla. (El-Rayyes and Nahas, 1976, p.9).

There can be no reduction in tension nor an increased stability within the Middle East until the refugee problem is faced squarely, and until a just, equitable and lasting solution obtained for all parties.

Potential scenarios and territorial settlements

Table 6 outlines some possible scenarios of territorial changes that could be achieved following further major conflict, Scenario 4 representing the position as of 1983, Israel approximating the areal extent of Eretz Yisrael and a united Jerusalem under Israeli control. Further permutations on the various combinations in the table are quite feasible. It should now be patently obvious that the Israelis will never freely surrender the occupied territories—those areas occupied in 1967; the fate of the region will continue to be determined by power and not by rationally considered options.

To assess the likelihood for change from Scenario 4 the defence expenditures and military manpower patterns in the Middle East in the early 1980s must be taken into account. The startling arms built-up in the region in general has been aided and abetted by the major weapons exporting countries, in rank order, the U.S., the U.S.S.R., France, the U.K., Italy and West Germany. Information issued by the Stockholm International Peace Research Institute (S.I.P.R.I.) indicates that world trade in arms is now equal to that of transfers of food. In the period 1973–80 the Middle East and South Asian countries received from the major exporters 4,050 combat planes; 25,250 tanks, self-propelled guns and artillery; 21,680 armoured personnel carriers; 26,020 surface-to-air missiles; and countless rifles and machine guns. In per capita terms the Middle East is still the biggest spender on arms in the Third World, with approximately $250 per capita in 1977, about the per capita average for industrialized countries and far in excess of Africa and Latin America with about $20 per capita or Asia with $10 per capita (S.I.P.R.I., 1979, pp.1–2).

The mind boggles at this seemingly uncontrolled trade in and build-up of arms apparently impelled, in large part at least, by economic factors of the supplying countries. These growing arsenals do not augur well for peace in the Middle East.

Table 7, compiled from data contained within *The Military Balance 1981–1982* (London, International Institute for Strategic Studies), provides a quantitative assessment of military power and defence

TABLE 6. Possible territorial settlements within Israel–Palestine

Scenarios:	1	2	3
Israel	No Israel	Mini state of Israel (U.N. plan of 1948)	Israel as of 1948–67
Jerusalem	Entirely under Arab control	International control or under Arab control	Divided between east (Arab) and west (Zionist)
West Bank	Part of greater Palestine	Core area of a Palestinian state	Palestinian political entity centred on West Bank
Palestine	Greater Palestinian state, pressure on Jordan, Egypt and Syria	Palestinian state	Occupied by Arabs under Jordanian control or limited indepencence
Overall position	International Zionist action— position of U.S. crucial	U.N. involvement as peace-keeping agency— friction among Arab states, especially with Jordan— attempts to overthrow Hashemites	International guarantees of sovereignty, territorial integrity and political independence of all states within area

4	5	6
Eretz Yisrael	Greater Eretz Yisrael	Enlarged Israel beyond Jordan and into south Lebanon
Under Israeli control	Major eviction of Arabs	Under Israeli control—increasing disregard of Muslim holy places
Under Israeli occupation	Formal annexation by Israel	Occupation of West Bank, western Jordan, southern Lebanon and southwest Syria by Zionists
Israeli control plus 'Autonomy plan'	No Palestine	No Palestine and mass eviction of Arab population
Problems: Palestinians, peaceful relations and territory	U.N.-international opposition—position of U.S. crucial but ineffective?	Defeated Arab states faced with annexations or occupations—position of U.S.S.R. crucial

TABLE 7. Population, Gross National Product, military manpower and defence expenditures within the Middle East, c. 1980

Key to columns:
1 Estimated Gross National Product (GNP) in U.S. $ million, unless specified as Gross Domestic Product (GDP): GDP is equal to GNP less income from abroad. 1979 is the year of the data unless otherwise specified. As a step towards greater comparability, wherever possible the U.N. System of National Accounts rather than national statistics is used. 2 Defence expenditure in U.S. $ million, for 1981 unless otherwise stated. 3 Population. 4 Total armed forces personnel (equal to the total of columns 5, 6 and 7). 5 Army personnel. 6 Navy personnel. 7 Airforce personnel. 8 Para-military personnel. 9 Combat aircraft.
Source of data: The International Institute for Strategic Studies (1981), pp.39, 47–59.

	1 $ million	2 $ million	3	4	5	6	7	8	9
Algeria	40,680 GDP (1980)	914	19,330,000	101,000	90,000	4,000	7,000	10,000	295
Bahrein	1,700 GDP	135	400,000	2,500	2,300	200	—	25,000	—
Egypt	17,800	2,170 (1980)	43,190,000	367,000	320,000	20,000	27,000	139,000	290
Iran	81,700	4,200 (1980)	39,665,000	195,000	150,000	10,000	35,000	75,000	100
Iraq	35,200	2,700 (1980)	13,835,000	252,250	210,000	4,250	38,000	4,800	335
Israel	23,000 (1980)	7,340	4,000,000	172,000	135,000	9,000	28,000	4,500	602
Jordan	2,690 (1980)	420	3,320,000	67,500	60,000	300	7,200	11,000	84
Kuwait	23,500	1,100 (1980)	1,460,000	12,400	10,000	500	1,900	18,000	50

Country								
Lebanon	2,900 (1977)	253	3,090,000	23,750	22,250	250	1,250	7,500	21
Libya	20,000	448 (1978)	3,125,000	55,000	45,000	5,000	5,000	5,000	408
Morocco	15,200	1,200	21,580,000	120,000	107,000	5,000	8,000	30,000	75
Oman	2,600 (1978)	879	930,000	14,500	11,500	1,000	2,000	3,300	38
Qatar	5,000	59.5	230,000	9,700	9,000	400	300	—	9
Saudi Arabia	94,600	27,700	10,395,000	51,700	35,000	2,200	14,500	36.500	139
Sudan	5,600 GDP	248 (1980)	19,310,000	71,000	68,000	1,500	1,500	3,500	44
Syria	9,200	2,390	9,150,000	222,500	170,000	2,500	50,000	9,800	448
Tunisia	7,000	262	6,670,000	28,600	24,000	2,600	2,000	8,500	11
Turkey	45,300 (1978)	3,100	46,263,000	569,000	470,000	46,000	53,000	120,000	325
United Arab Emirates	21,000	750	950,000	42,500	40,000	1,000	1,500	—	51
Yemen Arab Republic (N)	3,800	212	5,365,000	32,100	30,000	600	1,500	20,000	65
Yemen Peoples Democratic Republic (S)	500 (1978)	500	1,955,000	24,300	22,000	1,000	1,300	15,000	118

expenditures in the Middle East, including Turkey and North Africa. National defence expenditures, personnel numbers in the armed forces and the total number of combat aircraft in service are identified. Whereas the collective might of the Arabs far exceeds that of the Israelis, within twenty-four hours the Israeli army can mobilize from 135,000 to 450,000 men, the airforce from 28,000 to 37,000 and the 602 combat aircraft can be augmented by a further 150. About 85 percent of the 602 aircraft are U.S. built, including 246 A-4 Skyhawks, 138 F-4E Phantoms, seventy-five F-16 Fighting Falcons and forty F-15 Eagles. Israel has 4,000 U.S. M113 armoured personnel carriers and more than 3,500 tanks, of which 1,460 are from the U.S. including 810 of the advanced M-60s and sixty-five M-48s.

Whereas the broad strengths of potential alliances within the region may be evaluated from the data in Table 7, Table 8 demonstrates that Israel remains far ahead of any such alliances.

TABLE 8. Defence expenditures, and as percentage of GNP

Source of data: The International Institute for Strategic Studies (1981), pp.39, 47–59.

	Defence expenditure c.1980	% of GNP
Israel	$7,340,000,000	31.91
Egypt	$2,170,000,000	12.19
Syria	$2,390,000,000	25.98
Jordan	$ 420,000,000	15.61

Although Syria lost a significant number of combat aircraft and anti-aircraft missile launchers in the June 1982 war in southern Lebanon, it now appears that the U.S.S.R. has more than made good these losses. Even the remote possibility of direct Saudi involvement may not prove as dramatic as sometimes believed, for the Saudis appear to be particularly concerned with their internal security, with the National Guard and Counter Territorial units of the Ministry of the Interior of 36,500 exceeding the 35,000 army complement. Israel's prime military position within the region could only be undermined by a rapid and unexpected attack from its Arab neighbours.

In addition to the competition among the various countries of the region there also exists competition from outside. Figure 23 attempts to show the dispositions to and bilateral agreements with the two major world powers as of late 1982, with a five-part scale ranging from firm commitment to the U.S., through some commitment to the U.S.,

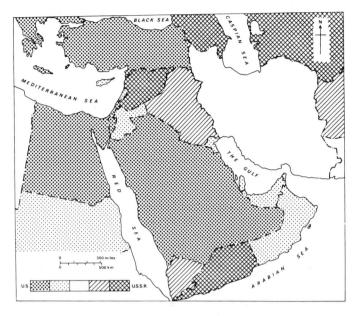

FIGURE 23. The Middle East, 1982: national dispositions toward the U.S. and U.S.S.R.

relative non-commitment and some commitment to the U.S.S.R., to firm commitment to the U.S.S.R. There also continues a certain British and French presence in the area; for instance, the British continue to sell arms in the Gulf, although the area is increasingly dominated by the U.S.–U.S.S.R. competition (International Institute for Strategic Studies, 1981, pp.47–8).

When considering possible territorial changes about the locale of Israel, it is well to recall Elizabeth Monroe's insightful comment that, 'Since 1967 the hard core of the Palestinian problem has never changed: the Israelis are unwilling to surrender enough territory to get the peace they want' (1977, p.397). The current Israeli view is that it is not feasible and quite out of the question to relinquish possession of the occupied territories; indeed, R.I. Isaac asserts that, 'Should Israel return to the old [pre-1967] borders she would greatly increase her vulnerability' (1976, p.159). In military parlance, West Bank space represents 'time' and thus an increased warning period against surprise attack, a prime concern of Israeli defence strategists (Israeli Defence Spokesman, *Judea and Samaria*, 1981).

The general lack of concern over Israeli annexation of the Golan Heights may have shown the Israelis that matters can be resolved by formally annexing the West Bank, although there are marked physical and human differences between the inhospitable Golan Heights and the settled West Bank. While visiting the West Bank in January 1982 I observed that no visible territorial markers or signs now delimit the boundary between the West Bank and Israel, nor that between the Gaza Strip and Israel. Annexation or absorption by default and stealth may well prove a less onerous proposition than public announcements. If, however, the annexation of the Golan Heights demonstrates that extensions of Israeli territory beyond the normally recognized confines of Eretz Yisrael can be justified on grounds of national security, an extension of full Israeli sovereignty over the West Bank, perceived by the Israelis as an integral part of Eretz Yisrael, may be only a matter of time.

In the present circumstances, however, it appears improbable that Israel would move toward a direct political annexation of the West Bank, as occurred in the Golan Heights; rather the developing Israeli strategy suggests an attempt to undermine the grassroot support of the P.L.O. through economic advancement, urbanization and integration of the occupied territories, particularly the West Bank, with Israel. By July 1981 almost 50 percent of the West Bank's 80,000 adult workers were employed within Israel, three times as many as in 1970; during 1980 the West Bank imported $400 million worth of goods, 80 percent coming from Israel, and exported $200 million, 50 percent of which went to Israel.

The emerging Israeli position is what they regard as a compromise: the occupied areas would be granted a form of local administrative autonomy, such as a Palestinian council for the West Bank, but overall Israeli control would be retained and a limited Israeli military presence would remain. The P.L.O. and the elected mayors of the occupied areas continue to resist the imposition of such a plan. This intention to bestow 'administrative autonomy' on the Arab population of the West Bank and the Gaza Strip while retaining basic responsibility for overall 'security and public order' is not a novel idea. Initially mooted in the Begin Plan of December 1977, this autonomy plan can in no way be interpreted as a step towards an independent Palestinian political entity. Rather the contrary is the case: Eliahu Ben Elissar, Director General of the Israeli Prime Minister's office, indicated in July 1979 that one objective of the Israeli settlement policy in the West Bank and of the Drobles Plan is to prevent 'Palestinian autonomy from ever developing into an independent Palestinian state' (Wall Street Journal, 25 July 1979, p.1). The autonomy plan would result in a foreclosure of the central political option for the occupied territories (Ott, 1980, p.75), and its implementation could be a step toward Israeli sovereignty over the occupied territories.

The unprecedented dismissal of several of the West Bank's twenty-three elected mayors in March 1982 was precipitated by the supposed behaviour of the mayor of El Bireh, an Arab township with a population of some 25,000. Ibrahim Tawil, who had been mayor of El Bireh since winning the Israeli-sponsored elections in 1976, and his seven-man local council were replaced by an Israeli lieutenant colonel, as were the mayors of Nablus and Ramalla. The mayor had repeatedly refused to deal with the Israeli civilian bureaucracy established in the West Bank in November 1981 to replace the military administration. This change from military to civilian rule was viewed by the West Bank Arabs as an Israeli policy and ploy that, while supposedly offering the 800,000 residents more autonomy, would lead to Israeli control and absorption into the Israeli state. The massive defeat inflicted upon the P.L.O. in the southern Lebanon in June 1982 may, however, enable Israel to reconsider the matter of direct annexation of the West Bank, or at least to proceed far more forcefully with implementation of an autonomy arrangement.

The advancing urbanization is also proceeding to destroy the general rural character of the West Bank. In time the Palestinian Arab *felahin* will become part of the urban proletariat. (Such attempts to acculturate the Arab population of the occupied territories do not directly affect Palestinians residing outside Israel and the occupied territories.) The Israelis continue to implement their land settlement policies, continue their 'annexations' within the occupied territories.

The following extract from a Drobles progress report provides an outline plan and strategy for the continuing Israeli settlement of Judea and Samaria to 1985:

In light of the current negotiations on the future of Judea and Samaria, it will now become necessary for us to conduct a race against time. During this period (1980–85), everything will be mainly determined by the facts we establish in these territories and less by any other considerations. This is therefore the best time for launching an extensive and comprehensive settlement momentum, particularly on the Judea and Samaria hilltops which are not easily passable by nature and which preside over the Jordan Valley on the east and over the Coastal Plain on the west.

It is therefore significant to stress today, mainly by means of actions, that the autonomy does not and will not apply to the territories but only to the Arab population thereof. This should mainly find expression by establishing facts on the ground. Therefore, the state-owned lands and the uncultivated barren lands of Judea and Samaria ought to be seized right away, with the purpose of settling the areas between and around the centres occupied by the minorities [sic], so as to reduce to the minimum the danger of an additional Arab state being established in these territories. Being cut off by Jewish settlements the minority population will find it difficult to form a territorial and political continuity. There mustn't be even the shadow of a doubt about our intention to keep the territories of Judea and Samaria for good. Otherwise, the minority population may get into a state of growing disquiet which will eventually result in recurrent efforts to establish an additional Arab state in these territories. The best and most effective way of removing every shadow of a doubt about our intention to hold on to Judea and Samaria forever is by speeding up the settlement momentum in these territories. . . .

Experience indicates that the situation must be averted of any one settlement being left isolated in whatever region, both owing to the need of relying on shared services together with neighbouring settlements and because of the security aspect. Thus, it is necessary to establish additional settlements near every existing settlement in Judea and Samaria, so as to create settlement clusters in homogenous settlement regions and to make it possible to develop shared services and means of production. It is not altogether unlikely that the expansion and development of these settlements will eventually result in some cases in their natural decision to merge and create a single urban settlement containing all the settlements of the same cluster.

Over the next 5 years it is necessary to establish 12–15 rural and urban settlements per annum in Judea and Samaria, so that in five years from now the number of settlements will grow by 60–75 and the Jewish population thereof will amount to between 120,000 and 150,000 people. (Drobles, 1980, pp.3–4)

Drobles' repeated use of the term 'minority' population in his references to the Palestinian Arab population of Judea and Samaria, which in 1980 totalled 800,000 as opposed to an Israeli Jewish population of 25–30,000, derives from his Zionist perspective that Judea and Samaria are integral parts of Eretz Yisrael.

The crucial problem for any general settlement is Jerusalem. Since 1967 both in the suburban areas to the north, east and south and in the Old City of Jerusalem, Jewish developments have continued to modify the disposition of the various communities. While Jewish commentators assume that Jerusalem will remain politically united and under Israeli control (Cohen, 1977), the status quo is likely to be resisted by the Palestinians. The U.N. General Assembly Resolution 303 (IV) of 9 December 1949 restated the decision that Jerusalem should be placed under a permanent international regime to be administered by the U.N., thereby preserving this particular recommendation from the aborted Partition Resolution of November 1947. U.N. Security Council Resolution 267 of 3 July 1969, passed unanimously, confirmed that 'all legislative and administrative measures and actions taken by Israel which purports to alter the status of Jerusalem, including expropriation of land and properties thereon, are invalid and cannot change that status'. U.N. Security Council Resolution 298 of 25 September 1971 'urgently calls upon Israel to take no further steps in the occupied section of Jerusalem which may purport to change the status of the City'. A consensus statement of the Security Council on 11 November 1976 expressed 'grave anxiety and concern over the present serious situation in the occupied Arab territories as a result of continued Israeli occupation' and condemned Israel's 'purported annexation' of East Jerusalem. U.N. Security Council Resolution 471 of June 1980 brings together a number of the separate resolutions on both the occupied territories in general and Jerusalem in particular:

The Security Council
Recalling once again the Fourth Geneva Convention Relative to the Protection of Civilian Persons in Time of War (1949), and in particular article 27 which *inter alia* reads: 'Protected persons are entitled, in all circumstances, to respect for their persons. ... They shall at all times be humanely treated, and shall be protected especially against all acts of violence or threats thereof';
Reaffirming the applicability of the Fourth Geneva Convention Relative to the Protection of Civilian Persons in Time of War (1949) to the Arab territories occupied by Israel since 1967, including Jerusalem.
Recalling also its resolutions 468 (1980) and 469 (1980) of 8 and 20 May 1980.
Reaffirming its resolution 465 (1980), by which the Council determined 'that all measures taken by Israel to change the physical character, demographic composition, institutional structure or status of the Palestinian and other Arab territories occupied since 1967, including Jerusalem, or any parts thereof, have no legal validity and that Israel's policy and practices of settling parts of its population and new immigrants in those territories constitute a flagrant violation of the Fourth Geneva Convention Relative to the Protection of Civilian Persons in Time of War and also constitute a serious obstruction to achieving a comprehensive, just and lasting peace in the Middle East' and strongly deplored the 'continuation and persistence of Israel in pursuing those policies and practices'.
Shocked by the assassination attempts on the lives of the mayors of Nablus, Ramallah and Al Bireh, *Deeply concerned* that Jewish settlers

125

in the occupied Arab territories are allowed to carry arms thus enabling them to perpetrate crimes against the civilian Arab population.

1. *Condemns* the assassination attempts on the lives of the mayors of Nablus, Ramallah and Al Bireh and calls for the immediate apprehension and prosecution of the perpetrators of these crimes;

2. *Expresses deep concern* that Israel, as occupying Power, has failed to provide adequate protection to the civilian population in the occupied territories in conformity with the provisions of the Fourth Geneva Convention Relative to the Protection of Civilian Persons in Time of War (1949);

3. *Calls upon* the Government of Israel to provide the victims with adequate compensation for the damages suffered as a result of these crimes;

4. *Calls again* upon the Government of Israel to respect and to comply with the provisions of the Fourth Geneva Convention of 1949, as well as with the relevant resolution of the Security Council;

5. *Calls once again* upon all States not to provide Israel with any assistance to be used specifically in connection with settlements in the occupied territories;

6. *Reaffirms* the overriding necessity to end the prolonged occupation of Arab territories occupied by Israel since 1967, including Jerusalem;

7. *Requests* the Secretary-General to report on the implementation of the present resolution. (United Nations Security Council, Resolution 471, 1980)

Using the section of Resolution 471 that reaffirms U.N. Security Council Resolution 465 of 1980 D. Ott has demonstrated that the law of belligerent occupation provides Israel with no basis for the establishment of permanent civilian settlements in occupied territory (1980, p.81).

Let us now consider potential changes from the present position, broadly scenario 4 of Table 6, to scenario 5, moving to the formal annexation of the occupied territories. A move in this direction was recommended in the Allon Plan of 1976, the overall aim of which was to establish settlement and to gain 'secure and defensible' borders for Israel along the eastern borders of Judea and Samaria. The Allon Plan included proposals for the formal annexation of the Golan Heights, the Gaza Strip and a belt of land running from north to south, to the west of the Jordan, which would virtually complete the Israeli encirclement of the West Bank (Allon, 1976; Schiff and Haber, 1976). The general territorial details of Allon are presented in Figure 24. One conclusion is to view this proposed territorial aggrandisement

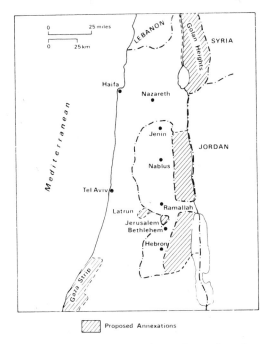

FIGURE 24. The Allon Plan of 1976 that envisages formal annexations of border territories

as a precursor either to formal annexation or some form of incorporation of the entire West Bank, that is Judea and Samaria, into Israel.

In opposition to various U.N. resolutions and international law relating to territorial expansion following war, Israel alters its demographic position with the 'annexation' of the occupied territories; further large scale Jewish immigration from Eastern Europe and the U.S.S.R., however, might modify such projections. Nadav Safran examines the demographic profiles of the Arab population which in 1971 amounted to just under 15 per cent of the population of Israel, as defined by its pre-1967 boundaries plus East Jerusalem (Safran, 1979, pp.99–101). If Israel annexed the West Bank and Gaza Strip, Safran asserts, the Arabs would comprise approximately 35 percent of the national population but, due to great differences in the natural rates of population growth between Arabs and Jews, the Arab population of this enlarged Israel, including the West Bank and Gaza, would rise constantly and equal almost half the total population by 1990. Even within pre-1967 Israel plus East Jerusalem it is predicted that the Arab proportion will rise to 20 percent by 1990. Friedlander

127

and Goldscheider (1979) suggest that if Jewish immigration is minimal, an assumption they say is not unrealistic, the numerical minority-majority statuses would reverse within the next thirty years. These computations, of course, presuppose that no expulsion or 'mass emigration' of the Arab population occurs; certain Zionist extremists, such as Rabbi Meir Kahane in October 1981, have demanded the expulsion of all Palestinians from Israel, including the 574,000 who are Israeli citizens.

The second and further form of Israel expansion would see an extension across the Jordan to the East Bank, as in scenario 6 in Table 6, into an Israeli occupation of buffer positions along its eastern border, thereby pushing Israels' boundaries out beyond what is usually considered to be Eretz Yisrael. Such an augmentation of territory would need a war, probably sparked off by mounting Arab frustration at developments under scenario 5. Israel might justify the expansion on two grounds. Firstly, while Eretz Yisrael may be defined as that area to the west of the Jordan valley extending to the Gulf of Aqaba and Wadi-el-Arish in the southwest and northwards to the present border with the Lebanon (Rowley, 1981), Eretz Yisrael can also be defined to encompass the lands of the Twelve Tribes with the land of Reuben to the east of the Dead Sea and the land of Gad eastwards of that part of the Jordan valley between the Sea of Galilee and the Dead Sea (Fig. 12). Compare the Twelve Tribes' lands to the areal extent of the kingdom of the Maccabees in 100 B.C. (Fig. 7). Indeed the 1977 election manifesto of the Likud emphasized that in any forthcoming peace negotiations the Likud would not concede any 'parts of western Eretz Yisrael' whose eastern boundary was the River Jordan, implying that an 'eastern Eretz Yisrael' lay to the east of the river. Mr Begin has continued to reiterate this concept of western Eretz Yisrael, as quoted in *The New York Times* of 3 May 1979 (p.A5). Secondly, the creation of an enlarged buffer zone to the east would give Israel a greater flexibility and a longer warning period of attack from its Arab neighbours. This extension beyond the Jordan would encompass the entire breadth of the Jordan valley and the commanding East Bank Highlands of, from north to south, Jebel Ajlun and Jebel Munif, rising to 1,198 metres, to the southwest of Irbid; Jebel Yusha, over 1,000 metres above sea level, to the west of Amman; and Jebel el Ata'ita, 1,641 metres above sea level, and Jebel Mubarak, 1,727 metres, west of Ma'an. A further permanent Israeli expansion to the north into southern Lebanon, south of the Litani River, does appear possible and would be particularly attractive for both strategic-political reasons and for the supply of Litani water southwards to Israel (Hudson, 1970).

A position less favourable to the current Israeli territorial stance is scenario 3 in Table 6, wherein a pre-1967 Israel exists alongside a Palestinian state comprised of the West Bank, the Gaza Strip and East Jerusalem. This scenario could be attained through concerted and united international pressure, some type of Israeli defeat or even a further inconclusive war as occurred in 1973. It is, unfortunately, most unlikely that any generally acceptable agreement could ever develop peacefully from within the Arab-Israeli camp. Indeed, Israel continues to assert that both Israel and the P.L.O. are fundamentally opposed to the two-state solution, although in the first section of this chapter I have shown that the attitude of the P.L.O. has shifted toward acceptance.

For many scenario 3 is viewed as a just compromise. Israel would remain, protected by international agreements—including U.S. and U.S.S.R.—with U.N. policing. Astor and Yorke, in their evaluation of the possibilities for joint U.S.-U.S.S.R. guarantees to a territorial settlement along these lines conclude that 'The question is whether the Super Powers are sufficiently committed to a Middle East peace and regional stability to co-operate to the extent required' (Astor and Yorke, 1978, p.149). Such co-operation would represent a major step towards institutionalizing détente at the regional level.

For the adjacent Arab states, a small Palestinian state would be a controllable Palestine; certain fears of Egypt, Jordan and Saudi Arabia would thereby be allayed. This Palestinian state, for example, would receive aid for economic development which, from the Egyptian and Jordanian and Saudi Arabian perspectives at least, would serve to counteract the revolutionary, socialist fervour that in the longer term could threaten not only Israel but the neighbouring Arab states as well.

In 1967 prior to the June war, the late Moshe Dayan, in considering a settlement akin to scenario 3, envisaged that a solution to the 'Arab-Israeli problem' could lie in some form of regional confederacy that would include Israel, Jordan and Palestine:

In Dayan's view, the two nations in the area formerly called Palestine could function within a single economy, even though they belonged to different cultures and sovereign states. The basic principle in his approach was neighborliness, or in his phrase, 'a joint way of life. . . . Dayan saw the country as an integral part of a region and only its geographic and economic borders were identical. They contained two distinct demographic and cultural entities whose political demarcation did not follow strictly demographic lines. Thus an Arab from Jerusalem and an Arab from Nablus, though belonging to the same demographic and cultural group, could belong to different political entities. Both would work in the same

129

economy but would vote for representatives in different countries and enjoy different civil rights. Dayan's overall aim was to blur the identification between the geographic and the demographic lines of demarcation. . . . The Jewish State Dayan envisaged was not defined by a geographical border but by demographic and cultural criteria. The same applied to the Palestinian entity, although he had not yet decided whether it should be a state in its own right or a part of the Hashemite Kingdom of Jordan whose inhabitants live in Israel. (Teveth, 1972, pp.348, 380–1)

In essence Dayan's proposals endeavoured to weaken the conventional tie between citizenship and geographic space, but only for the Palestinian Arab population, while elsewhere he reasserted such a relationship for the Israeli Jew through the notion of Eretz Yisrael. Perhaps Dayan's response must be considered against the prospect of the growing Palestinian Arab minority population that threatens to become a majority population (Isaac, 1976, pp.120–1). There is also the basis for comparison of Dayan's view of Israeli policy towards the Palestinian Arabs to the South African apartheid views on planned segregation and spatial reorganization through the creation of 'African Homelands' in rural areas (Smith, 1977, pp.242–4). Many Palestinians reject the idea of an 'independent' West Bank in the same way that South African blacks dismiss the notion of the black tribal 'homelands'. The West Bank, like the 'homeland policy' is regarded by many Arabs as only a transitional phase that would lead to a unitary multi-racial democracy. But Dayan's views on some form of confederacy were not generally acceptable.

By 1972 King Hussein of Jordan was seeking, characteristically, to assert the advancement of his country with a plan for a federation of Jordan with the West Bank, subsequent to Israeli withdrawal. However the Knesset reacted sharply to his plan by recording that, 'The Knesset reaffirms and confirms the historic right of the Jewish people over the Land of Israel' (*Jerusalem Post*, 4 March 1972, quoted in Isaac, 1976, p.128). This statement effectively represents Israel's view against a confederacy and opposition to a scenario 3 type settlement.

The Soviet Union and its partners clearly and unequivocally expressed their position on the Middle East in a Warsaw Pact Declaration of 14–15 May 1980:

Lasting peace in the Middle East could have been established long ago. The road to this is well known ... it is the road of a comprehensive Middle East political settlement with the direct participation of all sides concerned, including the Arab people of Palestine in the person of its representative, the Palestine Liberation

Organization, on the basis of respect for the lawful interest of all states and peoples of the Middle East, including Israel.

Such a settlement requires the withdrawal of Israeli troops from all Arab territories occupied in 1967, restoration of the right of the Arab people of Palestine to self-determination, including the creation of their own independent state, ensuring the sovereignty and security of all states of that area. A political settlement in the Middle East also requires that no actions impeding the attainment of these aims be taken, that no state shall interfere in the internal affairs of the countries and peoples of the area, should not try to prescribe to them what socio-political systems they should establish, nor lay claim to, or encroach on, their natural resources. . . .

This declaration laid particular emphasis upon the rights of all states within the Middle East, including Israel, and stressed the need for full P.L.O. involvement in the move towards the realization of an independent Palestinian state.

Other suggestions have been advanced for territorial settlements broadly under scenario 3. A recommendation outlined by Lord Caradon in *The Guardian*, 27 August 1979, suggested that, 'There should be an Arab Jerusalem and an Israeli Jerusalem each exercising full sovereignty within its own territory but with no barriers between them and no impediment in freedom of movement between them'. This suggestion apparently presupposes the creation of a Palestinian state alongside the Israeli state.

The EEC Venice Declaration of June 1980, deriving largely from a British initiative, expressed a particular concern for Palestinian rights, stressing the need to include the P.L.O. in any Middle East 'peace initiative'.

EEC Statement on the Middle East 13 June 1980
1. The heads of state and the ministers of foreign affairs . . . agreed that growing tensions affecting this region constitute a serious danger and render a comprehensive solution to the Israeli–Arab conflict more necessary and pressing than ever.
2. The nine member-states of the European Community consider that the traditional ties and common interests which link Europe to the Middle East oblige them to play a special role and now require them to work in a more concrete way towards peace. . . .
5. All of the countries in the area are entitled to live in peace within secure, recognized and guaranteed borders. . . .
6. A just solution must finally be found to the Palestinian problem, which is not simply one of the refugees. . . .
7. The achievement of these objectives requires the involvement and support of all the parties concerned in the peace settlement

... and the P.L.O., which will have to be associated with the negotiations.

8. The Nine stress that they will not accept any unilateral initiative designed to change the status of Jerusalem and that any agreement on the city's status should guarantee freedom of access for everyone to the holy places.

9. The Nine stress the need for Israel to put an end to the territorial occupation which it has maintained since the conflict of 1967, as it has done for part of Sinai. They are deeply concerned that the Israeli settlements constitute a serious obstacle to the peace process in the Middle East. . . .

10. Concerned as they are to put an end to violence, the Nine consider that only the renunciation of force or the threatened use of force by all the parties can create a climate of confidence in the area. . . .

11. The Nine have decided to make the necessary contacts with all the parties concerned. . . .

The Israeli response was quick and sharp and is summed up in a 'Statement by the Israeli Cabinet on the EEC Middle East Declaration 15 June 1980':

Nothing will remain of the Venice decision but a bitter memory. The decision calls on us and other nations to bring into the peace process that Arab SS which calls itself 'the Palestine Liberation Organisation'. . . .

Israel asks no European nation to guarantee its security. Israel has known in the past, and will continue to know in the future, how to defend itself.

The initiators and draftsmen of the Venice document even tried to meddle with the status of Jerusalem, our eternal capital which is indivisible, and our right to settle in the Land of Israel. . . .

All men of good will in Europe, all men who revere liberty, will see in this document another Munich-like capitulation to totalitarian blackmail and a spur to all those seeking to undermine the Camp David accords and derail the peace process in the Middle East. . . .

This rhetoric does not veil the uncompromising and belligerent attitude being expressed by the Israelis.

The Saudi Arabian plan put forward by Crown Prince Fahd in an interview with the official Saudi Press Agency in August 1981 was a variant of such proposals and did not differ basically from the general position maintained by the moderate Arab states since the summit of the Arab League held in Rabat in 1974 that recognized the P.L.O. as the sole legitimate representative of the Palestinian people. The Saudi plan envisaged an independent Palestinian state centred on the West Bank with East Jerusalem as its capital; furthermore, it called for a broader discussion than the Camp David peace process, which the Saudis consider doomed to failure particularly because of its perceived singular concern with a rapprochement between Israel and Egypt only. The specific Saudi proposals suggested:

1. Israeli withdrawal from all territory that it had occupied since the war of 1967.
2. Removal of Israeli settlements in the West Bank and other occupied areas.
3. Guarantees of freedom of worship for all religious groups within these areas.
4. Recognition of the rights of two million Palestinian refugees, from both the war of 1948 and the 1967 war, and for their repatriation and compensation.
5. U.N. trusteeship over the West Bank and the Gaza Strip during a transitional period of several months.
6. The establishment of an independent Palestinian state with East Jerusalem as its capital.
7. The agreement would assure the right of all states in the area to live with each other in peace.
8. All these principles are to be guaranteed by the U.N. or some of its members.

The Saudi plan was subsequently endorsed by Yasser Arafat during a visit to Riyadh in October 1981; the leader of the P.L.O. thereby again implicitly reiterated the right of all states in the area, including Israel, to live with each other in peace.

However at the Twelfth Arab Summit held in Fez, Morocco, in November 1981, the Fahd plan was firmly rejected by an overwhelming majority. Whereas certain of the moderates within the P.L.O., typified by Yasser Arafat, were apparently willing to adopt the Saudi plan as a basis for discussion to achieve some form of Palestinian state centred on the West Bank and Gaza, the leaders of the more radical and Marxist groups within the P.L.O., notably Dr George Habash, were joined on this occasion by Farouk Khadoumi, moderate 'Foreign Minister' of the P.L.O. and, like Arafat, a representative of Al Fatah on the P.L.O. Council. The Arab Summit thus, in essence, concluded that it could not recognize Israel under any circumstances. This outcome fits into the Marxist notion of continuing revolutionary struggle (*see* the third section of Chapter 4).

To be realistic, there was no real chance that Israel would accept the Fahd plan. While point 6 is the crux of the Saudi plan, the Israelis reject an independent Palestinian state entirely and the suggestion of a divided Jerusalem is anathema to them. One outside possibility as a base for some form of future compromise may lie in a Palestinian confederation with Jordan, with specific guarantees of complete Palestinian independence and statehood left for the future.

While point 7 of the Saudi plan probably alluded to the participation of the U.S. in guaranteeing the agreement, the U.S.S.R. in October 1981 formally granted full diplomatic status to the P.L.O. mission in Moscow and the P.L.O. gave its support to the Soviet proposal for a new Middle East peace conference. The highly unlikely Israeli acceptance of a Palestinian state would require both a great deal of faith and a willingness to compromise. However, the inability of the Israelis to seek compromise, according to Mordecai Kaplan, is based in part upon the dominant self-conception of Judaism as an 'organic' cell in which religion and nation cannot be separated; thus Kaplan suggests that Israel represents a unity that stands in opposition to modern concepts of both religion and nationhood (Kaplan, 1963; Lucas, 1974, Ch.17). Any search for compromises acceptable to the Israelis appears to be doomed to failure.

Ott (1980, Ch.7) develops an interesting but misplaced analogy between the Austrian and West Bank–Gaza situations, recounting how Austria was able to resume its independent status in 1955. But Austria is a European country; Vienna had been the capital and administrative centre of the Habsburg empire and possessed the outline structures and personnel to come forward to run the country's affairs. By contrast, the Israelis gained their victory in 1948 not only because of military superiority but also due to their organizational-administrative infrastructure that had gradually developed into a parallel quasi-governmental enterprise from the early 1920s. The British did almost nothing to advance the Arab position within Palestine. Today the development of a Palestinian bureaucracy would require much time, interest, patience and good will from all parties, including the broader international community.

A number of writers have focussed attention upon the viability of a Palestinian 'state'. Bull's assessment of the potential viability of the West Bank with economic and political links to both Israel and Jordan represents a far too localized, myopic viewpoint which lacks breadth, vision and imagination (Bull, 1975). In contrast Ward, Peretz and Wilson (1977) focus upon the viability of a mini-state, assuming support from the 'oil-rich' Arab states and free access to Israeli and Jordanian markets through a form of customs union arrangement.

At an even broader level Middle Eastern economies, like the world economies in general, are characterized by substantial financial imbalances. The major oil-exporting countries have been running large current account surpluses and the oil-importing nations—in the Middle East, Egypt, Israel and Jordan—are running current account deficits so high that future financing by external borrowing will become too great to be met by any conceivable expansion of export earnings. The potential for inter-linkage of all Middle Eastern countries through interdependence and long-term development financing could lead to regional economic growth and advancement on a quite unprecedented scale. Furthermore the gigantic tourist bonanza that would follow a general peace settlement would also contribute to that growth.

There is of course a possibility that the affairs of the Middle East could be overtaken by events on an even broader scale. During the 1970s certain Arab O.P.E.C. states moved into what may be defined as an adversary posture. If Western living standards are further eroded and the political stability of Western societies threatened by economic crises and dislocations a redefinition of positions may occur and force may then be used, as in 1956, for taking over Arab oil fields. Israel could be the base for such operations.

However times are changing. Whereas crude oil prices rose from $3 to as high as $41 per barrel in the eight years between 1973 and 1981, in 1983 the thirteen-member O.P.E.C. is in apparent disarray amidst plunging oil prices, oversupplies, excessive production, drooping consumption, world economic recession and fears of future depression. O.P.E.C. production has fallen from a high of 31.3 million barrels a day in 1977 to 22.5 million barrels in 1981 and to an estimated 14 million barrels in March 1983 with a planned 17.5 million barrels per day rate for 1983. Furthermore, non-O.P.E.C. countries, including Britain, Canada, Mexico and the U.S. now produce about 50 percent of the free world's crude. Saudi Arabia alone accounts for 40 percent of O.P.E.C.'s total production.

The position of the U.S.S.R., the world's largest oil producer, is crucial. Of its daily production of 12 million barrels in March 1983, a quarter was exported mostly to Eastern Europe and Cuba. However, 1.5 million barrels a day was sold to Western Europe, an amount that is increasing. Each $1 decline in oil prices deprives the U.S.S.R. of between $600 and $760 million in hard currencies; to compensate the U.S.S.R. has sold more oil to the West, often at knock-down prices, initiating a further round of price reductions.

O.P.E.C., supposedly a cartel, a combination of independent enterprises designed to limit competition, should by definition be able to control production between its members and thereby set prices in good or bad times. Yet some may suggest that the greediness of O.P.E.C. in the late 1970s killed the goose that laid the golden egg, leading the U.S. and Western Europe to adopt major energy conservation programmes and produce more of their own oil and power from alternative sources and for the U.S.S.R. to boost its production (Banks, 1981; Hallwood and Sinclair, 1981). In the longer term it is probable that it will again be the geopolitical realities of the Middle East rather than oil which will prove of prime importance to the West. Perhaps those fundamental properties of the region have been uppermost all along and oil has temporarily deflected Western perceptions! A mounting U.S.-U.S.S.R. conflict in the region might see attempts to submerge the Palestinian problem under a U.S.-backed coalition between Israel, Saudi Arabia, Egypt and, possibly, Jordan, against the supposed imperialistic objectives of the U.S.S.R. in the Middle East (Dawisha, 1980).

Returning to the potential scenarios set forth in Table 6, even with a massive Arab victory the attainment of a scenario 1 type settlement appears most unlikely, particularly because of the effect it would have on conservative Arab states of the region. For example, the position of Jordan would be untenable: it would seem probable that this creation of imperialism would quickly disappear and be re-integrated into the greater region from which it was torn. Syria would face a similar confrontation. Thus, even though Israel were destroyed it is unlikely that peace would ensue, at least in the immediate aftermath. As Elie Kedourie (1970, p.1) has insightfully noted, disorder is endemic to the region. The emergence of a greater Palestine, in a number of ways, is feared as much by Jordan, Syria, Saudi Arabia and Egypt as by Israel. However, the potential for conflict remains as an incentive to attain some type of agreement as under scenario 3, or even scenario 2.

Yet while the Israelis remember that since 1948 there have been major confrontations between Israel and its Arab neighbours in 1956, 1967 and October 1973, they continue to fear 'the nightmares of a murderous, bloody defeat and counteroccupation' of Israel by the Palestinians (Davis, 1977, p.122). At times of particular danger, according to Don Segre (1980), the entire state of Israel feels itself plunged into an historic, Jewish existentialist state of solitude, fears of imminent annihilation and 'no choice situations', what some term the 'holocaust mentality'. They fear that Israel only has to lose once to be wiped out. The reality is that Israel, a non-signatory to international anti-nuclear proliferation agreements, possesses a proven nuclear capability and delivery system with a secret nuclear plant located in the northern Negev at Dimona.

Dimona lies in a small basin with Hare Dimona (689 metres above sea level) to the north and Har Zayyad (656 metres) to the south, about thirty-five kilometres (22 miles) southeast of Be'er Sheva on the road to Sedom, located on the southwest shore of the Dead Sea. The Dimona research reactor, imported from France in 1963, is supplied with Norwegian heavy water and is a type similar to the Circus reactor in India which produced that country's nuclear explosion. The plutonium produced by the Dimona reactor is widely assumed to be extracted at the adjacent reprocessing plant and used for military purposes (Stockholm International Peace Research Institute, 1979, p.313).

One scenario must be considered whereby an almost vanquished Israel, facing imminent extinction by invading Arab armies, uses its nuclear potential to 'turn the tide at a stroke', and produce a chance for survival of the Israeli state. The employment of the Israeli nuclear capability could well lead to immediate and direct intervention by at least one of the superpowers with the possibility of general escalation into a cataclysmic war. Finally, the sobering thought is that the Bible (Revelations 16: 16) refers to Armageddon, the hill of Megiddo, as the scene of the great final battle leading to world destruction. Megiddo lies some thirty kilometres to the southeast of Mount Carmel and Haifa on the plain of Yizreel, *Emeo Yizre'el*.

CHAPTER 7

Towards the Mounting Crisis

Two dominant viewpoints on its national space and territorial expansion are now becoming apparent within Israel. The first sees Jordan as eastern Eretz Yisrael and looks forward to an eventual territorial expansion beyond the Jordan valley to encompass the highlands, at least, immediately to the east of the Jordan. A second view appears as a developing Israeli insistence on the dichotomous division of the former mandated territory of Palestine between Israel and Palestinian Jordan. This is the so-called 'Jordan is Palestine' position which emphasizes that almost 70 percent of the 2.2 million population of Jordan is Palestinian and, thus, seeks quite dexterously to deny the entire refugee problem. Alternatively, however, it can be suggested that Palestine was partitioned amongst outside interests by Western imperialists, between the Zionists to the west into what has become Israel and the parvenu Hashemites to the east in Transjordania (Fig. 25). The seeds of this division can be traced back to the administrative plan of the pro-Zionist British Mandate whereby the East Bank in Transjordania would 'serve as a reserve of land for use in the resettlement of Arabs once the National Home for Jews in Palestine ... became an accomplished fact' (Childers, 1971, p.173).

The first of these viewpoints, that of an Eretz Yisrael encompassing at least the hills to the east of the Jordan, now appears to be in the ascendant and reflects the Israeli belief that a durable peace with the Palestinians, even within Jordan, is quite beyond the realms of imagination. Against this background we will consider both the lack of progress toward a general peace within the Middle East as envisaged within the Egyptian-Israeli peace initiatives of 1978–79 and the June 1982 Israeli invasion of the southern Lebanon.

The failure of the move towards a comprehensive peace

The Egyptian–Israeli peace treaty was signed by President Sadat and Prime Minister Begin in ceremonies in Washington, D.C., on 26 March 1979. The Preamble to the *Treaty of Peace between the Arab Republic of Egypt and the State of Israel* recognized that 'the conclusion of a Treaty of Peace between Egypt and Israel is an important step in

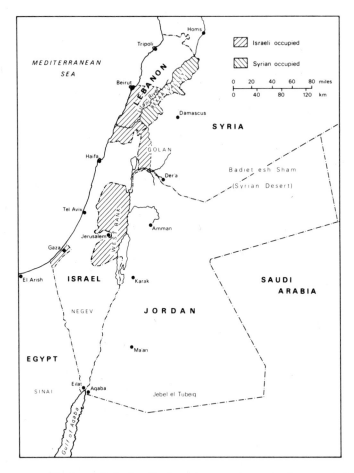

FIGURE 25. Israel–Palestine–Jordan, showing the territories occupied
in 1967 and 1982

the search for comprehensive peace in the area and for the attainment
of the settlement of the Arab–Israeli conflict in all its aspects'. To the
furtherance of this accord and its longer term 'search for comprehensive peace' a letter to the U.S. President was appended to the Treaty
and signed by both President Sadat and Prime Minister Begin. From
this letter a clear statement emerges on the intentions to maintain a
continuing peace process towards a comprehensive Arab–Israeli
settlement, not only an Egyptian–Israeli accord:

Dear Mr. President,   March 26, 1979

This letter confirms that Egypt and Israel have agreed as follows:

The Governments of Egypt and Israel recall that they concluded at Camp David and signed at the White House on September 17, 1978, the annexed documents entitled 'A Framework for Peace in the Middle East Agreed at Camp David' and 'Framework for the conclusion of a Peace Treaty between Egypt and Israel'.

For the purpose of achieving a comprehensive peace settlement in accordance with the above-mentioned Frameworks, Egypt and Israel will proceed with the implementation of those provisions relating to the West Bank and the Gaza Strip. They have agreed to start negotiations within a month after the exchange of the instruments of ratification of the Peace Treaty. In accordance with the 'Framework for Peace in the Middle East', the Hashemite Kingdom of Jordan is invited to join the negotiations. The Delegations of Egypt and Jordan may include Palestinians from the West Bank and Gaza Strip or other Palestinians as mutually agreed. The purpose of the negotiation shall be to agree, prior to the elections, on the modalities for establishing the elected self-governing authority (administrative council), define its powers and responsibilities, and agree upon other related issues. In the event Jordan decides not to take part in the negotiations, the negotiations will be held by Egypt and Israel.

The two Governments agree to negotiate continuously and in good faith to conclude these negotiations at the earliest possible date. They also agree that the objective of the negotiations is the establishment of the self-governing authority in the West Bank and Gaza in order to provide full autonomy to the inhabitants.

Egypt and Israel set for themselves the goal of completing the negotiations within one year so that elections will be held as expeditiously as possible after agreement has been reached between the parties. The self-governing authority referred to in the 'Framework' for Peace in the Middle East' will be established and inaugurated within one month after it has been elected, at which time the transitional period of five years will begin. The Israeli military government and its civilian administration will be withdrawn, to be replaced by the self-governing authority, as specified in the 'Framework for Peace in the Middle East'. A withdrawal of Israeli armed forces will then take place and there will be a redeployment of the remaining Israeli forces into specified security locations.

This letter also confirms our understanding that the United States Government will participate fully in all stages of negotiations.

Sincerely yours,

140

For the Government of Israel:

Menachim Begin

For the Government of the Arab Republic of Egypt:

Mohamed Anwar El-Sadat

The President
The White House*

*Explanatory Note
President Carter, upon receipt of the Joint Letter to him from President Sadat and Prime Minister Begin, has added to the American and Israeli copies the notation: 'I have been informed that the expression "West Bank" is understood by the Government of Israel to mean "Judea and Samaria".' This notation is in accordance with similar procedures established at Camp David.

The third paragraph of the letter specifies that the West Bank and Gaza Strip Palestinians were to obtain autonomy. However, as we discussed in the third section of Chapter 6, the Israeli delegation upon its return to Israel in March 1979 immediately clarified its definition of the term 'Palestinians' as Palestinian Arabs rather than what might have been inferred as the Palestinian people. Furthermore the fourth paragraph set a transitional period for the realization of 'the self-governing authority referred to in the "Framework for Peace in the Middle East"'. Clearly, these suggestions have come to nought; with the advancing Israeli settlement, particularly in the West Bank and East Jerusalem, a comprehensive settlement and a real Palestinian autonomy have deteriorated and receded. The sense of hope embodied within the Framework has now passed away.

The Israeli invasion of the southern Lebanon, June 1982

The massive Israeli invasion of the Lebanon in early June 1982 was specifically triggered by the attempted assassination of Israel's Ambassador to Britain, Shlomo Argov, in London on 3 June 1982, although the attack against the Lebanon had been under active preparation since August 1981 when Ariel Sharon was appointed Israeli Defence Minister. Preparations for a major Israeli offensive into the Lebanon were well underway and gaining momentum in January 1982 when I toured the Israeli–Lebanese borderland. At that time, however, the intended Israeli action was to have begun about April or May 1982. The Israeli invasion of the southern Lebanon, referred to by Israel as 'Operation Peace for the Galilee' but generally now termed the Sixth Middle Eastern war, was the largest conflict within the region since the Yom Kippur War of 1973, far exceeding the 1978 Israeli incursion into the Lebanon.

Briefly to recapitulate, in May 1948 the first Middle Eastern war saw the emergence of the Israeli state. The Suez conflict of 1956 was the second war; the third war, the Six-Day War of June 1967, witnessed the Israeli occupation of the West Bank and East Jerusalem, the Gaza Strip and the Golan Heights. An Egyptian–Syrian pact led on to the indecisive Yom Kippur War of October 1973. The fifth war, confined to the Lebanon, raged throughout most of 1976 and was terminated by the Egyptian–Syrian agreement at the Arab summit in Riyadh in October 1976. Much of the southern Lebanon came under the influence of Israel through its 'Good Fence' policy from the summer of 1976.

The publicly stated aims of the Israeli invasion of the Lebanon in June 1980 were not only the destruction of the P.L.O. and the removal of its stronghold in the Lebanon, especially about Tyre, Sidon and in western Beirut (*see* Fig. 13 in Chap. 5), but also the creation of a larger, firmly based buffer territory nominally under the Christian Militia of Major Sa'ad Haddad to provide a more secure future for Israeli settlements within the Galilee. Prior to the invasion the so-called Fatahland extended over 155 square miles about Tyre while the territory controlled by the Christian Militia of Major Haddad, with Israeli support, was a 600-square-mile buffer zone along the Israeli border in the southern Lebanon.

The Israeli invasion of the Lebanon from June 1982 was marked by savage and indiscriminate slaughter and maimings of ordinary Palestinian refugees. A rapid advance, bypassing the ineffective and inconsequential United Nations Interim Force in the Lebanon (U.N.I.F.I.L.) brought Israeli forces into contact with P.L.O. positions, and the Israelis succeeded in taking Tyre and Sidon from the P.L.O. Further east the Israelis waged battle against and inflicted heavy losses upon Syrian air and ground forces about the Bekaa Valley, although this specific Israeli–Syrian contest was brought to an uneasy conclusion by an agreed cease-fire on 11 June. In the Israeli attempt to destroy finally the P.L.O., the battle in the southern Lebanon raged on mercilessly.

Whereas U.S. public reactions deplored the renewed outbreaks of violence in the southern Lebanon consequent upon the Israeli invasion and the U.S. backed two U.N. Security Council resolutions calling for an immediate cease-fire by all parties, the U.S. vetoed an important, far more significant resolution that threatened sanctions unless Israel withdrew from Lebanese territory. U.S. Ambassador to the U.N. Jeane Kirkpatrick emphasized that the U.S. veto was cast because this U.N. resolution was 'not sufficiently balanced'. The U.S. position maintained that, 'Israel will have to withdraw its forces from the Lebanon, and the Palestinians will have to stop using Lebanon as a launching pad for attacks on Israel.' Yet it was Israel that had broken the relative calm of the cease-fire along the Israeli–Lebanese border, a cease-fire that had existed between Israel and the P.L.O. since its formalization by the U.S. Special Envoy to the Middle East, Philip Habib, in July 1981. According to U.N. sources in the southern Lebanon no P.L.O. cross-border shellings had occurred since 24 July 1981 except in direct response to Israeli bombings.

Israeli expansion into the Lebanon is not simply for the destruction of the P.L.O. but is the result of an uncompromising Israeli irredentist policy for an enlarged state with controlled buffer positions that could, effectively, redraw the map of Lebanon. The Israelis would wish to see such a Lebanon controlled by the right-wing Maronite Christian Phalange, the Kata'eb, probably led by the Gemayel family, as a buffer-puppet of the Israeli state. For an appreciation of the *prime* objectives of the Israeli offensive, however, we must return to our view on Israeli intentions for Eretz Yisrael, particularly the future of the West Bank and the Gaza Strip and the adamant Israeli opposition to any vestige of a real Palestinian autonomy for the West Bank and Gaza.

Ariel Sharon has viewed the destruction of P.L.O. infrastructures as a fundamental prerequisite for isolating external P.L.O. support for the Palestinian Arabs within the occupied territories of the West Bank and the Gaza Strip and as a precursor to the implementation of an updated Israeli 'autonomy/annexation' initiative for those territories of Shomeron and Yehuda in particular. In his position as Minister of Agriculture in the Likud coalition government between 1977 and 1981, Sharon, whose ruthlessness was feared even by Moshe Dayan, had orchestrated the plans for the increased rate of new Israeli settlements in the West Bank.

The eradication of the core of the P.L.O. residing within the Lebanon, could lead to a unification of Palestinians within a Jordan firmly under the control of the Hashemites, seen as posing a far lesser threat to Israel, and could isolate Palestinian Arabs within Israel and the West Bank and Gaza. This aim to cut off the West Bank from outside P.L.O. influence contributed significantly to the decision of Israel to invade the Lebanon in June 1982.

The results of a PORI-TIME poll, conducted during a period of considerable unrest throughout the West Bank in general and Jerusalem in particular between 4 and 15 April 1982, however, are indicative of the mounting radicalization and disillusionment among West Bank Arabs. The poll, which adhered to the usual professional standards of such enquiries and contained a sample of 441 individuals

143

residing within fifty-eight West Bank towns, villages and refugee camps, weighted according to age, sex and geographical location, has an estimated error factor of 4–5 percent. The results of the poll, published in late May 1982, refute the current Israeli view that if West Bank Palestinians could be isolated from the P.L.O. they would settle for an Israeli version of an 'autonomy agreement': the findings show that 86 percent of the respondents favour a Palestinian state run solely by the P.L.O. Half the respondents believed that Yasser Arafat should lead the Palestinians, 12 percent selected the radical Naif Hawatmeh and 7 percent would have Marxist George Habash; still 25 percent appeared to favour local West Bank leaders such as Bassam Shaka'a, the former mayor of Nablus deposed by the Israelis earlier in 1982. 56 percent said they wanted a 'secular-democratic' Palestinian state, whereas 35 percent favoured an outright Islamic one. 18 percent wanted a mixed economy but only 3 percent supported a purely capitalistic system. The continuing radicalization of the West Bank Palestinian population is further demonstrated by the 72.1 percent who chose the U.S.S.R. as the country they most admired (only 1.6 percent gave the U.S. and 25.4 percent said neither) and the 82 percent who said the U.S.S.R. was the 'most helpful to the Palestinian cause' (5 percent for the U.S.).

The affirmative response to the direct question, 'Are you in favour of an independent Palestinian state was nearly complete (98.2 percent), yet only 59 percent believed such a state should encompass 'all of Palestine' including Israel; 27 percent appeared ready to accept a Palestinian state comprised of only the West Bank and the Gaza Strip. There is no Palestinian belief in present and envisaged peace initiatives: only 2 percent thought the Egyptian–Israeli peace accord had helped the Palestinian cause while 88 percent said it had been a hindrance. Finally, when questioned about peace between Israel and the Palestinians, 71.4 percent of the sample considered that it would never happen and only 24.9 percent believed that it would happen 'someday'. The PORI poll thus confirms the disillusionment and apparent desperation of West Bank Palestinians, suggesting that we could witness continuing conflict and mounting crises within the West Bank even without external P.L.O. assistance. The ominous question then arises as to what the Israelis will do with this Palestinian population of the West Bank.

There is one further objective for continuing Israeli interest in the southern Lebanon. Israel is short of water, not only to undertake the envisaged development of the northern Negev and the West Bank but for general requirements. The diversion of Litani waters is now of particular and increasing relevance to the advancing settlement policy. During the Israeli 'War of Independence' Israeli Defence

Forces had captured the Naftali Hills in Operation Hiram of October 1948 and established the cease-fire line along the Litani River; however, with the signing of the Israeli–Lebanese Agreement of March 1949 the border was once again re-established at the former British Mandatory line. The importance of Litani waters has to be considered on two grounds—not only water *quantity* but also *quality*. Figure 26 sets forth the dominant water flow characteristics within and in the area about Israel; while the Litani flow at 100 million cubic meters per annum (m.c.m.) may not mean a great deal, it translates to 3.17 m³ per second. The important point to recognize is that this flow

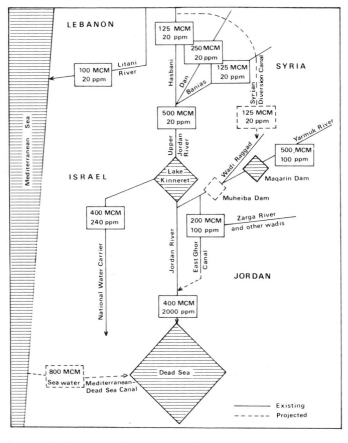

FIGURE 26. Schematic diagram of the Jordan and lower Litani catchment areas, showing the approximate annual flows in million m³ (m.c.m.) and salinities in parts per million (p.p.m.)

145

apparently equals 25 percent of the flow within the much heralded Israeli National Water Carrier. In addition the low salinity levels of Litani waters, only twenty parts per million (p.p.m.) compared to 240 p.p.m. of the water within the National Water Carrier, are important. Transfer of Litani water southwards to the National Water Carrier would greatly boost that system's water flow and facilitate irrigation planning in the northern Negev and extensions into the West Bank. Such transfers would reduce overall salinity levels within the National Carrier considerably, to below 200 p.p.m.

A census, undertaken in the southern Lebanon in March 1983 on the authority of the Israeli Defence Force Military Governor, provides a possible pointer to longer term Israeli intentions for the southern Lebanon. Through a twenty-seven page questionnaire circulated to village mukhtars (leaders), more than 250,000 civilians residing in the Israeli-occupied southern Lebanon were surveyed in detail. The collection of such a range of information—on populations, occupations, village infrastructure, public utilities and services—suggests the data would be of use in a permanent occupation, either by Israel itself or its Lebanese Christian Militia ally, rather than in returning the area to an integrated Lebanese political entity.

The Israelis seem set on maintaining their 'right' to enter the Lebanon at any time to search and arrest; but agreement on such proposals would make a mockery of any semblance of Lebanese sovereignty and independence.

Rage, rage against the dying of the light (Dylan Thomas)

The Camp David framework envisaged a continuing and broadening dialogue between Israel and Egypt and looked forward to extending negotiations to include Jordan and even 'Palestinians from the West Bank and Gaza Strip'. However, the Israeli invasion of and actions within the Lebanon from June 1982 and attempts to link up with the Christian Phalangists north of Beirut pointed to the real and continuing problem: Israel will veto any move towards compromise with the Palestinians as envisaged within the Camp David framework, will refuse to recognize or discuss a Palestinian problem, and will continue to refuse to discuss matters with the Palestinians.

The inability of a hamstrung and inept U.S. to oversee events—indeed her apparent acquiescence in continuing to provide arms to Israel to use in the summer 1982 attacks on civilian refugee camps in the southern Lebanon—also represents both a continuing and developing crisis. Perhaps the U.S. saw the destruction of the P.L.O. as a necessary condition for the establishment of more peaceful conditions in the region at a time when the Arab world was once again experi-

146

encing major internal divisions: the major rift between the moderate states of Egypt and Saudi Arabia and Jordan resulting from the Camp David accord, the long standing Iraqi-Iranian hostilities, and such internecine rivalries as those about the Gulf, the Yemen and Libya.

As mentioned above, the U.S.-Israeli agreement concluded at the second Sinai disengagement between Israel and Egypt in 1975 stipulated that as a precondition for Israeli participation in that disengagement the U.S. would agree not to undertake any direct contacts with the P.L.O. However, in October 1977 President Carter sought to develop an initiative by seeking P.L.O. agreement to U.N. Security Council Resolution 242 of 1967 that implicitly accepted Israel's right to exist. That initiative came to nought.

Yasser Arafat, in a meeting in Beirut on 25 July 1982 with six U.S. congressmen that included the California Republican Paul N. McClusky Jr., signed a document personally accepting all U.N. resolutions relevant to the Palestinian question, recalling a somewhat similar conciliatory meeting with U.S. Congressman Paul Finley in November 1978. The negative reaction from the U.S., indeed the outright and offhand rejection of the Arafat pledge which essentially accepted Israel's right to exist was not surprising. Although such a cursory rejection does not square with the U.S. position to effect a just settlement, it nevertheless conforms to the continuing steadfast U.S. support of Israel.

Despite twelve years of a virtual autonomous Palestinian 'state' within the Lebanon, as a guerrilla organization the P.L.O. was never singularly or specifically attached to its bases there. A considerable number of Palestinians are scattered throughout the Middle East and elsewhere, and when Israel destroyed much of the established P.L.O. infrastructure in southern Lebanon, P.L.O. units dispersed to Algeria, Iraq, Jordan, Syria, Tunisia, North and South Yemen, and northern and eastern Lebanon. The P.L.O. will regroup, probably with more vigour and pertinacity than after similar setbacks in Jordan in 1970–71 and Syria in 1976.

Israeli actions aimed at reducing tensions by the removal of the P.L.O., although in the short term greatly reducing guerrilla support raids into Israeli space, may have achieved a quite opposite effect. Any chance of a permanent political settlement that must of necessity precede a durable peace has been delayed. The essentially moderate policies of Arafat may now be firmly rejected for the ruthless, hard tactics of the far more radical P.L.O. groups. We could witness a return to the conditions of the early 1970s with its P.L.O.-induced acts of political terrorism, hijackings, the seizing of hostages, widespread assassinations and occasional forays into Israel. Indeed, the further setbacks for P.L.O. moderates may provide a filip for those advocating direct action against Israel after the lull in hostilities prior to the Sixth Middle Eastern war. On the other hand, the P.L.O. victory in western Beirut in which a beleaguered, outgunned P.L.O. force with the Lebanese leftist militia faced and kept at bay a ferocious onslaught by a U.S.-backed and armed modern Israeli military machine, may have engendered a renewed faith in the existing, moderate P.L.O. hierarchy symbolized by Arafat. Support may grow for his willingness again to seek a compromise towards a durable settlement that would include Israel's right to exist.

One of Israel's greatest fears is that the U.S. and P.L.O. may move toward direct negotiation. Israel sought by defeating the P.L.O. and its moderate leadership in the Sixth Middle Eastern war to set back any such direct U.S.-P.L.O. dealings over the occupied territories, and to proceed to absorb those territories into Israel. However, the war of 1982 may have set in motion a rapprochement, especially between Egypt and Saudi Arabia, that can re-establish a central ground for moderates in the Arab world, particularly with the loss of face by Libya, Syria and the South Yemen when they were unable or unwilling to aid the P.L.O. in the summer of 1982. But one over-riding point is that the spirit of Palestinian nationalism has not been extinguished; in the longer term the Sixth Middle Eastern war may have done much both to deepen and broaden the struggle.

The departure of the P.L.O. from southern Lebanon will not in itself herald any reduction in strife within that once traditionally tolerant and freedom-loving country, and any semblance of a real Lebanese independence has most likely been postponed for a decade. The minority Christian Phalangist and its military arm will continue to co-operate with Israel, to wage civil war against the majority Muslim population and such of its armed factions as the Moribitoum Nasserite militia. It is also probable that both the Israelis and Syrians will maintain a presence within the Lebanon to effect a virtual partition of the country, and that any further major confrontation between Israel and Syria might bring intervention from the Soviets, either directly or via action through their 1980 treaty obligations with Syria.

Until recently, the U.S.S.R. has exercised quite a remarkable restraint in its relations within the region; such restraint might almost suggest a defined U.S.-U.S.S.R. *modus vivendi* and the mutual acceptance of the other's sphere of influence within the general theatre.

President Reagan's 'new' Middle Eastern peace initiative published on 1 September 1982, the day the P.L.O. was completing its withdrawal from west Beirut, reiterated the general principles of a settlement along the lines of the Camp David framework. Indeed, President Reagan, upon assuming office in January 1981 and again in his 1982 initiative, emphasized that the general framework of U.S. Middle

Eastern policy should continue to follow the broad guidelines laid down by his predecessors. The preamble to the September 1982 statement records:

> There were two basic issues we had to address. First, there was the strategic threat to the region posed by the Soviet Union and its surrogates, best demonstrated by the brutal war in Afghanistan: and, second, the peace process between Israel and its Arab neighbors.

An insight into U.S. policy is afforded by the order given to the 'basic issues' set forth by President Reagan: the 'strategic threat to the region' and the Israeli–Arab 'peace process'.

The 1982 Reagan initiative owed much both to Mr George Shultz, the U.S. Secretary of State, and the aftermath of the Israeli invasion of the Lebanon in June 1982 and the ensuing Sixth Middle Eastern War that raged through June–August 1982. The crucial sentence of the Reagan statement is:

> The question now is how to reconcile Israel's legitimate security concerns with the legitimate rights of the Palestinians.

Three particular features of the Reagan initiative deserve attention and evaluation: the proposal for a freeze on Israeli settlement in the occupied territories, a movement towards a limited Palestinian autonomy under Jordan and the future status of Jerusalem.

The Reagan plan recognized the need to freeze further Israeli settlement within the occupied territories; it suggested that 'the immediate adoption of a settlement freeze by Israel, more than any other action, could create the confidence needed for wider participation in these talks'. President Reagan moved beyond Camp David, suggesting a broader participation in the peace process than just the U.S., Egypt and Israel. Such talks, most immediately between Jordan and the Palestinians and later between Israel and the Palestinians, will come to nought since it remains unlikely that Israel will ever enter freely into discussions with the Palestinians. A moot question is whether the Israeli perception of Palestinian nationalism could move toward negotiation from the present automatic Israeli response of military force when Palestinian nationalism is put forward. Since the Reagan initiative, Israeli settlement in the West Bank, the Gaza Strip and East Jerusalem has continued. No such public utterances as the Reagan formula can limit developments. The future settlement envisaged within the Drobles plan for the West Bank and dramatic redevelopments in East Jerusalem cause us to conclude that a point of no return has been reached, at least for settlement of the West Bank and East Jerusalem.

It may also be asserted that, despite the Reagan stance, it is largely U.S. finance that supports the Israeli settlement momentum. In October 1982 when the U.S. Government Accounting Office (G.A.O.) undertook a full-scale investigation of U.S. foreign aid to Israel, it discovered large amounts of 'hidden aid'. The G.A.O. estimated that since 1974 total U.S. aid to Israel may be as high as $30,000 million—that is $9 million a day over the past nine years. Such an amount represents more than 34 percent of the total U.S. foreign aid bill.

Dilip Hiro (1982, pp.375–76) has pointed to a particular irony: although Israel is firmly committed to upholding and extending Western interests against Communist and Soviet pressures, by conquering and colonizing the West Bank and Gaza Strip Israel has created conditions under which tens of thousands of young Palestinians have turned to radical Marxism.

The second aspect of the Reagan initiative that requires comment relates to a limited Palestinian autonomy under Jordan, which suggests that the 1.3 million Palestinians residing within the West Bank and Gaza Strip should attain only a 'domestic authority'. Following free elections a self-governing Palestinian authority would be established for a five-year probationary period, 'to prove to the Palestinians that they can run their own affairs, and that such Palestinian autonomy poses no threat to Israeli security'. Yet, even after this five-year period, the reality of a truly independent Palestine would still not be realized, for President Reagan asserted:

> Beyond the transition period, as we look into the future of the West Bank and Gaza, it is clear to me that peace cannot be achieved by the formation of an independent Palestinian state in those territories. Nor is it achievable on the basis of Israeli sovereignty or permanent control over the West Bank and Gaza. So the United States will not support the establishment of an independent Palestinian state in the West Bank and Gaza, and we will not support annexation or permanent control by Israel. There is, however, another way to peace. The final status of these lands must, of course, be reached through the give-and-take of negotiations. But it is the firm view of the United States that self-government by the Palestinians of the West Bank and Gaza in association with Jordan offers the best chance for a durable, just and lasting peace.

This position accords with the U.S. veto of U.N. Resolution 3236 of November 1974, which sought to affirm the inalienable right of the Palestinian people to self-determination, including the right to establish an independent state in Palestine in accordance with the charter of the U.N. It is quite feasible that the P.L.O. could accept such a proposal for a limited autonomy as outlined within the Reagan formula as one small step towards the realization of a full Palestinian nationhood, whereas the Israelis would continue to reject it for the same reason. This notion of an 'independent' Palestinian entity 'in association with Jordan', mooted previously by King Hussein of Jordan, was firmly rejected by the Knesset in March 1972.

The third issue raised by the Reagan peace formula relates to the future of Jerusalem, which appears to have crept into the document almost as an afterthought. The sensitive and crucial question of Jerusalem is stated as, 'Finally we remain convinced that Jerusalem must remain undivided, but its final status should be decided through negotiations.' Such a brief, loose and trivial statement is open to so many interpretations as to be quite ineffective; furthermore, it suggests that the enormity of the Jerusalem problem is not appreciated by the U.S. and that a bitter conflict will continue over the future political status of the Holy City.

In the latter part of 1982 President Reagan's hopes for a broader Arab participation in the peace process appeared to be receiving encouragement on two fronts. First, at the Arab summit in Fez in September 1982, some interest was shown in aspects of the Reagan plan; by guaranteeing peace for 'all states in the region', the Fez summit went a long way toward acknowledging Israel's right to exist while also calling for an independent Palestinian state with East Jerusalem as its capital. Secondly, an agreement was reached by Yasser Arafat and Jordanian Prime Minister Mudar Badran prior to the visit of King Hussein to Washington in late December 1982. This agreement pledged 'joint political moves at all levels' and called for 'a special and distinctive relationship' between Jordan and a 'liberated Palestine' to be created from the occupied West Bank and Gaza Strip. Whereas the Palestinians have not deviated from their basic goal of an independent Palestine, the emerging Palestinian–Jordanian accord could be seen as a constructive attempt to break the deadlock between the U.S., Israel and the P.L.O. that had been reinforced by Israel's continued rejection of the Reagan initiative. To this end the Palestinians agreed to be represented by a delegation that included Jordanians and non-P.L.O. Palestinians who could be authorized by the P.L.O. to represent Palestinian interest.

During his December 1982 visit to Washington, King Hussein was assured by President Reagan that if Jordan expressed its willingness to join the U.S. peace process, which directly conflicted with the Fez plan, the U.S. would obtain, prior to the commencement of negotiations, an Israeli freeze on settlements in the occupied territories and a complete Israel withdrawal from the Lebanon. It was thus disappointing to President Reagan and Secretary of State George Shultz that

151

King Hussein expressed his reluctance to enter into negotiations on the West Bank and Gaza Strip. It should be remembered, however, that King Hussein, unlike Sadat in 1979, is in a particularly vulnerable position: the Hashemite kingdom relies upon Saudi Arabia and the Gulf States for more than $1,000 million a year in economic assistance; there are a large number of Palestinians residing within Jordan; and the Israelis are beginning to threaten to take Jordanian territory along the east bank of the Jordan. Amidst all this King Hussein's prime aim is for the survival and continuity of the Hashemite kingdom.

While the U.S. was offering positive inducements to Hussein to enter the U.S. peace process, they were also exerting real pressure upon the Jordanians: in April 1983, a U.S. Congressional House Foreign Affairs sub-committee voted to make further U.S. arms sales to Jordan conditional upon Hussein's willingness to enter the Camp David peace negotiations and Jordan's granting diplomatic recognition to Israel. At the same meeting, the sub-committee recommended the addition of $365 million to President Reagan's request for $2,450 million in economic and military aid to Israel in the fiscal year 1984.

Real doubts must remain on the ability of the U.S. to deliver on her promises to King Hussein about the freezing of Israeli settlement in the occupied territories and a complete Israeli withdrawal from the Lebanon. In a forceful and uncompromising address to the Thirtieth World Zionist Congress in December 1982, Mr Begin re-emphasized Israel's right to Eretz Yisrael, including the occupied West Bank and Jerusalem, and asserted that no compromise on this fundamental matter would ever be contemplated by the Israelis. In addition, the activities of Ariel Sharon highlight the difficulties the U.S. faces in this regard.

Although the indictment of Sharon by the Commission of Inquiry into the Arab massacres by Lebanese Phalangists at the Sabra and Shatila refugee camps in Beirut during September 1982 led to his resignation as Israeli Defence Minister in February 1983 (Kahan, Barok and Efrat, 1983), within ten days, at the instigation of Mr Begin, the Israeli Cabinet had reinstated Sharon to the two key ministerial committees on the Lebanon and defence. Under the terms of his appointment to the latter committee, Sharon was charged with the responsibilities of maintaining the momentum in the settlement of the West Bank as he had done while Minister of Agriculture prior to August 1981.

It is opportune to mention at this point the *Thirty-Year Plan for the Settlement of Judea and Samaria*, published in April 1983 by the World Zionist Organization and the Israeli Ministry of Agriculture. In brief the plan provides for a continuation to the year 2013 of the Israeli settlement procedures given specific direction by the Drobles plan.

The new, extended settlement plan details a budget of £347 million a year, of which 60 percent would derive from Israeli government finances and the remainder from the private sector. In the first five years (1983–88), it is intended to construct fifty-seven settlements in the West Bank. Particularly ominous, under the terms of the plan, was the inauguration of a new Israeli settlement in April 1983 that over-looks Nablus, the most heavily populated Palestinian town in the West Bank and the core of the Samarian agricultural heartland. Further-more, the plan specifies settlement sites on Arab owned and cultivated West Bank lands, where direct and major confrontations will undoubt-edly develop.

Sharon's membership on the Israeli Cabinet committee responsible for negotiations with the Lebanese may have helped maintain the deadlock on that front through the Israeli–Christian Phalangist special relationship—an impasse that focused world attention on the Lebanon while the West Bank and East Jerusalem settlement plans proceed apace. The overall ploy of the Israelis, abetted by the Reagan initiative, appears to be to set up two sides in Western eyes—an Israeli as opposed to an Arab—while any independent Palestinian view is ignored. Hussein of Jordan, an Arab and in Western eyes perceptually akin to the Palestinians, is cast as the noble representative of the Arab side, despite his own avowed territorial ambitions towards the West Bank.

The Israelis are thus able to stall on the Reagan peace initiative until Hussein agrees to enter into negotiations to link the Israeli-occupied West Bank and Gaza Strip to Jordan without associating it with some longer term independent Palestinian entity. Israel would hope that the peace initiative fails because Hussein refuses to partici-pate rather than because Israel has refused to negotiate. Whatever the outcome, as time is of the essence the Palestinians are the losers. U.S. attention will soon be diverted to the 1984 presidential campaign, while Israel proceeds methodically with settlements in the occupied territories. By 1985 settlement procedures will be further advanced according to the Drobles and the Thirty-Year plans, and over 100,000 Jewish settlers will be residing in the West Bank alone.

Whereas the Reagan peace initiative represented a statement of U.S. intentions, there appear to be no penalties for Israeli non-com-pliance. The likelihood is that this peace formula will, in time, pass away. The cynic might even suggest that some form of U.S. statement had to be made following the conclusion of the Sixth Middle Eastern war; the U.S. has issued such a statement and matters can now proceed with little real change until the next emergency. We have been here before.

In conclusion, we mention again the overall and pervasive importance of the Hebrew notion of Promised Land, a theme that is almost a geography of the soul, that has followed the Jews from Abraham, Moses and Joshua to its modern manifestation in Zionism and the related idea of Eretz Yisrael. Now, even for those supposedly non-religious Jews, the recognition of Israel as storied place and historical referent obtains, despite an erosion of the fundamental beliefs that gave rise initially to the basic philosophy. The literal acceptance of the Eretz Yisrael idea can brook no compromise.

During the massive Israeli bombardment of west Beirut and the besieged P.L.O. force entrapped in the city in the summer of 1982, certain Western European countries and even the U.S. began to question anew the Israeli threat and wonder at the receding prospect of a permanent settlement as envisaged within the Camp David agreement. The crux of the matter continues to be a truly independent Palestinian political entity. Yet where could such a state locate? Not, it appears, in the West Bank where Israel is settling that area of Eretz Yisrael. Indeed, the emerging Israeli intention now appears to create a greater Eretz Yisrael (Joshua 13: 6 and 8), protected by buffer positions in the Southern Lebanon and, ultimately, east of the Jordan River itself.

Finally, we stressed in the preface that any potentially durable and peaceful settlement within this sensitive region must embrace the four cardinal features: Palestinians and their nationality, Israel's right to exist, the territory, and peaceful relations. Until that agenda is completed, this region of the Middle East will continue as 'the cockpit of global tensions'.

Bibliography

Adams, H. *Prison of Grass: Canada from the Native Point of View*. General Publishing, Toronto, 1975.

Air University, *Military Aspects of World Geography*, Vols 2–3, A.F.R.O.T.C., Montgomery, Alabama, 1954.

Allon, Y. *The Making of the Israeli Army*, Weidenfeld and Nicolson, 1970.

Allon, Y. 'The Case for Defensible Borders', *Foreign Affairs*, Vol. 55, (1976), pp.38–53.

Almond, G. A. and Powell, G. B. (eds.), *Comparative Politics: A Developmental Approach*, Little, Brown, Boston, 1966.

Amin, S. *The Arab Nation: Nationalism and Class Struggles*, Zed Press, London, 1978.

Antonius, G. *The Arab Awakening: The Story of the Arab National Movement*, Hamilton, London, 1938.

Arieh, S. *Planning Jerusalem: The Old City and its Environs*, Weidenfeld and Nicolson, Jerusalem, 1973.

Ash-Sha'ab Daily Newspaper, 9 December 1975.

Astor, D. and Yorke, V. *Peace in the Middle East: Super Powers and Security Guarantees*, Corgi, London, 1978.

Astragal, 'Israel', *The Architects Journal*, Vol. 168, No. 48, 29 November 1978, pp.1019–21.

Avi-Yonah, M. *The Jews of Palestine: A Political History from the Bar Kokhba War to the Arab Conquest*, Blackwell, Oxford, 1976.

Ayçoberry, P. *The Nazi Question: An Essay in the Interpretation of National Socialism, 1922–75*, Routledge, Kegan and Paul, London, 1981.

Bain, K. R. *The March to Zion: United States Policy and the Founding of Israel*, Texas A. and M. University Press, College Station, Texas, 1969.

Baldwin, P.M. 'Liberalism, Nationalism, and Degeneration: The Case of Max Nordau', *Central European History*, Vol. 13 (1980), pp.99–120.

Beaumont, P., Blake, G.H., and Wagstaff, J.M. *The Middle East: A Geographical Study*, Wiley, London, 1976.

Begin, M. *The Revolt*, Steimatzky, Tel Aviv, 1970.

Benevenisti, M. *Jerusalem: The Torn City*, Isratypest, Jerusalem, 1976.

Bethell, N. *The Palestinian Triangle: The Struggle between the British, the Jews and the Arabs 1935–48*, Andre Deutsch, London, 1979.

Birnbaum, P. 'Les Pogromes Russes et la Naissance du Sionisme,' *Le Monde*, 9 May 1982.

Blake, G.H. 'Immigration and Dispersal of Population', in Clarke, J.I. and Fisher, W.B. (eds.), *Population of the Middle East and North Africa: A Geographical Appraisal*, University of London, London, 1972.

Blake, G.H., 'Israel' in H. Bowen-Jones, P. Beaumont, et al (eds.) *Middle East Yearbook*. I.C. Magazines, London, 1978.

Bonné, A. *State and Economies in the Middle East: A Society in Transition*, Routledge, Kegan and Paul, London, 1960.

Braudel, F. *La Mediterranée et le Monde mediterranéen a l'époque de Philippe I*, Armand Collin, Paris, 1949.

Brecher, M. 'Jerusalem: Israel's political decisions, 1947–1977', *Middle East Journal*, Vol. 32 (1978), pp.13–34.

Brenner, L. *Zionism in the Age of the Dictators*, Croom Helm, London, 1982.

Briscoe, L.R. *For the Life of Me*, Longmans, London, 1959.

Brown, D. *Bury my Heart at Wounded Knee: An Indian History of the American West*, Pan, London, 1972.

Brueggemann, W. *The Land: Place as Gift, Promise and Challenge*, Fortress Press, Philadelphia, 1977.

Bull, V.A. *The West Bank—Is it Viable?* Lexington Books, Lexington, Massachusetts, 1975.

Burns, E.A. *Handbook of Marxism*, Gollancz, London, 1935.

Carlton, D. *Anthony Eden: A Biography*, Allan Lane, London, 1981.

Carmi, S. and Rosenfeld, H. 'The Origins of the Process of Proletarianization and Urbanization of Arab Peasants in Palestine', in E. Krausz (ed.), *Studies of Israeli Society. Volume I: Migration, Ethnicity and Community*, Translations, New Brunswick, N.J., 1980, pp.183–98.

Carré, O. *Le Mouvement National Palestinien*, Editions Gallimard-Julliard, Paris, 1977.

Childers, E.B. 'The Wordless Wish: From Citizens to Refugees', in I. Abu Lughod (ed.), *The Transformation of Palestine: Essays on the Origin and Development of the Arab–Israeli Conflict*, Northwestern University Press, Evanston, Illinois, 1971, pp.165–202.

Clout, H.D. *Rural Geography: An Introductory Survey*, Pergamon, Oxford, 1972.

Cohen, E.A. *Human Behaviour in the Concentration Camp* (trans. by H.H. Braaksma), Jonathan Cape, London, 1954.

Cohen, S.B. *Geography and Politics in a World Divided*, Random House, New York, 1963.

Cohen, S.B. *Jerusalem: Bridging the Four Walls; A Geographical Perspective*, Herzl Press, New York, 1977.

Cressey, G.B. *Asia's Lands and Peoples: A Geography of One-Third of the Earth and Two-thirds of its People*, McGraw Hill, New York, 1963.

Daiches, D. *Moses*, Weidenfeld and Nicolson, London, 1975.

Davies, J.C. 'Towards a Theory of Revolutions', *American Sociological Review*, Vol. 27 (1962), pp.5–19.

Davies, M.R. and Lewis, V.A. *Models of Political Systems*, Macmillan, New York, 1971.

Davies, R.W. 'Jewish Military Recruitment in Palestine, 1940–43', *Journal of Palestinian Studies*, Vol. 8, (1979), pp.53–76.

Davies, W.D. *The Gospel and the Land*, University of California, Los Angeles, 1974.

Davis, U. *Israel: Utopia Incorporated*, Zed Press, London, 1977.

Dawisha, K. 'Soviet Policy in the Arab World: Permanent Interests and Changing Influence', *Arab Studies Quarterly*, Vol. 2 (1980), pp.19–37.

Dayan, M. *Ha-Aretz*, 4 April 1969, Jerusalem.

De Blij, H.J. *Systematic Political Geography*, Wiley, New York, 1967.

De Jouvenal, B. *Sovereignty* (trans. J.F. Huntingdon), University of Chicago, Chicago, 1957.

Derogy, J. and Carmel, H. *The Untold History of Israel*, Grove Press, New York, 1979.

Divrei Ha-Knesset, Official Records of the Knesset (1949).

Drobles, M. *The Master Plan for the Development of Settlement in Judea and Samaria*, Jewish National Fund, Jerusalem, 1978.

Drobles, M. *Strategy, Policy and Plans for Settlement in Judea and Samaria*, World Zionist Organization, Jerusalem, 1980.

Duchacek, I.D. *Power Maps: Comparative Politics of Constitutions*, American Bibliographical Center—Clio Press, Santa Barbara, California, 1973.

Eichrodt, W. *Theology and the Old Testament*, The Westminster Press, Philadelphia, 1961.

El-Rayyes, R. and Nahas, D. *Guerillas for Palestine*, Croom Helm, London, 1976.

Epstein, I. *Judaism: A Historical Perspective*, Penguin, Harmondsworth, 1959.

Fairgreave, J. *Geography and World Power*, University of London, London, 1915.

Fischer, C.S. *The Urban Experience*, Harcourt Brace, Jovanovich, New York, 1976.

Fisher, S.N. *Social Forces in the Middle East*, Cornell University Press, New York, 1955.

Fogg, W. 'Southwest Asia', in W.G. East and O.H.K. Spate (eds.),

The Changing Map of Asia: A Political Geography, Methuen, London, 1950, pp.51–118.

Frankenstein, E. *Justice for My People*, Nicholson and Watson, London, 1943.

Friedlander, D. and Goldscheider, C. *The Population of Israel*, Columbia University Press, New York, 1979.

Geographical Handbook Series, *Palestine and Transjordan*, British Naval Intelligence, London, 1943.

George, A. 'Making the Desert Bloom: A Myth Examined', *Journal of Palestinian Studies*, Vol. 8 (1979), pp.88–100.

Gessner, R. 'Brown Shirts in Zion: Jabotinsky—The Jewish Hitler', *New Masses*, 19 February 1935, pp.5–10.

Gerson, A. *Israel, the West Bank and International Law*, Frank Cass, Totowa, N.J., 1978.

Ghilan, M. *How Israel Lost its Soul*, Penguin, Harmondsworth, England, 1974.

Gilbert, M. *The Arab Conflict: Its History in Maps*, Weidenfeld and Nicolson, London, 1975.

Gilbert, M. *Winston S. Churchill*, Vol. IV, Heinemann, London, 1975

Gilmour, D. *The Ordeal of the Palestinians, 1917-1980*, Sidgwick and Jackson, London, 1980.

Glubb, J.B. *A Short History of the Arab Peoples*, Hodder and Stoughton, London, 1969.

Goiten, S.D. *Jews and Arabs: Their Contact through the Ages*, Schoken Books, New York, 1967.

Gordon, T.E., 'The Problems of the Middle East', *The Nineteenth Century*, Vol. 37 (1900), pp.409–418.

Greenberg, H.I. and Nadler, S., *Poverty in Israel: Economic Realities and the Promise of Social Justice*, Praeger, New York, 1977.

Greenberg, M. 'Hab/Piru and the Hebrews', in B. Mazar (ed.), *The World History of the Jewish People*, Vol. 2, W.H. Allen, London, 1970, pp.188–200.

Grigg, D. *The Harsh Lands: A Study in Agricultural Development*, Macmillan, London, 1970.

Grindea, M. (ed.) *The Holy City in Literature*, Kahn and Averill, London, 1982.

Habas, B. *The Gate Breakers: A Dramatic Chronicle of Jewish Immigration into Palestine*, Herzl Press, New York, 1963.

Halevi, I. *Question Juive*, Editions de Minuit, Paris, 1981.

Halevi, N. and Klinov-Malul, R. *The Economic Development of Israel*, Praeger, New York, 1968.

Hall, E.T. *The Hidden Dimension*, Doubleday, Garden City, New York 1966.

Harris, W.W. *Taking Root: Israeli Settlements in the West Bank, the*

Golan and Gaza-Sinai, 1967–1980, Research Studies Press, Chichester, 1980.

Hazlewood, A. *The Emergence of Kenya: the Kenyatta Era*, Oxford University Press, London, 1979.

Hebrew University of Jerusalem, *Israel and the United Nations: Report of a Study Group set up by the Hebrew University of Jerusalem*, Manhattan Publishing, New York, 1956.

Herzl, T. *Complete Diaries*, ed. by R. Patai (trans. H. Zohn), Herzl Press, New York, 1960.

Hess, M. *Rome and Jerusalem*, (trans. M. Waxman), Herzl Press, New York, 1943.

Hick, J.H. *Philosophy of Religion*, Prentice-Hall, Englewood Cliffs, N.J. 2nd ed. 1973.

Hicks, D. *Tetum Ghosts and Kin: Fieldwork in an Indonesian Community*, Mayfield, Palo Alto, Calif., 1976.

Hilan, R. *Culture et Développement en Syrie et dans les Pays Arabes*, Anthropos, Paris, 1969.

Hilberg, R. *The Destruction of the European Jews*, Quadrangle, Chicago, 1967.

Hiro, D. *Inside the Middle East*, Routledge and Kegan Paul, London, 1982.

Hirst, D. 'Rush to Annexation: Israel in Jerusalem', *Journal of Palestine Studies*, Vol. 3 (1973–4), pp.3–31.

Horowitz, D. and Lissak, M. *Origin of the Israeli Polity: Palestine under the Mandate*, University of Chicago Press, Chicago, 1978.

Howie, C.G. *Teach Yourself the Old Testament Story*, English University Press, London, 1967.

Hudson, H. 'The Litani River of Lebanon: An Example of Middle Eastern Water Development', *The Middle East Journal*, Vol. 25 (1970), pp.1–14.

Hussein, G.M. *La Crise de l'Impérialisme*, Minuit, Paris, 1975.

International Institute for Strategic Studies, *The Military Balance 1981–1982*, London, 1981.

Isaac, R.I. *Israel Divided: Ideological Politics in the Jewish State*, Johns Hopkins University Press, Baltimore, 1976.

Israeli Defence Spokesman, *The Lebanese Border*, Ministry of Defence, Jerusalem, 1981.

Israeli Defence Spokesman, *Judea and Samaria*, Ministry of Defence, Jerusalem, 1981.

Issawi, C. (ed.), *The Economic History of the Middle East 1800–1914: A Book of Readings*, University of Chicago, Chicago, 1966.

Issawi, C. 'The Frontiers of Settlement 1800–1950', in C. Issawi (ed.), *The Economic History of the Middle East 1800–1914: A Book of Readings*, University of Chicago, Chicago, 1966, pp.258–9.

Jakle, J.A., Brunn, S. and Roseman, C.C. *Human Spatial Behavior: A Social Geography*, Duxbury Press, North Scituate, Massachusetts, 1976.

Jerusalem Master Plan Bureau, *The Master Plan 1968: Interim Report*, Jerusalem, 1968.

Jiryis, S. 'The Arabs in Israel, 1973–79', *Journal of Palestinian Studies*, Vol. 8 (1979), pp.31–56.

Jones, S.B. 'Global Strategic Views', *Geographical Review*, Vol. 45 (1955), pp.492–508.

Kafih, J. *Halikhot Teman* (Yemeni Paths), Ben Zui Institute, Jerusalem 1961 (in Hebrew).

Kahan, Y., Barok, A., Efrat, Y. *The Final Report of the Commission of Inquiry into the Events at the Refugee Camps in Beirut*, Israeli Government, Jerusalem, 1983.

Kaplan, M.M. *Basic Values in Jewish Religion*, The Reconstructionist Press, New York, 1963.

Karmon, Y. *Israel: A Regional Geography*, Wiley, New York, 1971.

Kayyali, A.W. *Palestine: A Modern History*, Croom Helm, London, 1978.

Kedourie, E. *The Chatham House Version and Other Middle-Eastern Studies*, Praeger, New York, 1970.

Kenen, I.L. *Israel's Defense Line: Her Friends and Foes in Washington*, Prometheus Books, Buffalo, N.Y., 1981.

Kenyon, K.M. *Digging up Jericho*, Benn, London, 1970.

Kimche, J. and D. *The Secret Roads: The Illegal Migration of a People 1938–1948*, Secker and Warburg, London, 1954.

Knapp, W. *The Middle East and the United States: Perceptions and Policies*, Transaction Books, New Brunswick, N.J. 1980.

Knopp, J. *The Trial of Judaism: Contemporary Jewish Writing*, University of Illinois Press, Urbana, Illinois, 1975.

Koenig, I. 'The Koenig Report', *SWASIA*, Vol. 3 (1976), pp. 16–21.

Koppes, C.R. 'Captain Mahan, General Gordon and the Origins of the Term "Middle East"', *Middle Eastern Studies*, Vol. 12 (1976), pp.95–8.

Kroyanker, D. *Developing Jerusalem 1967–1975*, Jerusalem Foundation and David Kroyanker, Jerusalem, 1975.

Kutcher, A. *The New Jerusalem: Planning and Politics*, M.I.T. Press, Cambridge, Mass. 1975.

Lacey, R. *The Kingdom*, Hutchinson, London, 1981.

Lawrence, T.E. *Seven Pillars of Wisdom: A Triumph*, Penguin, Harmondsworth, 1978.

Lehn, W. 'The Jewish National Fund', *Journal of Palestine Studies*, Vol. 3 (1973–4), pp.74–96.

Lesch, A.M. 'Israeli Deportation of Palestinians from the West Bank and the Gaza Strip, 1967-78', *Journal of Palestinian Studies*, Vol. 8-2 (1979), pp.101-31, and Vol. 8-3 (1979), pp.81-112.

Le Strange, G. *Palestine under the Moslems: A Description of Syria and the Holy Land from A.D. 650 to 1500. Translated from the Works of Medieval Arab Geographers*, Reprinted Khayati, Beirut, 1965.

Lewis, B. and Holt, P.M. *Historians of the Middle East*, Oxford University Press, London, 1962.

Lewis, N.N. 'The Frontier of Settlement in Syria, 1800-1950', *International Affairs*, Vol. 31 (1955), pp.48-60.

Lilienthal, A.M. *The Zionist Connection: What Price Peace?* Dodd, Mead, New York, 1978.

Lucas, N. *The Modern State of Israel*, Weidenfeld and Nicolson, London, 1974.

Luke, H.C. and Keith-Roach, E. *The Handbook of Palestine*, Macmillan, London, 1922.

Lustick, I. *Arabs in the Jewish State: Israeli Control of a National Minority*, University of Texas Press, Austin, 1980.

McDonald, J. *My Mission to Israel*, Simon and Schuster, New York, 1951.

Mackinder, H.J. *Democratic Ideals and Reality*, Henry Holt, New York, 1942.

Maier, E. 'Torah as Movable Territory', *Annals of the Association of American Geographers*, Vol. 65 (1975), pp.18-23.

Mallison, W.T. and S.V. 'The Right to Return', *Journal of Palestine Studies*, Vol. 9 (1980), pp.125-36.

Mandel, N.J. *The Arabs and Zionism before World War I*, University of California Press, Berkeley, 1976.

Ma'oz, M. 'New Attitudes of the PLO regarding Palestine and Israel', in G. Ben-Dor (ed.), *The Palestinians and the Middle East Conflict*, Turtledove Publishing, Ramat Gan, Israel, 1978, pp.545-52.

Mardor, M.M. *Strictly Illegal*, Robert Hale, London, 1964.

Mathias, M.McC. 'Ethnic groups and foreign policy', *Dialogue*, Vol. 57 (1982), pp.30-3.

Mazlish, B. *Kissinger: The European Mind in American Policy*, Basic Books, New York, 1976.

Meinig, D.W. 'Heartland and Rimland in Eurasian History', *Western Political Quarterly*, Vol. 9 (1956), pp.553-69.

Migdal, J.S. *Palestinian Society and Politics*, Princeton University Press, Princeton, N.J., 1980.

Monroe, E. *Britain's Moment in the Middle East 1914-56*. Chatto and Windus, London, 1963.

Moore, B. *Soviet Politics—The Dilemma of Power: The Role of Ideas in Social Change*, Harvard University Press, Cambridge, Mass., 1959.

Murphy, A. *The Ideology of French Imperialism, 1817–1881*, The Catholic University of America Press, Washington, D.C., 1947.

Nakhleh, K. 'The Ethnic Problem of Israel', *Journal of Palestinian Studies*, Vol. 8 (1979), p.111.

Nathan, R.R., Gass, O. and Creamer, D. *Palestine: Problem and Promise*, Public Affairs Press, Washington, D.C., 1946.

Nazzal, D.N. *Warriors of Suez*, Linden Press—Simon and Schuster, New York, 1981.

Nazzal, N. *The Palestinian Exodus from Galilee 1948*, Institute for Palestinian Studies, Beirut, 1979.

Neff, D. *Warriors at Suez*, Linden Press—Simon and Schuster, New York, 1981.

Newman, M.L. *The People of the Covenant: A Study of Israel from Moses to the Monarchy*, Abingdon Press, New York, 1962.

Nisan, M. *Israel and the Territories: A Study in Control 1967–1977*, Turtledove Publishing, Ramat Gam, Israel, 1978.

Ochsenwald, W. 'Saudi Arabia and the Islamic Revival', *International Journal of Middle East Studies*, Vol. 13 (1981), pp.271–85.

Orni, E. *Forms of Rural Settlement*, Jewish National Fund, Jerusalem, 1963.

Ott, D. *Palestine in Perspective: Politics, Human Rights and the West Bank*, Quartet, London, 1980.

Palestine Central Bureau of Statistics, *Palestinian Statistical Abstract*, Palestine National Fund, Damascus, 1979.

Peretz, D. 'Israel's 1969 Election Issues: The Visible and the Invisible', *The Middle East Journal*, Vol. 24 (1970), pp.31–46.

Perry, S. 'Security Resolution 242: The Withdrawal Clause', *The Middle East Journal*, Vol. 31 (1977), pp.413–33.

Porath, Y. *The Emergence of the Palestinian Arab National Movement*, Vol. 1 of 2 Vols (1918–29 and 1929–39), Frank Cass, London, 1964.

Porath, Y. 'The Land Problem as a Factor in Relations among Arabs, Jews and the Mandatory Government', in G. Ben-Dor (ed.), *The Palestinians and the Middle East Conflict*, Turtledove, Ramat Gan, Israel, 1978, pp.143–63.

Rabinovich, A. 'On Building a Fortress around Jerusalem', *Jerusalem Post Magazine*, 8 November 1974.

Rodinson, M. *Israel and the Arabs* (trans. M. Perl and B. Pearce), Penguin, Harmondsworth, 2nd ed. 1982.

Rowley, G. 'Israel and the Potential for Conflict: A rejoinder', *The Professional Geographer*, Vol. 22 (1970), pp.248–51.

Rowley, G. 'Israel and the Palestinian Refugees: Background and Comments', *Area*, Vol. 9 (1977), pp.81–9.

Rowley, G. and El-Hamdan, S.A. 'Once a Year in Mecca', *The Geographical Magazine*, Vol. 49 (1977), pp.753–59.

Rowley, G. 'The *Land* in Israel', in A.D. Burnett and P.J. Taylor (eds.), *Political Studies from Spatial Perspectives: Anglo-American Essays on Political Geography*, Wiley, Chichester, 1981, pp.443–65.

Safran, N. *Israel: The Embattled Ally*, Belkamp Press—Harvard University Press, Cambridge, Massachusetts, 1979.

Said, E. *The Question of Palestine*, Routledge and Kegan Paul, London, 1980.

Sayigh, R. *The Palestinians: From Peasants to Revolutionaries*, Zed Press, London, 1979.

Schiff, Z. and Haber, E. *Israel Army and Defence: A Dictionary*, Zmora Bitan Modan, Tel Aviv, 1976.

Schleunes, K.A. *The Twisted Road to Auschwitz: Nazi Policy Toward German Jews, 1933–39*, University of Illinois Press, Urbana, Illinois, 1970.

Seaver, R. 'Introduction' to M. Nyiszli, *Auschwitz: a Doctor's Eye Witness Account* (trans. by T. Kremer and R. Seaver), Panther, London, 1962.

Segre, D.V. *A Crisis of Identity: Israel and Zionism*, Oxford University Press, Oxford, 1980.

Selzer, M. *The Aryanization of the Jewish State*, Black Star Books, New York, 1967.

Sharon, A. *Planning Jerusalem: The Old City and its Environs*, Weidenfeld and Nicolson, Jerusalem, 1973.

Shilhav, Y. 'Communal Conflict in Jerusalem: The Spread of Ultra-Orthodox Jewish Neighbourhoods', paper presented at the International Seminar in Political Geography, University of Haifa, Israel, January 1982.

Sicron, M. *Immigration to Israel: 1948–1953*, Falk Project and CBS, Jerusalem, 1957.

Singer, I. (ed.) *The Jewish Encyclopaedia*, Funk and Wagnalls, New York, 1939.

Smilianskaya, I.M. 'The Disintegration of Feudal Relations in Syria and Lebanon in the Middle of the Nineteenth Century', in C. Issawi (ed.), *The Economic History of the Middle East 1800–1914: A book of Readings*, University of Chicago, Chicago, 1966, pp.227–47.

Smith, C. and Andrews, J. *The Palestinians*, Minority Rights Group, London, 1977.

Smith, D.M. *Human Geography: A Welfare Approach*, Arnold, London, 1977.

Special Correspondent, 'How the Iraqi Jews came to Israel', *Middle East International*, Vol. 19 (1973), pp.18–20.

Spykman, N.J. *The Geography of Peace*, Harcourt Brace, New York, 1944.

Stay Kosher in Israel, Kollek, Jerusalem, 1981.

Stevens, R.P. 'Smuts and Weizmann', *Journal of Palestinian Studies*, Vol. 3 (1973–4), pp.35–59.

Stevenson, R.L. *Virginibus Puerisque*, Nelson, Edinburgh, 1881.

Stockholm International Peace Research Institute, *World Disarmament SIPRI Yearbook, 1979*, Taylor and Francis, London, 1979.

Sykes, C. *Cross Roads to Israel*, Collins, London, 1965.

Talal, H.B. *A Study on Jerusalem*, Longmans, Amman, Jordan, 1979.

Teveth, S. *Moshe Dayan*, Weidenfeld and Nicolson, London, 1972.

Tingsten, H. *The Problem of South Africa*, Gollancz, London, 1955.

Toms, W.H. *Geographia Antiqua*, Toms, London, 1758.

Tuan, Y.F. *Landscapes of Fear*, Blackwell, Oxford, 1979.

Ultizur, A. *National Capital and the Building of Palestine*, Palestine Foundation Fund, Jerusalem, 1939 (in Hebrew).

United Nations, *Report of the Commissioner-General of the United Nations Relief and Works Agency for Palestinian Refugees in the Near East*, United Nations, New York, 1974, 1978 and 1981.

United Nations, *General Assembly Records: Thirty-First Session, Supplement 13*, United Nations, New York, 1976.

United Nations, *The Committee on the Exercise of the Inalienable Rights of the Palestinian People: Its Establishment, Mandate, Recommendations*, United Nations, New York, 1978.

United Nations Relief and Works Agency, *Definitions and Statistics*, United Nations, Geneva, 1979, 1980 and 1981.

von Waldov, H.E. 'Israel and her Land: Some Theological considerations', in Breamond, H.N. and Moore, C.A. (eds.), *A Light Unto My Path*, Temple University, Philadelphia, 1974, pp.493–508.

Ward, R., Peretz, D. and Wilson, E. *The Palestinian State: A Rational Approach*, Kennikot Press, Port Washington, N.Y., 1977.

Wasserstein, B. *The British in Palestine: The Mandatory Government and the Arab-Jewish Conflict 1917–1929*, Royal Historical Society, London, 1978.

Weinstock, N. *Zionism: False Messiah* (trans. and ed. by A. Adler), Ink Links, London, 1969.

Weitz, J. *My Diary and Letters to the Children*, Massada, Tel Aviv, 1965.

Weizmann, C. *Trial and Error: The Autobiography of Chaim Weizmann*, Harper and Row, New York, 1959.

Williams, G. *The Welsh in their History*, Croom Helm, London, 1982.

World Zionist Organization, *The Community Settlement—Organizing Structure*, W.Z.O. Rural Settlement Department, Jerusalem, 1977.

Zander, W. *Israel and the Holy Places of Christendom*, Weidenfeld and Nicolson, London, 1971.

Zeidan, G. *The Arabs before Islam*, Al-Hilal Press, Cairo, 1922 (Arabic).

Appendix I

Excerpts from the opinion of
the Acting President of the Israeli Supreme Court,
22 October 1979

In this petition we are asked to judge the question of the legality of the establishment of a civilian settlement at Elon Moreh, adjacent to the town of Nablus, on land which is privately owned by Arab residents. This court dealt with a similar issue in which judgement was handed down on 13 March 1979. We ruled there that the establishment of two civilian settlements on private land at Beit-El near Ramallah, and at Bekaot B near Tubas, did not infringe upon either Israeli municipal law or customary international law, which constitutes part of the municipal law, because those two settlements were established for military purposes, as we defined that term . . .

Since then, the acuteness of the dispute has not faded in the international arena; and it has, moreover, intensified also among the Israeli public domestically. This time it has been reflected also in the very decision to establish a civilian settlement at Elon Moreh, which was adopted by majority vote in the Israeli Cabinet. . . .

MILITARY JUSTIFICATION

On 7 June 1979, in the morning, Israeli citizens, with the help of the Israel Defence Forces (IDF), launched a settlement operation on a hill lying about 2 km east of the Jerusalem–Nablus road, and about the same distance south-east of the junction of that road with the road descending from Nablus to the Jordan Valley. . . . The impression is created that the settling of the site was organized like a military operation, taking advantage of the element of surprise and in order to ward off the 'danger' of this court's intervention in the wake of landowners' applications even before work in the field could begin.

The petitioners applied to this court on 14 June 1979, and on 20 June 1979 an order was issued against the respondents, the Government of Israel, the Minister of Defence (Ezer Weizman), the military Commander of the Nablus Subdistrict, ordering them, *inter alia*, to show cause, why the requisition orders issued should not be declared null and void, and why the site should not be cleared of the instruments and the structures erected on it and why the establishment there of a civilian settlement be prevented. . . .

In his affidavit in reply, the Chief of Staff (Lt Gen. Raphael Eitan) explains that he arrived at the view that the establishment of the civilian settlement in that place was required for security reasons, and that his position concerning the security importance of the area and of the establishment of the settlement on it was brought to the knowledge of the Ministerial Defence Committee, which in its sessions of 8 May 1979 and 10 May 1979 decided to approve the seizure of the area with a requisition order for the establishment of the settlement. . . . But he does not hide the fact that there are those who dispute his conclusion concerning the crucial importance of the establishment of a civilian settlement at the site chosen for Elon Moreh. In his affidavit he states: 'I am aware of the view of Respondent No. 2 (the Minister of Defence) who does not dispute the strategic importance of the region under discussion, but believes that the security needs can be realized by a means other than by the establishment of a settlement at the said site. . . .

Lt Gen. (Res.) Haim Bar-Lev (former Chief of Staff) expresses his professional assessment that Elon Moreh makes no contribution to Israel's security, neither in the war against hostile terrorist activity during times of tranquillity, nor in the event of a war on the eastern front, because a civilian settlement, situated on a hill some 2 km from the Nablus-Jerusalem road, cannot facilitate the safeguarding of this traffic axis, the more so since close to this road itself is located a large Army camp, which dominates the traffic axes southward and eastward. In fact, says Lt Gen. (Res.) Bar-Lev, because of hostile terrorist activity in time of war, IDF troops will be tied down to guard the civilian settlement instead of engaging in the war against the enemy's army. . . .

The opinion of Maj-Gen. (Res.) M. Peled is detailed and its conclusion is that 'the claim regarding the security value of the Elon Moreh settlement was not put forward in good faith and was made with only one end in sight: to give a justification for the seizure of land which cannot be justified in any other way. . . .

ISRAELI SOVEREIGNTY

Now the . . . main question: can the establishment of a civilian settlement at the site under discussion be justified legally, if for that purpose privately owned land was requisitioned? In the Beit-El case we gave an affirmative answer to a similar question, both according to internal municipal, Israeli law and according to customary international law, because we were convinced that the requirements of the Army obligated the establishment of the two civilian settlements discussed in that case at the places where they were established.... Each case must be examined to determine whether military purposes, as this term must be interpreted, in fact justify the seizure of the private land.

In this hearing we have—unlike in the Beit-El case—the argument on behalf of two settlers at the 'Elon Moreh' site.... In their affidavit and their pleadings these additional respondents painted a broad picture, far beyond what was argued on behalf of the original respondents. Their affidavit ... explained that the members of the nucleus settled at Elon Moreh because of the Divine commandment to inherit the land which was given to our forefathers and that 'the two elements, therefore, of our sovereignty and our settlement, are intertwined': and that 'it is the settlement activity of the People of Israel in the Land of Israel which is the concrete, the most effective and the truest security action. But the settlement itself does not stem from security reasons or physical needs but from the force of destiny and from the force of the Jewish people's return to its land.' He goes on to declare:

> Elon Moreh is the very heart of the Land of Israel in the profound sense of the word—also, it is true, from the geographical and the strategic points of view, but first and foremost it is the place where this land was first promised to our first forefather, and it is the place where the first property transaction was made by the father of the nation after whom this land is named—The Land of Israel.
>
> This being the case, the security reason, with all due deference and about whose genuineness there is no doubt, makes no difference to us....

Even one who does not hold the views of the respondent and his colleagues will respect their deep religious belief and the devotion spurring them. But we, sitting in judgement in a State based on law in which the Halakha is employed only to the degree that this is permitted by the secular law—must employ the law of the State. As to the respondent's view concerning ownership of land in the Land of Israel, I assume that he does not wish to say that according to the Halakha anyone who is not a Jew may be deprived of private property at any time....

The authentic voice of the Zionism insists on the Jewish people's right of return to its land, as recognized also by the nations of the world—for example, in the preamble to the Palestine Mandate—but has never sought to deprive the residents of the country, members of other peoples, of their civil rights....

The argument is a forceful one, but must be rejected. The fact is that the Minister of Defence did not use his authority under Section I of that Ordinance to make any order in respect of the Judaea and

Samaria region (and the Government of Israel also refrained from applying Israeli law to the same region, as was done in relation to East Jerusalem, by an order on the basis of Section 11B of the Law and Administration Ordinance, 5708-1948). When we come to consider the legal bases of Israeli rule in Judaea and Samaria, our interest is in the legal norms which exist, in practice and not just those which exist potentially, and the basic norm upon which Israeli rule in Judaea and Samaria was based was, and is until today, the norm of a military administration, and not the application of Israeli law, which brings with it Israeli sovereignty.

There can be no doubt that in Lt Gen. Eitan's professional opinion the establishment of the civilian settlement at that site is consistent with the needs of regional defence, which is of special importance in safeguarding the axes of movement during the deployment of the reserve forces in time of war. But I have come to the view that this professional view of the Chief of Staff would in itself not have led to the taking of the decision on the establishment of the Elon Moreh settlement, had there not been another reason, which was the driving force for the taking of said decision in the Ministerial Defence Committee and in the Cabinet plenum—namely, the powerful desire of the members of Gush Emunim to settle in the heart of Eretz-Israel, as close as possible to the town of Nablus....

The question which is before this court in this petition is whether this view justifies the taking of private property in an area subject to rule by military government—and, as I have tried to make clear, the answer to this depends on the correct interpretation of Article 52 of the Hague Regulations. I am of the opinion that the military needs cited in that article cannot include, according to any reasonable interpretation, national security needs in their broad sense, as I have just mentioned them. I shall cite Oppenheim:

> According to Article 52 of the Hague Regulations, requisitions may be made from municipalities as well as from the inhabitants, but so far only as they are really necessary for the army of occupation. They must not be made in order to supply the belligerent's general needs.

Military needs in the meaning of Article 52 can, therefore, include the needs that the Chief of Staff spoke of in his affidavit of response, that is, the needs of regional defence and of defending axes of movement so that reserve forces can deploy uninterruptedly in time of war....

When it is military needs that are involved, I would have expected that the Army authorities would initiate the establishment of the settlement precisely at that site, and that it would be the Chief of Staff who would, in line with this initiative, bring the Army's request before the political level so that it could approve the settlement's establishment, should it find that there are no political reasons preventing this. . . . It emerges that the process was the very opposite: the initiative came from the political level, and the political level asked the Chief of Staff to give his professional opinion, and then (he) expressed a positive opinion, in accordance with the conception he has always held. . . .

It was the pressure of the Gush Emunim members that impelled the Ministerial Committee to take up, in that session, the subject of a civilian settlement in the Nablus area. The matter was subsequently passed on to the Ministerial Settlement Committee so that it could send its representatives for an advance survey in order to select the feasible sites for the establishment of a settlement for the 'Elon Moreh' nucleus near Nablus. They selected five sites, and of the five the IDF opted for the site under discussion. It emerges from this that the IDF had no hand in determining those five sites, but was confronted with the choice of selecting one of the five sites determined by the political level. This process is not consistent with the language of Article 52, which in my view necessitates the demarcation in advance of a certain area because precisely that land is needed for military needs. . . .

The political consideration was, therefore, the dominant factor in the Ministerial Defence Committee's decision to establish the settlement at that site, although I assume that the Committee as well as the Cabinet majority were convinced that its establishment *also* (emphasis in the original) fulfils military needs. . . .

I have still not dwelt on an additional reason which must bring about a revocation of the decision to seize the petitioners' land—a reason which stands on its own, without even taking into consideration the other reasons which I have so far detailed. . . .

The decision to establish a permanent settlement intended from the outset to remain in its place forever—even beyond the duration of the military government which was established in Judaea and Samaria—encounters a legal obstacle which is unsurmountable, because the military government cannot create in its area facts for its military needs which are designed *ab initio* to exist even after the end of the military rule in that area, when the fate of the area after the termination of military rule is still not known. This contains a *prima facie* contradiction which shows also, according to the evidence before us in this petition, that the decisive consideration which led the political level to decide on the establishment of the settlement under discussion was not the military consideration. In these circumstances the legal form of requisitioning the possession only and not expropriating rights of ownership, cannot change the face of things, namely the taking of possession, which is the main content of property, forever. . . .

Appendix II

Political programme of the
Fourth Fatah Conference 21–29 May 1980

Fatah is a revolutionary patriotic movement that aims to liberate the whole of Palestine and to establish a democratic Palestinian state on the whole of Palestinian soil. [Compare the Beirut daily *Al-Liwa'* version that reads in transliteration, 'Al-Fatah is an independent national revolutionary movement, whose aim is to liberate Palestine completely and to liquidate the Zionist entity politically, economically, militarily, culturally and ideologically'.] The political programme points out that armed popular revolution and armed struggle are the only way to liberate Palestine.... The following was decided by the Fatah fourth general conference.

AT THE PALESTINIAN LEVEL

Basing itself on the unity of the Palestinian people, territory and political representation; to consolidate the independent national will in order to ensure the continuation and victory of the revolution....
3. To step up the armed struggle inside the occupied land and across all confrontation lines against the Zionist enemy....
5. To support the steadfastness of our Palestinian people inside the occupied land at all levels.... to place special emphasis on strengthening links with our Palestinian masses in the territory occupied since 1948 in order to enable them to confront the plans aimed at disintegrating their Arab character....

AT THE ARAB LEVEL

1. Relations with the Arab masses are strategic, which makes it incumbent on these masses further to expand their participation in safeguarding the revolution and waging all forms of struggle against the imperialist-Zionist base in Palestine.
5. The Jordanian arena is of special importance to the Palestine revolution. It must be given special attention so that it may be restored as a basic springboard of struggle against the Zionist enemy. The potential of the masses must be employed to reach this aim.

6. We must strengthen the joint struggle with the Palestinian people, represented by their patriotic and progressive forces, in order to foil the Camp David plot and its consequences, and to restore Egypt to the Arab fold to take its natural position in the Arab struggle. . . .

RELATIONS WITH THE ARAB REGIMES

6. The revolution will exercise its responsibility for struggle at the pan-Arab level and across any Arab country towards the occupied Palestinian territory in order to restore that territory. It will act to pool the manpower and material resources of the Arab nation, especially the oil wealth, as a weapon to achieve these aims. . . .

THE FRIENDLY FORCES

1. To strengthen the strategic alliance with the socialist countries, especially the Soviet Union, since this alliance is necessary in order to confront effectively and seriously the US and Zionist plots against the Palestine question and the world liberation issues. . . .

THE U.S. POSITION

The United States stands at the head of the enemies of our people and nation. It is pursuing a policy hostile to our people, our revolution, our Arab nation and to all Arab and world liberation forces. The United States supports the Zionist entity and its agents in the area and establishes military alliances aimed at surrendering the area to its military influence so that it may continue to plunder our nation's resources. For this reason, the world front hostile to U.S. policy must be strengthened and must fight to foil this policy and strike at U.S. interests in the area.

WEST EUROPEAN COUNTRIES, THE EEC, JAPAN AND CHINA

1. To intensify political action in these countries and to benefit from the support of the democratic and progressive political forces in these countries so as to diminish and stop their support for the Zionist entity. To isolate the Zionist entity through their recognition of the P.L.O. as the sole legitimate representative of the Palestinian people, and to achieve maximum political and financial support for our cause, struggle and national rights. . . .

In conclusion, our movement's fourth conference stresses the need to safeguard and strengthen the political gains and achievements that have been attained at the international level, which make the Palestine question a vital issue that enjoys the largest international support, making it the vanguard of the world liberation movements and the holder of its banner. Revolution and victory. But surely revolution should continue after victory.

Index

Palestine Liberation Organization
(P.L.O.), 52, 96, 113, 122,
133, 142, 147
Palestinian Arabs, 83, 107
Palestinian rights, 106, 109, 131
Palestinian state, 96, 131, 134, 144,
151
peace initiatives, 101, 139, 144,
148
peace treaty, 100-6, 138
Peel Commission, The, 25-6
Phalange, The, 55, 148, 152
Popular Front for the Liberation
of Palestine, 52
population, Arab, 127
Promised Land, The, xix-xx, 3, 7,
49, 154

Reagan plan, 148-53
refugee camps, 152
refugee problem, 106-11, 113-14
regional confederacy, 129
religious settlements, 57
residential suburbs, 57, 60
revolutionary movement, 114,
170-1
riots, 25

Sabra refugee camp, 152
Safdie-Lansky project, 82
Saladin, 14
Salit Nahal, 58
Samaria, 60
San Remo Conference, 15
Saudi Arabia, 54
Saudi Arabian plan, 132-4
Semites, 1
separatism, 3, 8
settlement, 35, 149, 153
agricultural, 66
blocks, 63
combined, 66
community, 66
finance, 69
Israeli, 57-70, 123, 149
rural, 24-5, 36
urban, 66
Zionist, 31, 36, 43

Sham, 1, 16
Sharia, The, 81
Sharon, Ariel, 143, 152-3
Shatila refugee camp, 152
Shaw Commission, The, 25
Shaw Report, 35
Simpson Report, 35
Solomon, 9
South Africa, 39, 130
storied place, xx
Suez Canal, 15
Sykes-Picot Agreement, 15
Syria, 16, 55

Tabernacle, The, 5
Tammuz nuclear reactor, 102
Temple, The, 9, 11-12
Terah clan, 2
territorial changes, 115, 127-37
Thirty Year Plan, 152
Torah, The, xx
Transjordania, 16

U.S.S.R. interest in the Middle
East, 46, 120
United Jewish Appeal, 69
U.N. General Assembly
Resolution 194, 38
Resolution 303, 124
Resolution 3236, 55, 100, 109,
150
U.N. Relief and Works Agency for
Palestine Refugees, 108-11
U.N. Security Council
Resolution 242, 95, 147
Resolution 267, 125
Resolution 298, 125
Resolution 465, 126
Resolution 471, 125-6
Resolution 508, 104
Resolution 509, 104
U.S.A.
arms agreement with Israel, 103
arms sales, 151
interest in the Middle East, 98,
105, 142
Jewish lobby, 98, 100-1, 103
Middle Eastern policy, 148

176